Waterdrum Science

Science Through American Indian Arts and Culture

By Carolyn A. Petty

Larchmere Ltd. Bemidji, Minnesota, USA

Second Edition 1997

About the Author/Artist

Carolyn Petty is an artist and education consultant. Her focus is on multi-cultural connections of science and art. For more than 15 years she has been sharing her hands-on workshops with thousands of children and teachers -- from Alaska to Miami to Moscow. Workshops include: Bones, Fur And Feathers; The Chemistry Of Flower Petal Paints; Micro-World Geology; The Physics Of Eagles And Airplanes....

Carolyn is a Sequoia Fellow of AISES (American Indian Science and Engineering Society). She is President-Elect of the Council for Elementary Science International (CESI), and edits "Science Sparklers" for *Science & Children* magazine. She has earned numerous honors in both wildlife art and science education.

A quiet lake in Northern Minnesota is home to Carolyn, her forester husband, and their family. Deer, beavers, bears, loons, eagles, wolves and great blue herons make their homes here too. Carolyn can often be found outdoors -- flying a single-engine airplane or observing and recording nature from the ground with a sketchbook and children.

Library of Congress Catalog Card Number 94-78267

ISBN 0-9642898-0-6

Waterdrum Science
is for my parents,
Howard and Mildred Petty,
who opened their home and hearts
to people of Many Nations,
opening a child's horizons in the process.

Waterdrum Science
is dedicated to the memories
of three teachers who changed my life:

To Blackbear Bosin, my first art teacher.
He took my work seriously,
and believed it was possible,
to succeed in two worlds.

To Dr. Les Duly,
who was dedicated to serving,
who had an overwhelming kindness,
and quiet humor,
and caring for people.

To Mary C. McCurdy,
who was a great teacher
because she loved children.

Praise for WATERDRUM SCIENCE:

Waterdrum Science provides culturally relevant content and approaches to the study of science through the incorporation of American Indian science and art into the lessons."
Norbert S. Hill, Jr., Executive Director, AISES, The American Indian Science and Engineering Society.

"*Waterdrum Science* is a creative, innovative, hands-on learning resource that provides students in my classroom with exciting lessons through a multi-cultural perspective. I recommend this motivational tool, as it focuses on visual learning as well as Anishinabe culture. I like the book's flexibility of providing cooperative family activities as well as art projects."
Gayle Littlewolf, Classroom Teacher.

"...A practical manual for the classroom teacher packed full of ideas for learning science through interdisciplinary, hands-on activities, from a Native American perspective. *Waterdrum Science* is an International Exemplar."
Ann Vick, Director, Roger Lang Clearinghouse, Boston.

"...This project will continue to help improve the science aptitude skills and science processes, critical factors for success in high school science classes for our young Indian children's lives."
Joe Aitken, State of Minnesota: Indian Education Scholarship Director.

"It is an honor for the Bug-O-Nay-Ge-Shig School Staff and Students to be a part of *Waterdrum Science*. Teachers have had input on the project to meet the needs of their students. Students show success with this project because the materials are relevant to the culture as Ojibwe people. It is important now to implement this resource book into every classroom. The American Indian culture can be a very useful learning tool for all children when it is treated respectfully. *Waterdrum Science* accomplishes this."
Patty Cornelius, Superintendent, Chief Bug-O-Nay-Ge-Shig School.

Table of Contents

Earth Science

Physical Science

MEE GWECH -- THANK YOU

The Author gratefully acknowledges the support of all who have contributed to the excellence of **Waterdrum Science.**

Waterdrum Science is one of forty major projects funded through the Blandin Foundation's Native American Initiative for Northern Minnesota. Through the insight of the Board of Directors and under the guidance of Foundation President Paul Olson, educators are making a difference in the lives of Native American children in Minnesota.

Additional funding was generously provided by the Land-O-Lakes Foundation. Extensive in-service is supported by schools of Leech Lake Reservation. and the West Central / North West Educational Cooperative Service Units. Books used by the project are printed with funding by schools at Red Lake, Leech Lake, White Earth, and Bemidji.

I am grateful to several key people at Bemidji State University who made the initial project possible: Dr. Ranae Wolmack, Asst, Professor of Nursing, former Coordinator of Native Americans into Medicine (NAM); Dr. Linda Baer, Interim President, Sr. Vice Pres. for Academic and Student Affairs; and the late Dr. Les Duly, President, who saw some glimmer of potential in a student many years ago, on the Nebraska prairies.

Opportunities in Science Directors Drs. James and Laddie Elwell, founders of the Headwaters Science Center, added long-term stability and scientific advice.

Encouragement for expansion to other American Indian communities came from Dr. Emma Walton, Anchorage and Washington D.C.; Ann Vick, Boston; Dr. Walter Smith, Uni. of Kansas; Barb Miller, Bismarck, ND; Cathy Abeita, AISES, Colorado.

I appreciate the counsel of Vince Beyl, Bemidji Indian Education Coordinator, always ready to answer a question and offer help. His sound advice and careful review of the manuscript helped maintain the project's cultural integrity and respect.

I thank science teacher Chuck Auger for his science review of the material. His knowledge of physics, his example and outlook have been valuable to this project.

A picture is worth a thousand words. Roberta Lord's art classes at the Chief Bug-O-Nay-Ge -Shig School provided many of the exquisite illustrations that grace these pages. These young artists have given *Waterdrum Science* a beauty and strength not achieved by words alone. A special thank you to illustrator Lee White for his excellent detailed ink drawings of Ojibwe culture.

Thank you to Dr. Walter Smith and MASTERS students from the Uni. of Kansas -- dedicated people involved with American Indian education from Alaska to the Southwest -- for your input, enthusiasm, and encouragement to write *Waterdrum Science* as a book.

I appreciate the help of my friends at the American Indian Science and Engineering Society (AISES). Cathy Abeita recommended me for this project. Al and Leslie Qoyawayma share their vision of science, art and culture with me. Director Norbert Hill believes in the human potential to overcome the odds, and to excel.

To my Editors, Ben Duranske, Elizabeth Petty, and Serri Miller: Thank you for your clarity, your questions, and your encouragement.

THE WATERDRUM AT SCHOOL

The Waterdrum is a sacred drum.
Its message reminds the Anishinaabe
and the Wayaabishkiiwed
to respect our Mother Earth,
and to keep all things in balance.
It is a vastly important message
for all people.

The Purpose of *Waterdrum Science* is
to provide an American Indian balance
to the Euro-centric science lessons
of most school classrooms.
Waterdrum Science shares the lessons
of Mother Earth in ways that are
holistic, visual, spiritual, and respectful
of the wisdom of the elders.

The Purpose of *Waterdrum Science* is
to provide resources for teachers,
so they can incorporate American Indian
science, arts and culture into their lessons,
making the learning more meaningful
to all children who live on this continent today.

Cultural materials are treated with
respect and honor,
and with extensive cultural review.
The stories, language and beliefs
are retold from published records,
and from stories told to the author.
Variations are due to interpretation,
never to lack of respect.

Remembering that interpretations of
content and tradition exist within
all societies, teachers need to be
sensitive to the traditions and needs
of their own communities.

PREFACE

By Vince Beyl

This resource book is based primarily on the Ojibwe heritage and arts along with other tribes designed to provide students with a visual hands-on learning experience through a Native American traditional science perspective.

We invite you to share in the Ojibwe traditions, culture and language through traditional science to promote appreciation and awareness of the Native American Learning Cycle of Science.

Mee-Gwetch

USING *WATERDRUM SCIENCE*

Waterdrum Science Is...

Waterdrum Science is a resource book for teachers of all children. While the focus is on Woodland tribes, the book's many cultures add balance and interest. Teachers can easily adapt activities to their geographic area. One Navajo teacher said, "I can always add Navajo stories or language. What I want are these great activities!" *Waterdrum Science* helps non-Indian children understand the science-art connection of the First Americans.

The book is the result of a five-year project, beginning with extensive classroom needs assessment and in-service. Through teacher requests, the project grew into this book for upper elementary and middle school children, their teachers and parents.

Research shows that American Indian children learn more effectively when they learn visually, through their own culture, and by *doing* rather than memorizing. Working with thousands of children and their teachers each year, I find this is true of most children. Many elementary children engage in art projects after school for fun. What a wonderful opportunity to stimulate and reinforce science concepts at the same time.

Waterdrum Science is not "another new curriculum." It is not intended to replace existing science curricula. It is meant to enhance it with explorations and applications that relate to the culture of American Indian children.

Waterdrum Science and the Learning Cycle

The Learning Cycle shows us that kids learn best when they explore a concept BEFORE we start loading on the facts.

Start the Exploration phase by sharing The Stories with your students. Ask children to do one of the story-related Activities. Children will find they soon need The Facts.

In the Concept Introduction phase, **Waterdrum Science** offers fascinating facts that relate the science concept directly to Native American culture and arts. Students can use text books and trade books as valuable resources to find more facts they need. With the facts in use, children gain understanding, not memorization.

Concept Application is essential for real learning and assessment. Children can do one or several additional Activities. They will be challenged to apply what they have learned. The directions are often open-ended, so children can explore, be inventive, and learn the value of risk-taking in science and art processes.

Waterdrum Science and Thinking Skills

We want our students to learn HOW to think. Hands-on science sometimes seems to "take too much time." We worry, "Will we finish the book by the end of the year?" One educator responds, "What difference does it make, if we cover it, if the kids don't learn it?"

In every *Waterdrum Science* Activity, children are asked to think and process information instead of merely memorizing it. They observe, analyze, classify, compare, record, recall, infer, interpret, measure, experiment.... They learn by doing, by seeking and using information, by relating science concepts to familiar cultural experiences.

Waterdrum Science and Multi-disciplinary Themes

Each Waterdrum Science chapter is prefaced with a page of Themes, Concepts, Ideas, Questions, Processes and Integrations for quick reference. It's easy to build integrated bridges to other disciplines using this guide to identify common strands.

Chapter 1

Waterdrum Science

CONCEPT(S):
Survival, Balance

IDEA (DEFINING CONCEPT):
Conserving Resources

TOPIC & THEME:
Finding Balances

QUESTION(S):
1. What lesson does the waterdrum have for conserving our resources?
2. How can we conserve water, earth (soil), air, animals, and plants?

PROCESS & THINKING SKILLS:
Data
Analyze
Record
Infer
Interpret

INTEGRATIONS:
Science
Language arts
Math
Social studies
Art

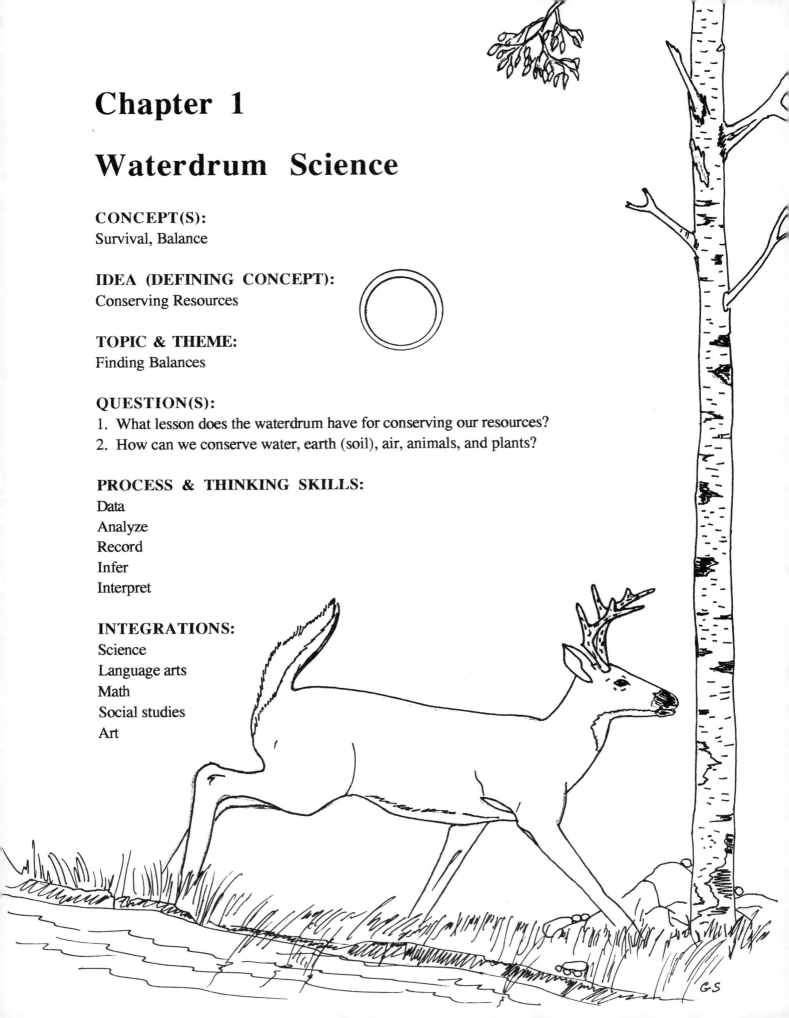

CONSERVING EARTH'S RESOURCES

The Waterdrum Song:

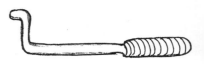

    The Ojibwe Waterdrum is a symbol of all things in balance.

    The Ojibwe call themselves Anishinaabe, First Nation.

    The Great Spirit's name is Gichi Manidoo, the Creator.

    The First Man's name is Winabozho, teacher of the Anishinaabe.

    The body of the drum is made from a hollow log.

    This reminds us to respect all members of the plant tribes.

    They give us life.

    Water is poured into the hollow.

    Water helps us honor Mother Earth. Water is her life blood.

    She gives us water, without which we cannot live.

    Tobacco is sprinkled on the water.

    With tobacco we honor the gift of speaking with the Creator.

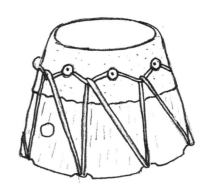

    The Waterdrum head is made from deer skin,

    Reminding us to honor the four-footed tribes.

    The sound is soft and quick.

    We should be gentle and quick like the deer.

    A hoop encircles the top of the drum.

    It is the Sacred Circle of birth, growth and death.

    It is the bond of love and respect between a man and woman.

    It is the movement of all water over the earth.

    All things in balance.

    Seven small round stones are tied to the drum head.

    They honor Mother Earth and the Seven Teachings

    Love, Respect, Honor, Obedience, Generosity, Humility, and Hope.

    The head can be tied onto the Waterdrum seven different ways.

    Each way has a special meaning for a special ceremony.

    The drum maker removes a plug from the drum.

    He blows his breath into the drum.

    This represents the breath of the Creator,

    -- life giving and life sustaining.

    All things in balance.

    A drum beater is carved from a live root.

    The curved neck of the drum beater reminds us of Crane and Loon.

    When the Waterdrum is finished, its voice is heard in four beats,

    Honoring the four directions.

G S

The Waterdrum brings songs of Beauty and Thanksgiving.
The Waterdrum reminds the Anishinaabe of the Seven Teachings:
Love, Respect, Honor, Generosity, Humility, Obedience and Hope.
The Waterdrum and the Midewiwin Lodge help people remember,
All things in balance.

THE ACTIVITIES:

1. Lessons of the Waterdrum

   What lesson does the Waterdrum have for conserving our resources?
   How can we conserve water, earth (soil) air, animals and plants?
   Many cultures conserved some resources and wasted others. Collect data showing examples
   of both conservation and waste in the same culture.

2. Balancing Use and Conservation

   For one day make a list of all the products you use made from the plants.
   Try this with earth resources (like rocks, soils, metals....)
   Try this with animal products (and animal medical/cosmetic testing.)
   How can you balance your needs with the future's needs?

3. The Waterdrum News

   Collect articles on environmental issues.
   Find articles and opinions on both sides of the issue.
   How many articles favor one side or the other? Make a graph to show your results.
   What conclusions can you draw about this?
   Ask yourself some questions:

   How easy or how hard is it to find both sides of the issue?
   Is there a real problem?
   How serious is the problem?
   How do I know? Are the sources credible?
   Where is the balance? Do both sides have some good points?
   Would a compromise work? (Why or why not?)

   Write two articles, use a computer if you can:

   One article should be facts only. (This is straight news.)
   One article should be opinion based on facts.

   Use your articles to create your own Waterdrum News newspaper.

   In your paper, be sure to keep facts and opinions on different pages. Facts are news
   stories; opinions are editorials. Illustrate your newspaper with drawings, cartoons,
   photos and pictographs.

   Design a newspaper logo based on the Waterdrum teachings of balance.

Chapter 2

Animal Adaptations

CONCEPT(S):
Survival
Patterns
Change
Cause and Effect

IDEA (DEFINING CONCEPT):
Adaptations aid survival.
Adaptations are caused by changes.

TOPIC & THEME:
Animal adaptation

QUESTION(S):
How do animals adapt to their environments?

PROCESS & THINKING SKILLS:
Observe
Analyze
Recall
Record
Classify
Compare

INTEGRATIONS:
Art
Language arts
Science

ANIMAL ADAPTATIONS

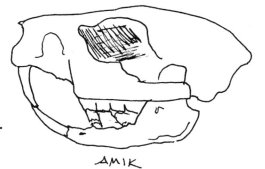

AMIK

THE FACTS:

Q. What IS a beaver?

A. Beavers are just big rodents.
    Like other rodents, they are especially adapted for gnawing.

Q. How are they adapted for gnawing?

A. Their long, curved incisors (front teeth) never stop growing.
    The front of these teeth is coated with hard orange enamel.
    Every time the beaver bites, the back of the tooth is worn down
    more than the front.
    It automatically sharpens the tooth into a chisel point, useful for eating trees!

Q. Why do they need water adaptations?

A. Beavers spend about 50% of their time in the water.
    Their dives can last up to 15 minutes before coming up for air.

Q. How "busy" are beavers?

A. No busier than they have to be! If the water stays at the same level, they don't build a dam.
    If they can, they dig a burrow into a bank instead of constructing a lodge.

Q. How do behavior adaptations help them survive?

A. When they need to, beavers can modify their environment more than any other animal (except
    for humans.) They live in small colonies so everyone can help gather food and keep warm.

Q. How else do they stay warm?

A. They comb oil into their fur to keep water from getting to the skin.
    On the back feet the second toenail is split, making a handy comb!
    Oil is stored in a special gland near the tail.

Q. Why don't they have to use ear plugs and nose plugs?

They have special muscles in their noses and ears.
These "valves" close to keep water out when the beaver dives.
Skin behind the teeth keeps water from going down the beaver's throat
when he swims with branches.

THE ACTIVITIES: (These can be done independently or in cooperative groups).

1. Game or Poster:
    "The Adaptations of Amik and Ajidamoo" (Beaver and Squirrel)
    Teachers can photocopy the following sheet of cards.
    Have students cut them out. They can make picture cards by drawing, or
    by adding magazine photos of beaver and squirrel adaptations.
    (For example: Squirrels have big eyes to watch for enemies.)
    Students can use observations and library materials to discover the
    What and Why of the adaptations shown on their cards.
    Students will record their observations on the cards.
    (If they are making a game, students may prefer to record on the back of the card.)
    Finally, students can compare the adaptations of each species
    and use the cards to make a game or poster.

    KEY : Remember, we are looking for multiple solutions and answers!
    There can be many different appropriate responses.

2. More Adaptation Cards!
    Cooperative Groups can make new sets of cards about other animals for
    the other students and groups to use. It's important to have students dig
    for the information themselves. Try to let them have as much time as
    they need. The best learning takes place when the students engage as
    long as they need to but can disengage when they are ready.

3). Invent an Animal!
    Describe or draw an environment for your animal.
    (It can be a real or imaginary place.)
    Describe or draw your imaginary animal.
    Identify the adaptations, telling why each is necessary for this animal's
    survival in its surroundings.
    Name your animal.
    Make up a How and Why Story about one adaptation.

4. Creating a Book for Fun and Profit!
    Students can write their stories on the computer, and do illustrations in black ink.
    They can copyright their work.
    Photocopy the pages, making a coloring/story book for younger children.
    Sell the book at PTA meetings or in a local store.
    Use the profit to take a field trip!

Body Part_____

picture

Adaptations: _____
_____
_____

Used for Survival:
_____
_____
_____

Body Part_____

picture

Adaptations: _____
_____
_____

Used for Survival:
_____
_____
_____

Body Part_____

picture

Adaptations:_____
_____

Used for Survival:
_____
_____
_____

Body Part_____

picture

Adaptations:_____
_____

Used for Survival:
_____
_____
_____

Chapter 3

Special Adaptations

CONCEPT(S):
Survival
Patterns
Change
Cause and effect
Structures

IDEA (DEFINING CONCEPT):
1. Special adaptations help some animals survive by blending in with their environment.
2. Some survive by being copy-cats (mimics).

TOPIC & THEME:
Special Adaptation

QUESTION(S):
How do special adaptations help certain animals survive?

PROCESS & THINKING SKILLS:
Interpret
Observe
Record
Classify

INTEGRATIONS:
Science
Language Arts
Math
Art

SPECIAL ADAPTATIONS

THE STORY: How Grasshopper's Tricks Almost Worked

Grasshopper (*Bapakine*) was a handsome young Ojibwe man. He was a fine dancer, whirling and leaping higher than anyone else. He loved to show off! But Grasshopper was lazy. "Why work? I am lucky at sticks and bones; I win by tricks what other men work for!" he laughed.

One day Winabozho came to the village to show people how to follow a good path in life. Soon they refused to play sticks and bones with Grasshopper. "Winabozho takes the fun and ease out of my life. I will play a trick on him and leave this boring village!" Grasshopper exclaimed.

One night, during a feast, Grasshopper crept into Winabozho's wigwam. He danced himself into a whirlwind and made a ruin of the beautiful baskets, bows, and buckskins. Leaping atop the wigwam, he strangled Winabozho's pet raven before running off into the night. Winabozho was very angry. "Lazy Grasshopper has played his last trick on this village!" he promised, slipping into his magic moccasins. The moccasins carried him a mile with each step.

Grasshopper had magic too. Whenever Winabozho closed in, he adapted into another form. In a pond, he gradually became a beaver, *amik*. On the prairie, he grew into an elk, *omashkooz*. Each time he grew so lazy and fat that the villagers killed him and made a feast, but Grasshopper's spirit, *jiibay*, escaped. Only Winabozho saw the whirlwind's shadow fly away with flock of geese, *na-kug*. When Winabozho caught up with the flock, lazy Grasshopper was too fat to fly fast. "Don't look down!" the other geese warned. But as Grasshopper flew over his old village, he bent his long neck to look at the villagers hard at work. "Fools!" he honked. Suddenly Grasshopper's heavy body was all out of balance. He tumbled out of the sky, landing in a cooking pot. The villagers were delighted with this enormous *na-kug* for dinner. Grasshopper's spirit drifted safely away through the forest, like smoke on the wind.

Winabozho, who saw the escape, followed closely so there was no time to adapt. Along the rocky cliffs of Gitchi Gumi, clever Grasshopper hid in the caves. Calling upon the lightning to shatter the rocks, Winabozho trapped him in the caves and finally killed him. "Grasshopper, you were foolish, but you did make people laugh with your tricks and dancing. I will let your spirit live in the whirlwind." Whenever a little whirlwind blows through the village, kicking up powdery snow or spilling a dish, people laugh. "There goes Grasshopper, still up to his old tricks!"

THE ACTIVITIES:

1. Write your own adaptation story. It can be real or imagined.
   Describe the environment. How does the adaptation help survival?
   What tricks could you play? How might your adaptations get you into trouble?
   Make a drawing to illustrate your adaptation and survival.

2. Make a book of Special Adaptations: Start by completing the following pages.
   Add more examples from magazines and your own drawings.
   Be sure to list the adaptation, and how it helps the animal survive.

Add the habitat of sharp pointed bullrushes and cattails. Color the picture.

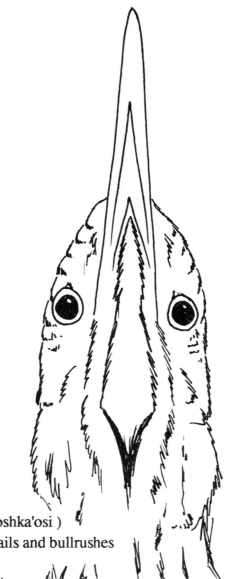

The Least Bittern (Mooshka'osi)
Habitat: swamps of cattails and bullrushes
Adaptations:
Its eyes are below its chin.
The long thin beak and legs are good for walking and eating in swamps.
Special adaptations:
When danger threatens, the bittern's protective resemblance helps him look like another bullrush.
He throws his beak up in the air and holds still.
Stripes on his neck help him blend in.

The Least Bittern Looking for Food
Add the habitat to this picture, too. Color the picture.
Take both bittern pictures across the room. Compare the camouflage!

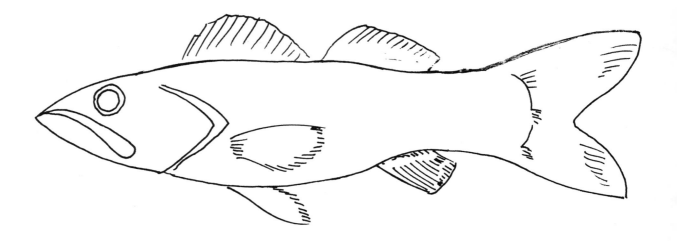

The Walleye (Ogaa) Has Counter Shading.

Color the walleye with counter shading, making it as real as possible.

Who are a walleye's enemies?

What is its food?

Add a habitat with predators and prey.

What color is seen from above?

What color is seen from below?

How does countershading help the walleye hide from predators?

How does it help him hide from its prey?

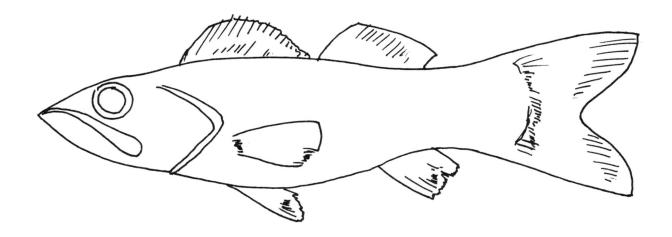

Color this walleye <u>without</u> countershading.
Take the two pictures across the room.
Compare them!

Rabbit is "waabooz".

The Snowshoe Hare's Special Adaptation is Protective Coloring.

Adaptation: How do his big feet help him get around in the winter?

Draw and color the hare and its habitat for three seasons -- summer, winter and either spring or fall. In spring and fall, the hare is brown and white spotted.

Spring and Fall (Patches of Snow)

Summer

Winter

Mimicry -- Can YOU Tell the Difference?*

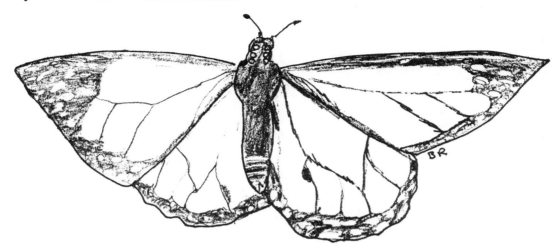

Warning coloration
The Monarch's color warns,
"I taste bad!" After a blue jay
tastes one monarch, he leaves
the rest alone.

Mimicry coloration
The Viceroy doesn't taste bad,
but the blue jay doesn't know that.
Because the Viceroy's coloring
mimics the Monarch's, jays don't
eat them either!

   Look up pictures of both butterflies in a guide book. Compare them.
   (Hint: Look for tiny differences of shapes, shading, color and number of spots)

Draw a cartoon! Show a blue jay learning that orange butterflies are yucky! Put Monarchs and
Viceroys in your cartoon. Can you use the words warning and mimicry?. In Ojibwe
"Maazhipogozi" means, "He tastes bad!" "Butterfly" is "memengwa."

Chapter 4

Northwoods Fossils

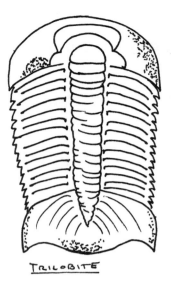

TRILOBITE

CONCEPT(S):
Change

IDEA (DEFINING CONCEPT):
Fossils tell us how the earth has changed over time.

TOPIC & THEME:
Special adaptation

QUESTION(S):
What fossils are found in the North woods?

PROCESS & THINKING SKILLS:
Recall
Record
Interpret
Observe
Analyze

INTEGRATIONS:
Science
Art
Math
Language Arts

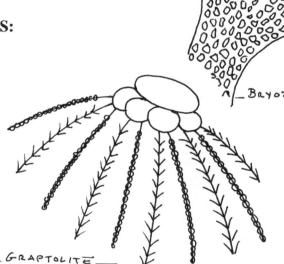

BRYOZOAN

GRAPTOLITE

CEPHALOPOD

MINNESOTA FOSSILS

THE PAINTINGS: Traditional Indian painting contrasts with traditional European painting. Today many artists mix the styles.

FOSSIL PLANT

INDIAN STYLE PAINTING
Colored paper
Dry Paper
Bright colors
Imaginary colors
Strong designs - no shadows
Opaque paints (tempera OR
white added to watercolors)

EUROPEAN STYLE PAINTING
White paper
Wet Paper
Soft colors
Real colors
Real shapes and shadows
Transparent paints (watercolors)

THE ACTIVITIES:

1. Geologic Time and Fossil Mural.
    Students will make a mural painting of geologic time, showing The Fossils in natural surroundings. Students can retell The Facts in big letters on another sheet of paper.
    Photocopy the next three pages for each student to use, and then take home.
    Every student or group is assigned one geologic time period from The Facts, so all time periods are covered. Time periods can be used more than once.
    HINT: Use geometric shapes to draw fossils.Tape the explanation under the painting.
    Hang the mural around the top of the blackboard, in chronological order so students can see the visual and verbal fossil record.
    Materials: White drawing paper, paints and brushes, 1 inch wide brushes or foam-tipped trim brushes (from hardware stores), masking tape. If you paint on wet paper, tape the edges down with masking tape, so the paper doesn't curl. You can remove it carefully when its dry (3 - 5 hours.)

2. Charge Ahead to the Past
    Write a story: Travel through Minnesota's Fossil Time.
    Be sure there is plenty of action and imagination combined with the facts.

3. Making Lines Into Circles
    Can you see patterns or cycles in the Fossil Facts?
    Identify cycles; make a circle painting showing one cycle.

NORTHWOODS FOSSILS -- THE FACTS

<u>4.5 Billion Years Ago</u>: The earth was formed from cosmic matter.

<u>For four billion years</u> across Minnesota volcanoes erupted and went extinct, mountains rose and eroded away, and huge seas advanced and receded.

<u>3.5 Billion Years Ago</u>: simple single-celled life forms began to develop from chemicals in the seas. They had no skeletons or shells, so it's not easy to find evidence of them. Very slowly -- over the next three billion years -- some of these life forms became more complex. Fossil algae (two billion years old) has been found on the Iron Range.

<u>500 Million Years Ago</u>: Southern Minnesota was covered by seas. Trilobites, Brachiopods, and Graptolites lived in the seas. These animals had shells, and we find their fossils today.

<u>400 Million Years Ago</u>: The land was low and covered with swamps, ancient ferns and trees. Straight cephalopods (relatives of the Chambered Nautilus), Bryozoans, snails, and corals lived in the seas that came and went across Minnesota. Sponges, crinoids, and conodonts (tiny tooth-shaped animals) lived in the warm waters too.

<u>300 Million Years Ago</u>: Fish, brachiopods and corals once lived in a great Minnesota sea. Their fossils are found today.

<u>200 Million Years Ago</u>: During this time pine trees evolved and covered the state. Minnesota had no seas, so there are no fossils here from this time. In other places there are fossils of Amphibians (like salamanders) and Reptiles (like dinosaurs).

<u>100 Million Years Ago</u>: Most of Minnesota was again covered by a huge sea, with sharks and sea reptiles! Fossil clams and oysters are also found. Dinosaurs probably roamed the eastern corners of Minnesota. Flowering plants evolved during this time, too.

<u>60 Million Years Ago</u>: Minnesota was above sea level. Mammals evolved.

<u>2 Million Years Ago</u>: The climate cooled, and glaciers formed, melted, and formed again across Minnesota. The fossil record of plants and animals tells the glacial story in detail.

13 Thousand Years Ago: Animals grew bigger to cope with the glacial climate. Bigger animals don't lose body heat as fast as smaller animals. For example, modern polar bears, which live in the Arctic, weigh much more than black bears, which live in Minnesota. Giant versions of elephants, (wooly mammoth and mastodons), musk-ox, sloths, beavers, short-faced bear, elk, and bison all lived on the edges of the glaciers. The giant sloth was as tall as a house, and the giant beaver weighed 500 pounds, as much as a modern black bear!

10,000 Years Ago: Humans first came to Minnesota about this time, although we don't know exactly when. They probably saw the last of the glaciers. Their beautiful stone tools are found among the bones and fossils of the big mammoths and bison they hunted.

7,000-9,000 years ago: Humans lived and hunted in organized societies. A hunting party of Indians killed 16 bison in Itasca Park about 9,000 years ago. A dog skeleton found at this sight is the earliest one found so far in Minnesota.

THE FOSSILS:

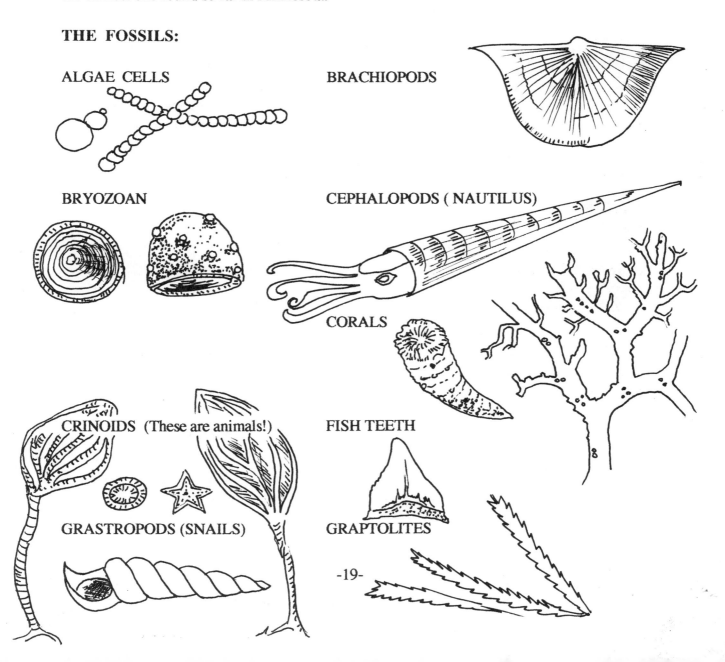

ALGAE CELLS

BRACHIOPODS

BRYOZOAN

CEPHALOPODS (NAUTILUS)

CORALS

CRINOIDS (These are animals!)

FISH TEETH

GRASTROPODS (SNAILS)

GRAPTOLITES

-19-

MAMMOTH TOOTH

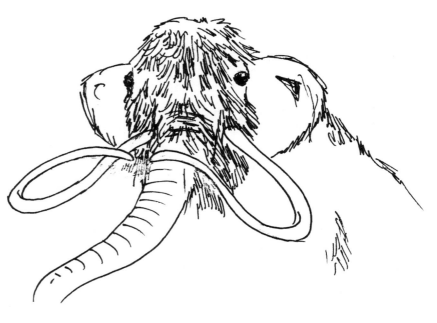

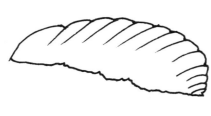

POLLEN

SPEAR POINT

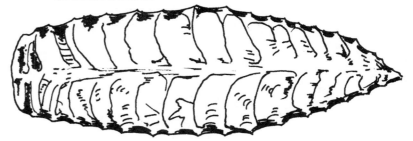

SPONGES

TRILOBITES

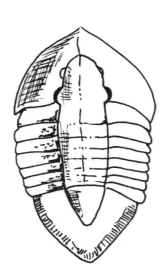

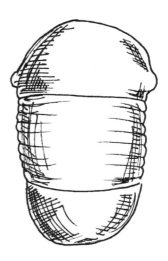

Chapter 5

Animal Behavior

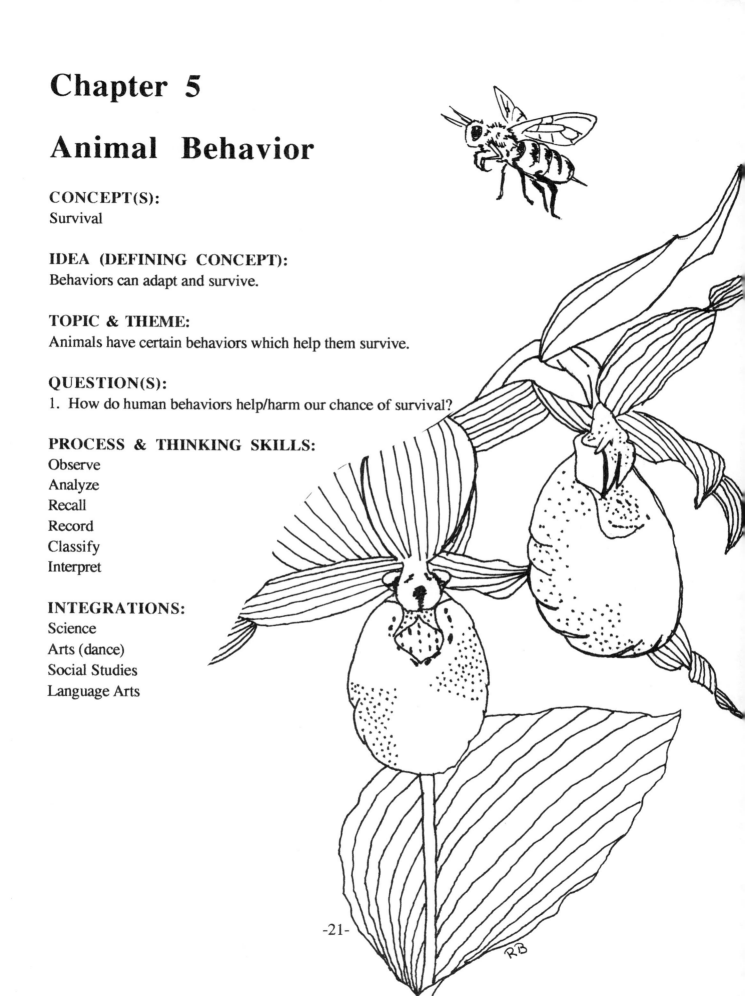

CONCEPT(S):
Survival

IDEA (DEFINING CONCEPT):
Behaviors can adapt and survive.

TOPIC & THEME:
Animals have certain behaviors which help them survive.

QUESTION(S):
1. How do human behaviors help/harm our chance of survival?

PROCESS & THINKING SKILLS:
Observe
Analyze
Recall
Record
Classify
Interpret

INTEGRATIONS:
Science
Arts (dance)
Social Studies
Language Arts

ANIMAL BEHAVIOR

THE STORIES:

Why the Loon Laughs and Cries --   An Ojibwe Legend

The Early Times were full of beauty and peace. The tribes of humans and animals had a single language. As First Man, Winabozho, walked among them, they all spoke together and understood each other perfectly. The language was beautiful. No creature hunted then.

The Great Spirit, Gichi Manidoo, gave a special gift to each animal for its own happiness. Fish swam in the cool lakes, birds flew in the warm air, wolves ran fast across the sparkling snow. The Anishinaabe, The People, made wigwams, looms, drums and flutes.

The creatures were happy at first. But soon they wanted more happiness and became greedy. The creatures squabbled all the time, fighting over each others gifts. Animals and people hunted each other, turning the beautiful world into a place of fear and death. Winabozho prepared a feast for all the creatures, hoping to make them happy again, but they even fought over who could sit in the places of honor. Each demanded, " I want to eat *first!*" Winabozho was disgusted.

He paddled his canoe out on the lake and thundered, "Silence!!! Gichi Manidoo has given each of you special gifts, but you don't appreciate them. You only want what the others have. He gave you one language so you could share ideas, and happiness. All you do is fight! You do not deserve this gift."

As the canoe drifted toward the horizon, Loon bravely swam after it. He pleaded, "Oh, please stay! Oh, give us another chance!"

Shaking his head sadly, Winabozho said, "Loon, when the all creatures have stopped fighting, then I will return. " And his canoe drifted away into the rising moon. After a terrible silence, all the creatures began talking. NO! NO! Each had a new and awful language. Bears growled, lynx screamed, owls screeched, people shouted, babies cried. They made horrible sounds.

Loon fearfully tried his voice. Oh! Astonishing! It sounded just the same! Winabozho had left Loon alone to sing in the beautiful original language. When Loon laughs he is enjoying his special gift. When Loon cries, he is remembering that Winabozho will never return until there is peace over all the earth.

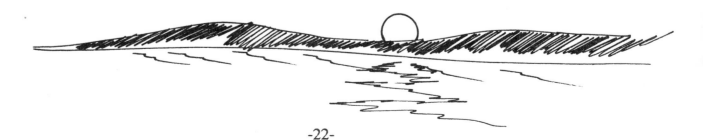

THE FACTS:

Communication: How does howling help wolves survive?
When two wolf packs meet accidentally on the edges of their territories, there is often a fight, and one or two wolves are killed. Howling can be heard six miles away and warns other packs not to come too close. Wolf packs usually don't want to waste energy fighting each other.

Symbiosis: How do hummingbirds and flowers help each other survive?
Hummingbirds get nectar from flowers. They live on the nectar. When they put their long beaks into the flowers their chests and throats become covered with pollen. So, when the hummingbird goes to the next flower, the flower is pollinated by the bird.

Caring for Young: How does care of young help "long ears" survive?
Snowshoe hares live in a harsh climate, so their babies are fully developed at birth--covered with fur, eyes open, and able to hop around. If the parents are killed, the babies still have a chance of survival. Females nurse five minutes a day. Within three days the baby hares can be on their own. Cottontail rabbits often live in a milder climate and have more time to care for their babies. These bunnies are born naked, blind and helpless. Mother rabbits take care of their babies for a month or more.

Group Living: How does the herd help deer survive?
A deer's eyes are set to the back of its head. The head is on top of a long neck. The whole thing works like a submarine periscope. When herd members raise their heads, there are many pairs of eyes to scan over the tops of brush and grasses -- to watch out for predators.
Caribou have leg joints that click as they walk. The sound probably helps keep the herd together.

Reflex, Instinct and Learned Behavior: How do reflex, instinct and learned behavior help blue jays survive?
When the bluejay flies, reflex makes the third eyelid brush across the eye, keeping it moist in the dry air currents.
Blue jays follow instincts in caring for young and nest building.
Bluejays can learn to mimic the songs of other birds, like red-tailed hawks and crows, to provide protection.

Inborn Social Behavior: How does inborn social behavior help walleye fish survive?
Walleyes live in schools, which protect the young by providing a good cover of large strong fish around them. Like the herd, there are many pairs of eyes to watch for danger.

THE ACTIVITIES:

1. Traditional Dance: Many cultures express a theme of animal survival in the arts. American Indian dances often feature nature's survival patterns in songs, outfits, drumming, and dance steps. African-Americans, Asians, Hispanics, and Europeans all express similar themes in different ways. An opera tells about the life and death of a fox. A ballet expresses the love between a beautiful swan and a prince. Maria Tallchief, Apache, was one of the most famous ballerinas to dance the part of the swan.

Watch a video of the American Indian Dance Theatre and/or Swan Lake.

Brainstorm a list of all the animal survival patterns you can find.

Create the plan for a dance that could be performed for the American Indian Dance Theatre or the Royal Winnipeg Ballet.

Choose predator and prey animals, and research the behaviors that help them survive. List all the survival behaviors they exhibit.

Classify them: Are they Reflex, Instinct or Learned?

Sketch outfits and sets for your production.

Select pre-recorded music or animal sounds, or make up your own music using simple instruments.

The plan can be for a short or long dance (three minutes or an hour).

Plan the steps and movements that will let the dancers "become" the animals.

A long dance could tell the story of a legend, like the loon.

Make a poster to advertise your Dance Company.

Make a Dance Program describing in words the behaviors you are expressing.

2. Extensions With Friends:

   Rehearse and perform your dances in outfits, with sets and music.

   Teach the dances to younger children.

   Photograph or video tape the dances.

   Sell calendars or tapes of the dances to earn money for a school animal project or field trip.

3. How and Why Stories:

   At the library, find a How and Why Story that explains animal behavior from your culture.

   Make a story board (like a big cartoon strip) to retell the story.

   At the end, write the animal behaviors that help it survive.

   Invent your own How and Why Story.

   Write and illustrate it. At the end, write the animal behaviors that help it survive.

Chapter 6

Life Cycles

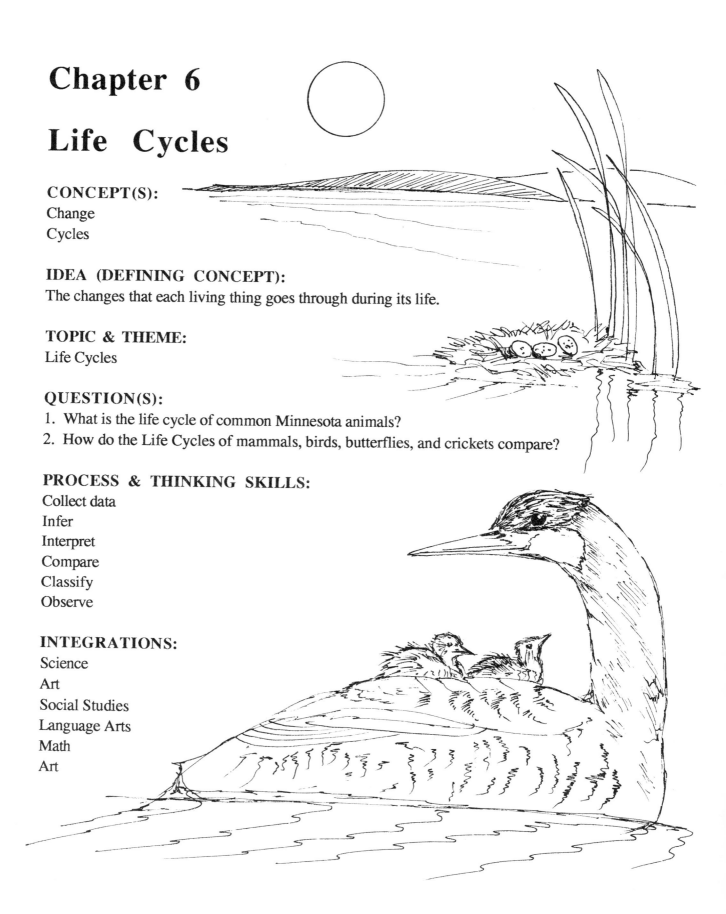

CONCEPT(S):
Change
Cycles

IDEA (DEFINING CONCEPT):
The changes that each living thing goes through during its life.

TOPIC & THEME:
Life Cycles

QUESTION(S):
1. What is the life cycle of common Minnesota animals?
2. How do the Life Cycles of mammals, birds, butterflies, and crickets compare?

PROCESS & THINKING SKILLS:
Collect data
Infer
Interpret
Compare
Classify
Observe

INTEGRATIONS:
Science
Art
Social Studies
Language Arts
Math
Art

LIFE CYCLES

THE SYMBOLS: Anishinaabe people invented symbols to express ideas.

Circle of the Earth

Circle of Heaven

Student and Teacher • Circle of
Heaven

Basket Design

Dream Catcher

Wigwam Floor Plan

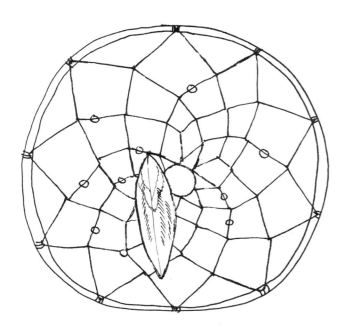

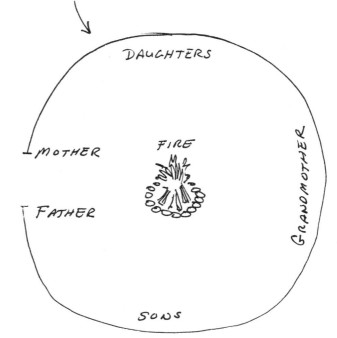

THE ACTIVITIES:

1. Invent your own Life Circle Symbols. Use them to tell a story.

2. Discover and compare the life cycles of familiar animals by making Life Cycle Circles.
   Making a Life Cycle Medicine Wheel
   a.) To the Teacher: Make one copy of the Animal List on Page 29 ; cut it into strips along lines.
   Make one copy of the Life Stages page for each student.

   b.) Students assemble in groups of four. Each group has a strip of four animals.
   Each student chooses a different animal from the strip.
   (Hint: To avoid conflicts over the choices, have students in each group select and write down a
   color -- red, yellow, black, or white, BEFORE they get the strip of animal names. Then say:
   Reds are mammals, Yellows are birds, fish and reptiles, Blacks are butterflies, and Whites are
   other insects."

   c.)Students research the life cycle of their animal in classroom books and field guides.

   d.) Making the Circle: Students cut out circles from construction paper.
   Mammals use red paper. Birds, Fish and Reptiles use yellow paper.
   Butterflies use black paper. Other Insects use white paper.

   e.) When research is complete. Students can sketch and color the life cycles
   onto the paper. -OR- They can use pictures from magazines. -OR- They can cut out sketches
   made on light paper, and paste them onto the circle. The Life Cycle should be labeled.
   Students may want to use an Ojibwe circle symbol around the edge. For example, the Eagle
   Life Cycle could be surrounded by the Circle of Heaven Symbol.

   g.) On the reverse side, students can write the Life Cycle with Ojibwe words and symbols,
   inventing any additional symbols as needed.

   h.) Students should fill in the Life Stages Chart, using information from all group members.

3) Hatch butterfly chrysalises or moth cocoons.
   a) Collect and record your observations. Make graphs to compare your results.
   b) Can you draw any conclusions?
   c) Draw and paint a design showing the life of one of these insects.

ANIMAL LIST

MAMMAL	FISH/BIRD/REPTILE	BUTTERFLY	OTHER INSECT
MARTEN*	CRANE*	MONARCH	GRASSHOPPER
BEAR*	CATFISH*	BLACK SWALLOWTAIL	BEETLE
WOLF*	PIKE*	SWALLOWTAIL	PRAYING MANTIS
LYNX*	LOON*	SULPHUR BUTTERFLY	CRICKET
MOOSE*	SNAKE*	CABBAGE BUTTERFLY	CICADA
OTTER*	EAGLE*	GT. SPANGLED BUTTERFLY	DRAGONFLY
BEAVER*	CORMORANT*	ISABELLA MOTH	DAMSEL FLY
DEER*	GOOSE*	LUNA MOTH	MAYFLY
MUSKRAT	SUCKER*	CECROPIA MOTH	HONEYBEE
OPOSSUM	STURGEON*	POLYPHEMUS BUTTERFLY	MOSQUITO
FOX	WHITEFISH*	GYPSY MOTH	LADYBUG/BIRD
PORCUPINE	GULL*	PROMETHA MOTH	FIREFLY
SKUNK	HAWK*	ADMIRAL BUTTERFLY	STINKBUG

LIFE STAGES PAGE

MY NAME _____

PEOPLE IN MY GROUP_____

FOR EACH ANIMAL IN YOUR GROUP, GIVE ITS NAME IN TWO LANGUAGES. YOU MIGHT CHOOSE OJIBWE, GERMAN, FRENCH, SPANISH, RUSSIAN...

I. MAMMAL'S NAME IN ENGLISH AND ANOTHER LANGUAGE.
_____

LIST THE LIFE STAGES FOR YOUR GROUP'S MAMMAL

2, BIRD, FISH, REPTILE: NAME THIS ANIMAL IN ENGLISH AND ANOTHER LANGUAGE. LIST THE LIFE STAGES OF THE ANIMAL.

3. BUTTERFLY/MOTH. NAME THS ANIMAL IN ENGLISH AND ANOTHER LANGUAGE. LIST THE LIFE STAGES OF THE ANIMAL.

4. OTHER INSECT. NAME THIS ANIMAL IN ENGLISH AND ANOTHER LANGUAGE. LIST THE LIFE STAGES OF THE ANIMAL.

Chapter 7

The Insect World

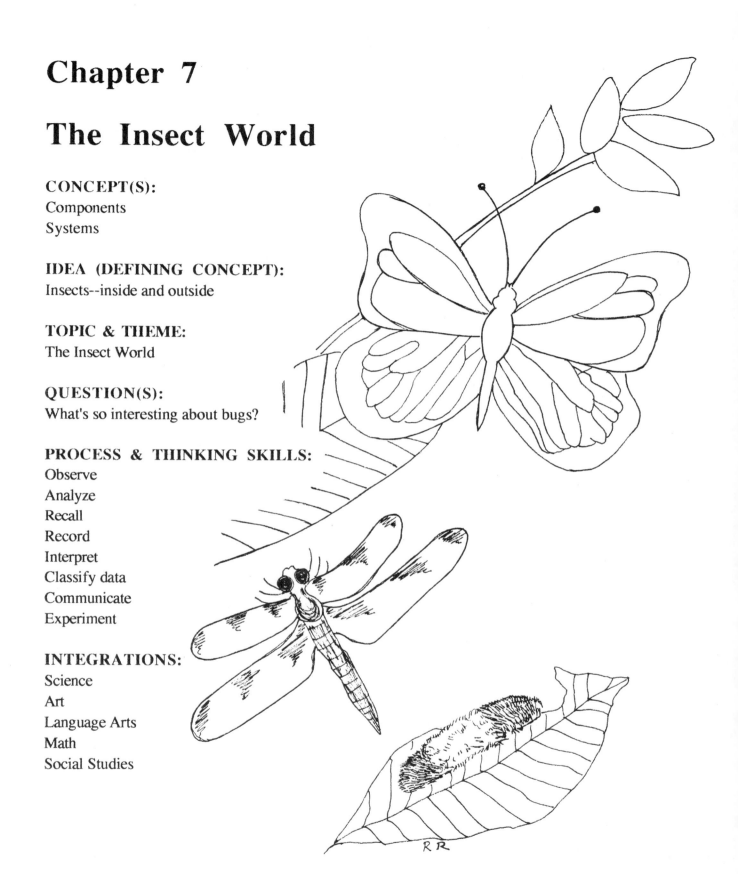

CONCEPT(S):
Components
Systems

IDEA (DEFINING CONCEPT):
Insects--inside and outside

TOPIC & THEME:
The Insect World

QUESTION(S):
What's so interesting about bugs?

PROCESS & THINKING SKILLS:
Observe
Analyze
Recall
Record
Interpret
Classify data
Communicate
Experiment

INTEGRATIONS:
Science
Art
Language Arts
Math
Social Studies

THE INSECT WORLD

THE FACTS:

Insects have no bones. Their skeleton is on the outside instead of the inside! They are covered with armor, which is like your fingernail. Armor doesn't grow. When the young insect (nymph) gets too big for its skeleton, the old armor breaks and the nymph crawls out, wearing a bigger skeleton.
Crickets grow in three stages: eggs, nymphs and adults.
(Nymphs look like little adults, growing into bigger armor all the time.)
Moths grow in four stages: eggs, larva , pupa (cocoon), adult.
(Larva look like worms or caterpillars, shedding their skin like nymphs.)

Inside the armor: Inside the <u>head</u> the tiny brain is connected to the eyes, antennae and mouth.
The <u>thorax</u> is loaded with muscles that move six legs and sometimes wings. Everything else is packed into the <u>abdomen</u>, including organs for digestion, reproduction, stinging, breathing, and even the heart!

Prehistoric insects lived more than 300 million years ago. One dragonfly fossil has a wing spread of 30 inches -- bigger than a wood duck!
Insects today range in size from the Fairy Fly (only one hundredth of an inch long) to the Atlas Moth, with a 12 inch wingspread (about like an oriole!)

About a million insect species are known in the world today. Insects have adapted to live nearly everywhere -- in the Himalayas (20,000 feet above sea level), in the polar regions, in deserts, on the surface of the oceans, in 120 degree water, frozen solid at 30 below zero, in almost pure salt, and in pools of crude oil.

Ants can haul stones that weigh 50 times more than they do. That's like a person carrying 7,500 pounds! If people could jump like a grasshopper, we could leap over two train engines -- lengthwise!

How fast can insects fly? A house fly flies as fast as a human on a brisk walk -- four -five mph. Butterflies and honey bees fly at more than twice that speed: 12-13 mph. Dragonflies zoom along as fast as a horse runs -- 25 mph! Their wings probably evolved from leg flaps of prehistoric crickets.

Fireflies are really beetles with soft bodies. Their body chemistry reacts with fatty tissue and air to make a very cool light. This is surprising, because most light is very warm. Scientists are still studying this.

Insects have to sleep with their eyes open because they have no eyelids.
They have compound eyes, composed of many hexagonal connected lenses.
They also have three small focusing eyes. We don't know what an insect <u>really</u> sees, but it's probably like pictures printed in magazine, made up of tiny separated dots.
(Look at a magazine picture and an insect eye under a magnifier!)

Insects see color differently than humans do.   Bees see yellow-green and blue-violet. They also see ultraviolet, which is beyond human sight. (Birds see infra-red.) Bright red looks black to an insect. Light that comes from the North, South, East and West has its own special quality. People can't see any difference, but insects can tell directions from the differences in this light.

Insect musicians fiddle and drum to make sounds that can be heard a mile away. A spiney scraper on the grasshopper's leg rubs across a thick vein on its wing. The insect's body amplifies the sound. It's like a violin. When the bow glides over the strings, the sound is amplified by the air inside the violin. Cicadas use muscles to vibrate the drum heads on their abdomens.

How do insects hear the sounds they make?
"Singing insects" like grasshoppers have hearing sensors on their legs or abdomens.
Mosquitoes sense vibrations at the base of their antennae.
Moths don't make any sounds, but they can hear the sonar sounds of the bats that hunt them.

Antennae are used for smelling, tasting, and feeling.
Insects don't have noses. They breathe through air tubes in the abdomen.
Some moths can smell a mate a mile away. Butterflies have their taste sensors on their feet.
If you were a butterfly and wanted to taste your birthday cake, you would have to step on it!

Mouth-parts show special adaptations too. Baby tiger beetles look like tiny sabre-toothed tigers. The mouth on an acorn weevil is as long as its leg, for drilling into acorn shells. Some moths and butterflies have a long tongue that rolls up into a neat coil. The tongue may be as long as the whole body!

Insect legs are adapted for use as paddles, baskets, nets, shovels, shears, and brushes. Two claws and moist bristles on each foot help insects walk on glassy surfaces.

THE ACTIVITIES:

1. Real Micro-World Insects: Collect insects, eggs, and insect homes. Look at them under a microscopes or magnifiers, draw and label what you see. Look at air tube openings, stingers, compound eye lenses, mouth parts, antenna, and wings.
   (See Resource List for Magnifiers and Magiscopes.)

2. Imagination Insects: Children will create their own insect that exhibits true insect structure: three body parts, jointed legs, compound eye and antennae.
   Materials: 2-4 oz. of modeling clay (half stick to a stick), glue, tape, brass paper fasteners, scissors, a collection of odds and ends: pebbles, shells, beads, paper scraps, glitter, seeds, pine needles, small twigs, tissue paper, foil, wax paper, sequins, feathers, bottle caps, pipe cleaners, straws ... .

   1. Imagine your insect. Try to visualize it in your mind.
   2. Make the insect's body from the clay. (Be sure it has all three parts!)
   3. Add jointed legs, mouth parts, compound and focusing eyes, antenna.
   4. Add special adaptations (wings, camouflage, stinger, sound structures....)
   5. Name your insect. (It might have the student's name as part of its name.)
   6. Write a Scientific Report about your insect, using the following pages.
   Be sure to include: Name, habitat, food, predators, shelter, life cycle,
   pupa, migrations, social habits, instinct....Tell about the adaptation of
   legs and mouth parts, if it sends or receives sound, how it attracts a
   mate, the purpose of antennae shape and size, use and/or harm the insect does.

3. Research/Debate : Looking at real issues in science.
   Talk about the following questions in class. Have each student choose a side to research.
   Give them at least a couple of days to research and talk to people. Students can write a
   paragraph to a page supporting their ideas. Each side can choose a few students to read their
   papers in class. Then have students research and argue the other side. It's good thinking
   practice!
   How do insects help or hurt people, pets or crops? How much damage can certain insects do?
   How much can they help people? Are some insects both helpful and harmful ? How did
   ancient people and early immigrants use helpful insects? How did they cope with harmful
   ones? How can people use and control insects without harming the environment? If the insect
   is very dangerous or very useful how much environmental harm is acceptable?
   How do insects and government interface?

IMAGINATION-INSECT REPORTING SHEET

My Imagination-Insect is called a _____,
because it

It lives in (habitat and environment)

It eats and drinks

It is prey for

It finds shelter in

This is my insect's life cycle. It has _____ stages:

It lays its eggs on

The larva and pupa or nymphs look like this:

My insect has this common behavior: (migration or social behavior). This is how it works for my
Imaginary Insect.

My insect has a strange behavior. It is

My insect's leg looks like this.
It has been adapted to
My insect's mouth parts look like this:
It has been adapted to:

This is how my insect makes sound.

This is how it "hears" sound.

This is how my insect's antennae look.
They are shaped for

My insect attracts it mate by:

My insect hides from or fights off predators by:

This is how my insect is helpful or harmful (or both) .

This is how scientists could use or control my insect.

Chapter 8

The Cell

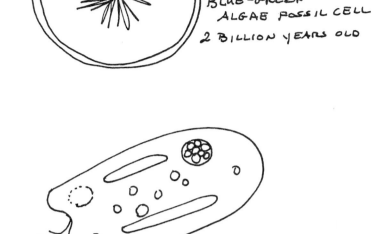

BLUE-GREEN ALGAE FOSSIL CELL 2 BILLION YEARS OLD

CONCEPT(S):
Components
Structures
Patterns

IDEA (DEFINING CONCEPT):
Cells and Homes have structures.

TOPIC & THEME:
The cell

GOLDEN ALGAE CELL

QUESTION(S):
Why is a cell like a home?

PROCESS & THINKING SKILLS:
Observe
Analyze
Recall
Record
Compare
Interpret

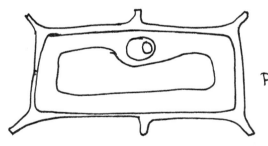

PLANT CELL

INTEGRATIONS:
Science
Art
Social Studies

BLOOD CELL

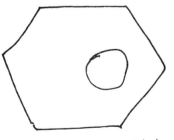

MOUTH CELL

THE CELL

The Architecture of Wigams and Cells:

Wigwams and cells have an outer covering.
Wigwams have **birch bark (wigwas)**. Cells have a **membrane**.

Most wigwams and cells have an important core.
Wigwams have a **fire (ishkote)** for family gatherings, cooking, and warmth.
Cells have a **nucleus** which is the control center for the cell's work.

The space between the outer covering and core is not "empty".
In the Wigwam the space has air, people, **food (miijim)** and **water (nibi)**.

In the Cell, the space has **cytoplasm**, food and water.

In wigwams, air, sound, and smells can pass through the birch bark. Food and water can be passed into the wigwam. Waste can be removed too.
In Cells, water carries food and waste through the membrane.

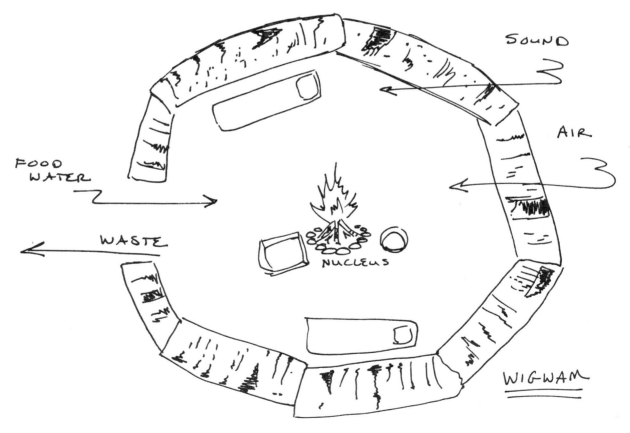

THE ACTIVITIES:

1. Make a sketch comparing the design of the wigwam and the Cell.

2. **Pictographic Cells**

   Dr. Lloyd Cooke, a Cherokee chemist, was diving in the ocean.
   What he saw when he emerged from the water amazed him:
   An ancient pictograph (rock picture) showing a perfect microscopic cell!

   --How could ancient people have known what it looked like?
   --What makes a magnifier?
   --What could the ancient people have used for a magnifier?
   --How do you think they explained the presence of the cell?

   Invent and Write a believable one-page story (more if you wish!) about a
   curious Young Ancient Person and his or her discovery of cells. The Young Ancient Person
   can be from your own culture.

3. **Make a magnifier** out of simple natural things. Experiment. Record your results.

4. **Look through a magnifier** at a drop of pond water. Find an animal or
   plant. Sketch what you see. Label the main parts. Try to identify it.

5. **Build Your own Cell Model.** Make it as creative as you can, while using
   the science facts.   Ideas: pictographs in plaster of paris, clay or jello.
   Compare to homes of other peoples (tipis, hogans, igloos, cabins, ancient
   European, African, or Asian dwellings.)

Chapter 9

Communities

CONCEPT(S):
Relationships
Interactions

IDEA (DEFINING CONCEPT):
All things are connected.

TOPIC & THEME: Connections.

QUESTION(S):
How are living things connected to each other and their environment?

PROCESS & THINKING SKILLS:
Observe
Analyze
Recall
Record
Collect data
Interpret
Sequence
Communicate

INTEGRATIONS
Science
Language Arts
Social Studies
Art
Math

COMMUNITIES

THE FACTS:

The Environment: everything that surrounds and affects a living thing.
Wild rice is surrounded by water, sun, air, fish, frogs, raccoons and people.

Ecosystem: a group of living things and their interactions with their non-
living environment. Wild rice needs light and the chemicals of earth, water and air to live.

Community: All living things that live and interact with each other in a place.
When high waters ruined the rice crop at Pilliger in 1849, the fish became scarce, too. The band of
1000 people moved onto the grasslands to hunt . Rice worms and carp damage the rice crop.
Predators eat worms and carp.

Population: A group of the same kind of living things in a community.
The walleye population depends on the minnow population.

Habitat: A special place in a community in which all living things live.
Wild rice habitat is clean, slow-moving water that is rich in minerals.

Niche: The role played by each living thing in its habitat.
Wild rice and muskrats live in the lakes and streams.

Population size is affected by many things. In a good rice year there is food for all. Duck
populations grow. When there are too many ducks for the food supply, they die off until the food
supply can support the population size.

Succession: A series of changes that take place in a community ecosystem.
A rice bed may eventually fill with silt until it becomes part of the forest.

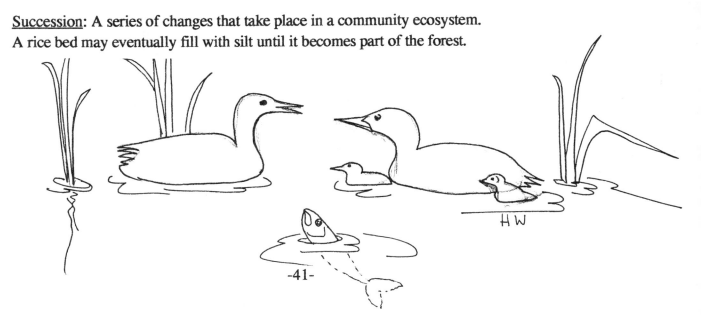

The Language of Communities :

air	ishpeming	**minnow**	giigoozens
beadwork	namidoominensikaan	**muskrat (s)**	wazhashk (wa)
clean	biinaagami	**people**	bemaadizidjig
ducks	zhiisiibag	**racoon**	esiban
earth	aki	**stream**	ziibiins
fish	giigoo	**sun**	giizis
forest	zazaakwaa	**walleye**	ogah
frog	omakakii	**water**	nibi
grasslands	mashkodi	**much water**	nibiika
inhabits	abiit	**deep water**	dimii
lake	zaaga 'igaans	**Wild rice**	mahnomen
lives	bimaadizi	**worms**	mooseg

ACTIVITY:

1. Write a fiction story or unrhymed poem about Communities using as many of <u>The Language Ojibwe</u> words as you can. For words that are not on this list, look them up in a book like <u>An Ojibwe Word Resource Book</u>, by Nichols and Nyholm. Or, you use English words. Or, you can draw a simple pictograph to represent the missing word or idea. Underline the Ojibwe words.

   If you draw pictographs, make a key, explaining what they mean.

   Other languages are welcome too!

   Be sure to show that you understand the ideas listed in The Facts on page 41.

BIOME CHARACTERISTICS:

BIOME: A large ecosystem containing similar populations and climate.

Tundra: Far north (or on tops of very high mountains) usual temperature is below freezing, little precipitation, no trees, permafrost.
Summer: a little thawing for two months, lichens, mosses, grasses, birds, reindeer, Arctic foxes, wolves, birds of prey, lemmings, voles, marmots.

Taiga: Forest ecosystems, just south of the tundra (or a little lower on the mountains) . Taiga has more rain than tundra. Trees are more than 20 meters tall --mostly evergreens with some aspen. There are moss and lichens. All year: deer, moose, bears, bighorn sheep, goats, rabbits, porcupines, small birds. Summers are longer; higher temperatures; wildflowers and waterfowl.

Temperate Forest: Have four seasons -- each about three months. The Temperate Forest has bears, deer, foxes, raccoons, opossums, squirrels, insects and birds, wildflowers, ferns and mosses.

Tropical Rain Forest: Located near the Equator where it rains every day. High temperatures all year. Plants can be 30-40 meters tall. There are palm and tree ferns, vines and fungi, large predator/prey populations including tigers, leopards, pythons, insects, spiders, tree frogs, monkeys, snakes and birds.

Grasslands: Most plants are grasses because there is little rain. There are a few trees along streams. Grassland animals are: hares, bison, antelope, badgers, prairie dogs, moles, ground squirrels, gophers, song birds, birds of prey.

Desert: Has a dry climate which means that the days are usually warm, and the nights are cool. Plants are cacti which have small leaves and thorns to conserve water. Animals of the desert are snakes, lizards, kangaroo rats, tortoises, jackrabbits, some birds, invertebrates...

Freshwater lakes and ponds have plants and protists: algae, water lilies, cattails, fish, snakes, crayfish and insects, frogs, muskrats and beavers.

Saltwater Biomes (marine) cover most of the earth's surface. Most organisms live near the surface (producers need light to make food for consumers) microscopic life, also whales, dolphins, seals, shrimp, fish, seaweed, jellyfish, lobsters, clams, starfish.

Ecotones: Blended Biome Boundaries. Minnesota is an ecotone of Taiga, Temperate Forest, Grassland, and Freshwater Biomes.

MORE ACTIVITIES:

2. Biome Diorama
    A. <u>Choose a biome</u>: Make a diorama of one habitat in the biome. You may want to choose a biome related in some way to your culture. (This can be done with a friend, by a small group, or by yourself. If you work with a group, you may each want to make your own diorama. Your dioramas can show different seasons, animals, or habitats of the same biome.)

    B. <u>Research your biome</u>:
    What kind of living and non-living things are found in this ecosystem? (Include people.)
    How are they connected in their ecosystem?
    How do the different populations interact within the community?
    What different habitats would you find in this biome?
    What niches do different plants and animals hold in the habitat?
    What things affect the size of different populations?
    What is the natural succession of your habitat?
    How do the living things interact? Your diorama should show the climate, plants, and animals. (Be sure the season and weather are clearly shown.)
    What are the cycles of water, nitrogen, carbon-dioxide?
    What are the producers, consumers, scavengers and decomposers?

    C. <u>Construct your diorama</u>. Use a box, natural things and human-made items.

3. <u>Communicating</u>: Write and illustrate a story based on your biome research.
    Include the information from the questions above. Use correct vocabulary.
    To show <u>Succession</u>: Draw 4 pictures to show the gradual changes in the habitat of your diorama. <u>Interaction</u>: (Explain or draw and label the interactions that take place in your habitat: competition, parasite/host, or cooperation?
    <u>Draw and label 4 cycles</u> in your biome: the water cycle, the Nitrogen cycle, the carbon-dioxide/oxygen cycles, the producer-to-decomposer cycle.
    (See sample cycles on pages 45 A and 45 B.)

4. <u>Draw a food chain</u>, food web, and energy pyramid for your habitat.
    Groups may want to make big chains, webs and pyramids for bulletin boards.

5. <u>Graphing</u>: As a class, make graphs to compare the biomes:
    summer and winter temperatures, average rain fall, biggest and smallest animals
    density of human population, and anything else can you think of...

6. Invent a game

    The class is formed into small groups.

    Each group invents a game based on a different Communities concept.

    Each group teaches the game to the class. Class members play all
    games. (You may want to laminate cards and game boards for durability.)

SOME IDEAS:

Rummy or Old Maid type card games:

    A "pair" is the science vocabulary word and its definition.

    Or a pair is a picture of an animal and its habitat,

    Or a pair can show relationships: host/parasite, or predator/prey.....

Board games are good for learning sequences or cycles:

Bingo/lotto games can be used when there are several parts to a concept:

    Biome Bingo might have a different Biome and nine traits listed on large
    Bingo cards. The matching biome characteristics are written on small
    cards, to be drawn by the caller. Three in a row or blackout wins.

Outdoor games can show predator/prey, food chains, food webs, pyramids....

7. Biome Beadwork

    Some of today's most exciting art is being created by people who are able to "connect all
    things" -- especially science, art, and math. They rely on the classic traditions of beads or
    bronze, clay or marble, ink or paint, but use them in new ways that feature strong designs.

Sketch a design based on the idea of a food web or energy pyramid.

Make the design with beads or with opaque paint on colored paper.

Use another medium if you wish.

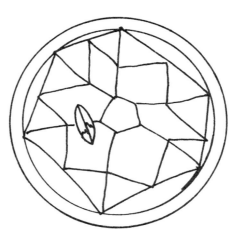

WATER CYCLE

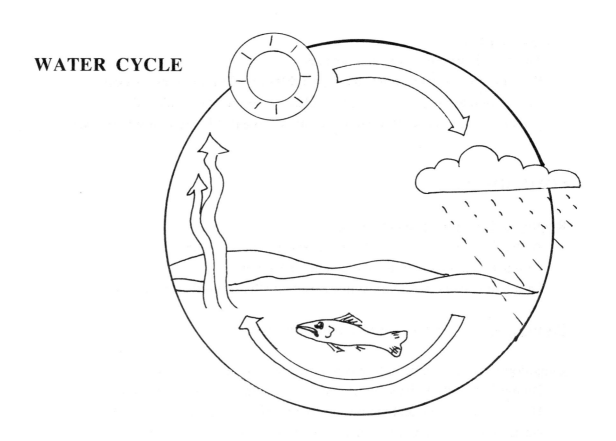

PRODUCER-CONSUMER-SCAVENGER-DECOMPOSER CYCLE

-45A-

CARBON DIOXIDE CYCLE

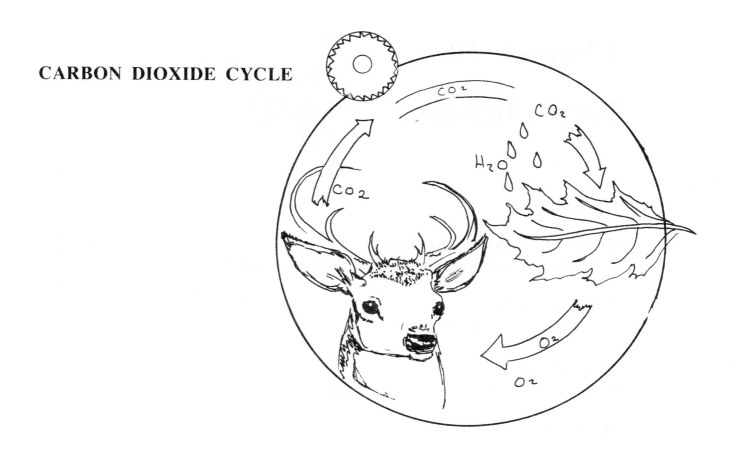

NITROGEN CYCLE

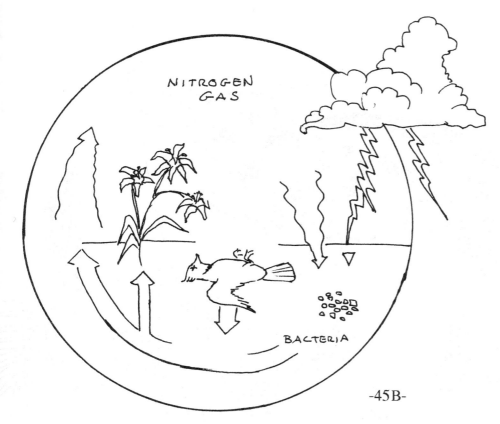

-45B-

Chapter 10

Reproduction

CONCEPT(S):
Systems
Structures

IDEA (DEFINING CONCEPT):
Living things reproduce, making offspring that are like themselves.

TOPIC & THEME:
Reproductions of plants and animals.

QUESTION(S):
How do some Minnesota living things reproduce?

PROCESS & THINKING SKILLS:
Classify
Compare
Observe
Record
Communicate
Interpret
Measuring
Experiment
Predictions

INTEGRATIONS:
Science
Math
Social Studies

REPRODUCTION

THE FACTS:

1. About 1820 an epidemic broke out among the Anishinaabe at Leech Lake. Someone wrote down their symptoms, which were like pneumonia. One hundred and fifty years later, the disease was identified as tularemia. The bacteria (a moneran) responsible for the disease lives in a habitat of water and mud -- exactly like wild rice! Bacteria is reproduced by mitosis (single cell-division.) This is one parent (asexual) reproduction.

2. Hydra are some of the teeming microscopic plant life that makes up the food for insect larva, which are eaten by insects, which are eaten by tadpoles and little fish, which are eaten by bigger fish, which are eaten by people! Hydra reproduce by budding, which is also asexual reproduction.

3. Sometimes tadpoles will regenerate (grow back) legs that have been lost. Earth worms will regenerate tails. Wild potatoes and bullrushes reproduce by regeneration.

4. The Anishinaabe used sasaparilla as medicine. European immigrants used it for making root beer. Sarsaparilla plants reproduce sexually with clusters of small white flowers. They can be found in dry and wet woodland forests. White flowers are often pollinated by bees.

5. Animals like fish and deer reproduce sexually with two parents.

6. Traditional Woodland Foods:

Vegetables:	Meat:	Seasonings:
wild rice	bear	mountain mint
corn	deer	maple sugar
pumpkins	duck	bearberry
squash	moose	wild ginger
wild potatoes	rabbit	
root of bullrush	beaver	Teas: leaves or twigs
acorns	(all trapped animals	raspberry
milkweed flowers	except marten)	wintergreen
berries and fruit	fish	spruce
	fish eggs	snowberry
		wild cherry

THE ACTIVITIES:

1. Reproduction of Traditional Foods. Divide the list of foods so each child has one item, or each cooperative group has a few items to research.
   Collect samples or find detailed pictures of the traditional food.
   Draw the food as it appears in nature. Use basic geometric shapes.
   Research the reproduction.
   Compile the class information into a bar graph.
   > How many foods are from different kingdoms?
   > How many reproduce sexually ? How many asexually?
   > How many reproduce by mitosis (single cell divsion)?
   > How many by meiosis (two parents) ?
   > How many reproduce by regeneration, budding, flower?
   > For each species, what are some factors that determine their numbers (the population?)
   > Brainstorm other information to be included.

   > How many other ways can you find to communicate this information?
   > What determines which is the best way? Is there more than one "best" way?

2. Traditional Foods Lab
   Collect seeds from traditional plant foods.
   Try to grow them inside by replicating natural conditions as much as possible.
   Keep daily records of amount of water, growth.
   Make predictions and draw conclusions about other plants. Experiment with them.

3. Cell Division Dances. Create two dances to demonstrate cell division.
   Create a Country line dance (with two lines) to demonstrate meiosis.
   Create a European or Anishinaabe circle dance to demonstrate mitosis.
   > Hints: Draw or write out the steps of cell division first.
   The dancers can be the cell membrane and nuclear membrane.
   > More dancers can be the chromatin and chromosomes.
   > How can outfits help show pairs of chromosomes?
   > Use traditional recorded music.
   > Rehearse and perform the dance.

4. Feast
   With a group of parents create a community feast or sampling of traditional foods from your school. Display your projects and dances at the feast.

Chapter 11

Heredity

CONCEPT(S):
Patterns

IDEA (DEFINING CONCEPT):
Heredity occurs when parents pass traits to their offspring.

TOPIC & THEME:
Heredity

QUESTION(S):
How are traits passed on?
What role did traditional people play in heredity?

PROCESS & THINKING SKILLS:
Observe
Record
Recall
Infer
Analyze
Compare
Classify
Interpret
Collect data
Predict
Experiment
Communicate

INTEGRATIONS:
Science
Art
Social studies
Language arts
Math

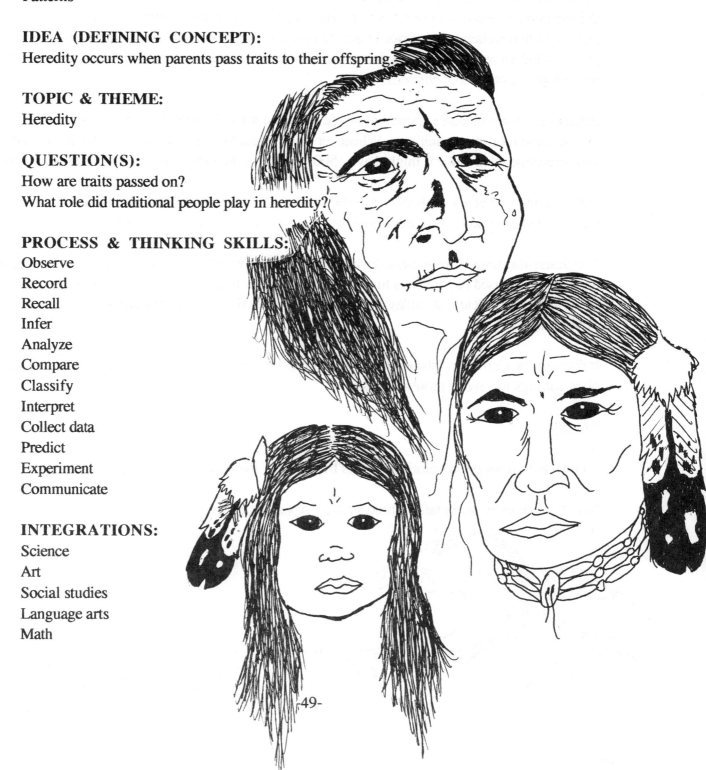

HEREDITY

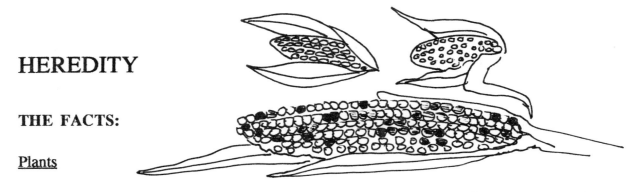

THE FACTS:

<u>Plants</u>

Much of modern genetic plant science is based on the practical efforts of the New World farmers. Ojibwe people spread wild rice from one lake to another so it could grow in new areas. Sometimes they identified certain traits of rice in order to grow different kinds of rice in different lakes and ponds. Modern research on wild rice might help identify even more potential food value, to help feed people of other cold climates.

Ancient Peruvian Indians experimentally developed corn and potatoes for many different soils, climates and moisture conditions. Whenever a new mutation was identified, they tried to develop it and determine what value it might have. 500 years ago, the Incas grew 3,000 kinds of potatoes!

Indian farmers selected seeds of corn to be planted. By placing pollen from one kind of corn onto the silk of another kind, they developed hybrids like sweet corn and popcorn!

The desert-dwelling Hopi Indians developed blue corn, which grew on a short stem. Its special trait was that it used the precious limited irrigation water to grow ears of corn, rather than long stems and leaves. Scientists today are trying to replicate the corn that the Hopi developed hundreds of years ago.

Indians of the Carribean Islands developed tropical plants, like pineapples and yams, by taking plant cuttings for over a thousand years.

<u>Animals</u>

Inuit (Eskimo) people domesticated dogs by breeding the tamest wolves over many generations.

Nez Pierce Indians successfully bred striking Appaloosa horses.

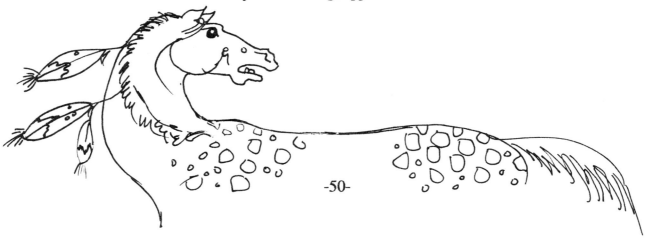

THE ACTIVITIES:

1. Genetics in the Traditional Foods Lab

   As a class or in small groups start genetics projects with the traditional food plants.
   Record your results on "family trees" or with Punnet squares.
   Plan on doing this for several generations, resulting in real research -- something new.
   Communicate your results in a science fair display. Use statistics and graphs.

   Be very clear. Make your display as attractive and professional as
   possible. You might want to use an Indian style painting to show the results.

   Participate in a science fair or school exhibit with your results.

2. Traditional woodland beadwork designs often have vines and plants.
   Create a beadwork design based on your research results.
   Use Punnet squares of family trees as the background of the design.
   Do the design first in pencil, then do the design with paint or beads.

3. Design a genetics family tree for yourself.
   Choose a trait of your family, and trace the genetics for at least two generations.
   Record the information with a drawing or painting of the family tree or Punnet box.
   Choose a trait that you notice in yourself: (fast runner, short chin....)
   See if you can predict how it might affect future generations.

4. Genetic Folk Stories
   Collect folk stories from your culture that explain mutations or different species.
   Retell them in your own words, and illustrate them.
   After each story add a page that may explain genetically what caused the species or mutation.

5. Languages
   Using a variety of language dictionaries, name traditional Ojibwe foods in Ojibwe and other languages. (See Reproduction Chapter.)

Example: Maple

Ojibwe	German	Norwegian	French	Spanish	Russian	Japanese
ininaatig	**Ahorn**	**lonn**	**erable**	**arce**	**kneH**	
in in ah tig	aa horn	luurn	er abl	ar say	klen	momiji

ACTIVITIES

Genetic (Inherited) Learning:
Select any animal. Find and list examples of genetic learning in that animal.
Transfer the information to 3x5 cards, using pictographs or simple poetry.
Invent a game to play using the cards.

For example: White Tailed Deer.

Reflexes: The tail flips up when the deer is alarmed.
Instincts: The deer "yard up" in winter.
Self-Preservation: Deer try to escape by swiftly leaping away.
Species Preservation: An Albino deer is a threat to the herd because it
   can be easily seen. The rest of the herd avoid this deer.
Social behavior: Herding allows many eyes to watch for predators.

Learned Behavior:
Search your own culture for examples of how your people learned and communicated knowledge.
Make poster paper to look like parchment or birchbark.
Make pictographs to tell a story of learning in your culture.

Example: Hispanic

Trial and Error: It took generations of trial and error to build earthquake -
proof buildings in Mexico. Many of these still stand centuries later.

Conditioning: Aztec families were strictly governed. An Aztec Codex illustrates punishment
for children. They were held over chile pepper smoke to make their eyes sting. Rewards in
Aztec society were honor and wealth. The rewards were based on ability as well as social position.

Habit: When children were about three years old, they were given toys like looms that
encouraged household help. By the time they were teen-agers, they were in the habit of
helping with family chores.

Reasoning: The Mayan people were one of only four ancient civilizations to discover the math
concept Zero. They used zero, reason and logic to make astronomy calculations. They
recorded this knowledge in a written language with hieroglyphs.

Chapter 12

Body Systems

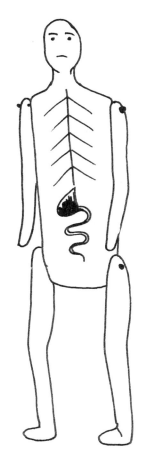

CONCEPT(S):
Systems
Components

IDEA (DEFINING CONCEPT):
Body systems work together.
Exercise strengthens body systems.

TOPIC & THEME:
Body systems

QUESTION(S):
How do the body systems operate?
What can modern medicine learn from ancient wisdom?

PROCESS & THINKING SKILLS:
Observe
Recall
Record
Compare
Interpret
Measure
Communicate
Special relationships

INTEGRATIONS:
Science
Art
Language arts
Social Studies
Physical education
Health
Math

THE BODY SYSTEMS

Bones, Muscles, Skin, Nerves, Senses, Digestion, Circulation, Respiration, Excretion, Endocrine

The Facts: People from many cultures have studied anatomy.

Inuit (Eskimo) people made anatomy puppets for their children. After carving the puppet in driftwood or whale bone, they painted a body system on the puppet. One puppet shows the ribs and spine, stomach and intestines.

Indian people inferred much about human anatomy from the animals they killed. They knew the placement and function of heart and veins, lungs and kidneys. Ancient Greeks dissected apes to learn about human anatomy.

A Norwegian immigrant woman was gored by the family's bull. She scooped up her intestines and carried them home in her apron. She washed them at the pump and put them back inside her body cavity. Then she sewed her muscle and skin closed with a needle and thread. Her family says she had supper waiting on the table when her family came in from the field.
She lived to be an old woman.

The Anishinaabe practiced skin surgery. If an ear was torn in an accident, the pieces of skin were cut straight, then sewed back into place with a needle and deer sinew. There is also a story about a skin graft of scalp.

They set fractured bones by washing and greasing the broken limb. Then it was wrapped in a splint of thin cedar strips. Other tribes made splints from clay, rawhide, and flexible cactus ribs.

Ancient Egyptians wrote a practical medical guide on papyrus, diagraming and explaining treatment for 48 injuries. They too used splints and sutures.

The ancient Chinese healed the mind and body together. They also dried and powdered the organs of animals as medicine. These contained valuable vitamins often missing from a steady diet of polished rice. Both Early Chinese and Central American doctors learned specialties like surgery and internal medicine. These ancient physicians also began experimenting with minerals as medicine.

American Indians invented syringes. The needle was made from a rattlesnake tooth, a cactus spine, or porcupine quill. The ball of the syringe was made from an animal bladder. In South America, the ball was made from rubber tree sap. The Potowatami and Ojibwe used porcupine quill syringes.

The Persians opened a medical school 1200 years ago. Some early surgeons in the Near East and the New World performed amputations and even brain surgeries. To perform these surgeries as painlessly as possible, the Persians relied on opium. Doctors near the Andes Mountains found cocaine to be effective.

The Aztecs had extensive knowledge of the circulatory system. They also identified and named all of the organs.

Indians of British Columbia drank a hot tea of a plant called Devils Club to control diabetes symptoms. Diabetes is a disease of the liver, in the excretory system.

In the 1800's, French doctors at the Surgeon's School learned anatomy at the dissecting rooms. They had the right to dissect any patient who died during surgery.

More than three hundred years ago, the English began using math to help predict disease epidemics.

Indian doctors sometimes took a patient's pulse. The heart rate could be slowed or speeded up with powerful herbs given in very small doses. French doctors used stiff paper cylinders for early stethoscopes.

The Ojibwe, Menomonie, Seneca, Zuni and Navajo had medical societies. Members of the Ojibwe Midewiwin (Grand Medicine Society) treated the patient's illness with mental and physical cures.

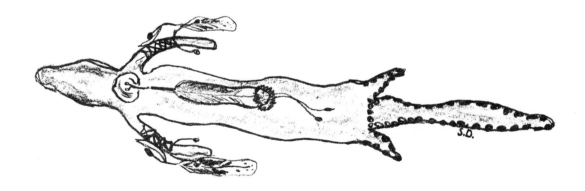

MEDICINE BAG

THE ACTIVITIES:

Maria Tallchief was a famous Apache ballet dancer. Afro-American Gene Washington is a former football star. Billy Mills is a famous Olympic Gold Medal runner. He is an American Indian. Kristi Yamaguchi, Asian-American, won a Gold Medal in figure skating for the United States. Scandinavian-American athletes like Pam Nordheim excel in Nordic skiing. What happens to the body systems of these stars when they perform?

Skeleton	Muscles
Nerves	Skin
Circulation	Respiration
Excretion	Endocrine

1. Create a Sports Puppet like Inuit parents made for their children.
   a. Research a sports or dance person you admire.
      Write a short report on the kind of work and preparation the person did to attain excellence at his/her sport. Explain how each body system is involved in this sport. Explain how the sport strengthens each system.

   b. Your puppet can be a life size body puppet or a play-size puppet. You can make your puppet from the front or side. Select a body system for your puppet to demonstrate. On one side, dress the puppet as he/she would look in his/her sports or dance outfit. On the other side construct a body system. You can use a variety of materials to make the system: straws, cotton swabs, small plastic bags or pipe cleaners. Use your imagination!

      HINT: Integrate math by having students make puppets to actual body proportions: (7-8 heads to the body, 2 1/2 heads to the waist and elbow, 4 heads to the fingertips. The femur is the longest bone in the body, with the knee at about 5 heads.)

2. Create a skit with friends using your puppets. The skit should include personal information about the person, the sport and the body systems.

3. Mapping Feedback Loops (Feedback Loops are message circuits that take information through the body to keep the processes in balance.)
      Put your anatomy puppet in an interesting pose and trace it onto a sheet of colored construction paper, and cut it out. Learn about one Feedback Loop. Then map the Loop onto the cut-out, using string or markers.
      Make a card for the cut-out to hold, telling how the Feedback Loop works.

4. More Feedback Loop Maps:

Ojibwe people made good maps for each other to follow. The maps showed lakes, streams, paths, turns, main landmarks, and the amount of time needed to travel the distances by foot or canoe.

Map a Feedback Loop as carefully as the early Ojibwe people did.
Show exactly how the system works. Pretend you are traveling in a cell instead of a canoe.

Write a story or unrhymed poem about your trip along the Feedback Trail.

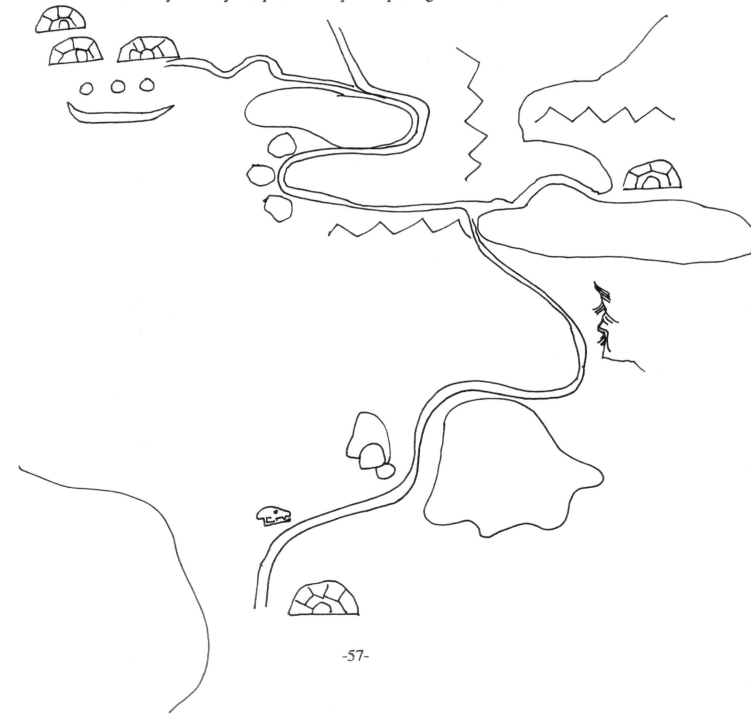

Chapter 13

Taking Care of Yourself

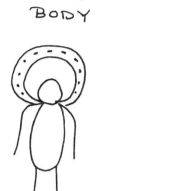

BODY

CONCEPT(S):
Change
Patterns

IDEA (DEFINING CONCEPT):
Changes have occurred in the human diet and exercise pattern.

TOPIC & THEME:
Healthy diets--yesterday and today.

MIND
(STUDENT)

QUESTION(S):
How can modern people maintain a traditional and healthy body?

PROCESS & THINKING SKILLS:
Collect data
Observe
Predict
Measure
Compare
Classify
Record
Communicate

HEART
(TEACHER)

SPIRIT
(MEDICINE)

INTEGRATIONS:
Science
Art
Language Arts
Social Studies
Math
Health

MEDICINE
BUFFALO

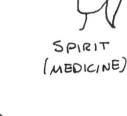

HEALTHY
MAN

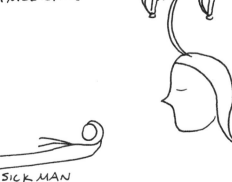

SICK MAN

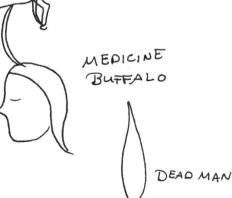

DEAD MAN

22. TAKING CARE OF YOURSELF

THE STORIES:

Shinguse is a folk-singer from Manitoba, Canada. His music and gentle humor reflect the problems that all people face, while focusing on his own people. One song says, "It's Hard to be Traditional When You're Living in the Nuclear Age." Another tells of the advantages of a "Natural Tan."

Dr. Cathy Annette is the first woman Ojibwe doctor. In a nation wide video, Dr. Annette explains that she studied medicine because she wanted to blend the best of traditional holistic medical learning with western medical knowledge. She says that body, mind, heart and spirit all go into making a healthy person.

THE FACTS:

The traditional diet of the Ojibwe was very healthy. Since it took a lot of exercise to hunt, gather and prepare food, exercise was part of daily living. Traditional Anishinaabe had a healthier diet and more exercise than we do.

Wild rice is an excellent source of nutrition and energy. It is low in fat too!
As a whole food, wild rice ranks higher than the oats and wheat brought from Europe. The people also stored large quantities of wild rice for winter.

In their gardens they grew corn, squash and pumpkins. Pumpkins and corn were dried for winter. The Ojibwe enjoyed fresh pumpkins and corn, roasted in husks. These plants are loaded with good carbohydrates and vitamins. Wild potatoes, acorns and nuts added vitamins and protein.

Blueberries, choke cherries, June berries and cranberries supplied more vitamins and made a balanced diet.

Protein came from fish, venison, ducks, and trapped animals like beaver, otter and muskrat. The fat meat of the bear and beaver was important in the winter, to keep people warm. They used no salt. Maple sugar, mint, wild ginger and bayberry were good seasonings.

THE ACTIVITIES:

1. Research and Art
   a. Write to a person from your culture who studies nutrition.
      Think up some good questions about traditional versus modern diets.

   b. Write or call your local County Extension Agent or County Home
      Economist for information about the nutrition of modern and traditional
      foods.

   c. For one month, keep a Food Diary. Write down everything you eat.
      Try to make your diet healthier every week. Record how you feel.
      (To have a healthy diet, cut fats, sugar, and salt. Eat lots of fruit
      and veggies. Drink low-fat milk. Whole grain breads and cereals and
      good, too.)

   d. Decide how to present your research.
      Do you need a graph? a chart? a poster?
      Present your research in the artistic style of your culture.
      Try to use traditional symbols and traditional colors.

2. Compare your diet with a traditional diet the elders might have eaten.
   Write down all the foods you eat in a week.
   Write down your main physical activities (playing baseball, jumping
         rope, or watching TV.)
   Write down a weekly menu for a traditional diet.
         (For more foods, see the list of Resource Books.)
   Write down the main physical activities of the traditional people.

   Compare your diet and exercise with the traditional diet.

   Make a graph, chart or poster showing the differences and similarities.

3.) Research and prepare a healthy feast of traditional foods from the
    cultures of the kids in the class.
    Make an illustrated cook book for a class project. Consider printing
    extra copies for sale. You could use the profit to take a field trip!

Chapter 14

Patterns in Plants

CONCEPT(S):
Patterns
Components

IDEA (DEFINING CONCEPT):
Plants show patterns.

TOPIC & THEME:
Science and arts patterns in plants.

QUESTION(S):
What plant patterns can be found in traditional folk arts like story telling, beadwork, and rosemaling?

PROCESS & THINKING SKILLS:
Observe
Analyze
Record
Classify
Compare
Interpret

INTEGRATIONS:
Science
Art
Language Arts
Social Studies
Math

PATTERNS IN PLANTS

THE STORY: How the Moccasin Flower (Lady's Slipper) Came to Be

In the long-ago time a little Ojibwe girl begged to go hunting with her older brother. "You are too little to be in the woods," he told her. "You might get lost and hurt. Stay with Grandmother and help her today."

But when he left, the little girl followed him, staying just out of sight. The brother knew the ways of the animals, and traveled very quietly. Soon his little sister could not see or hear him anywhere in the forest. She was lost.

When the young man returned late that night, he was frantic to discover his sister was missing. The villagers lit fires to light up the night, hoping the child would find the village from the firelight. One fire, blazing out of control, spread into the forest and burned wildly. All things in its path were lost to the smoke and flames -- plants, animals, and the little girl.

The seasons turned. When spring came, the people discovered a beautiful new flower, shaped just like the child's moccasin. Wherever she had stepped, a beautiful moccasin flower grew. Every spring the flowers remember the girl and grow in her footsteps.

THE FACTS:

Lady Slippers are perennials. They grow back year after year.
Lady Slipper flowers are specialized so bees can easily pollinate them: The flower only has one or two stamens attached to the pistil. Pollen hangs in a clump. The bee brushes up against the pollen when leaving the flower. Orchids have three petals. Lady slippers are monocots from the orchid family. Monocots are the most advanced flowers, and orchids are the most advanced monocots. Leaves are long and thin, with veins running down to the point. Vanilla is made from a orchid seed pods. (Anyone for orchid ice cream?)

European Lady Slippers are the world's largest orchids.
They are as big as dinner plates --10 inches across!

Seeds can live a long time. Two 2,000 year old lotus seeds were sprouted successfully by a Japanese botanist. They produced beautiful pink lotus flowers -- and more seeds! Arctic Lupin seeds from Canada sprouted and grew flowers, even though they were 10,000 - 15,000 years old!

Ferns (plants without seeds) come in all sizes. The smallest is only one-fourth of an inch across. It lives in water. The biggest fern lives on a tropical island. At 60 feet tall, it's as high as a stack of three houses!

Thorns on rose stems grow in a spiral pattern, based on a math formula. Leaves grow in a spiral too, so they don't shade each other. (A famous Polish musician, Bela Bartok, used the same formula to compose of piece of music about nature.)

Birch trees have slim yellow-green flowers (catkins) in the spring.
Each catkin makes more than 5 million grains of pollen!

Hummingbirds see infrared color, but do not have a very good sense of smell. Birds often pollinate red flowers. Bees see ultraviolet, and have a good sense of smell. Some white flowers have special ultraviolet marking, and have a strong sweet smell. Bees usually pollinate white flowers.

Pass the pie! The largest veggie ever raised was a 90 lb. pumpkin!

THE LANGUAGES:

English	Ojibwe	Norwegian	Spanish	French	Japanese
Flower	waabigwan	blomst	flor	fleur	hana
Lady's Slipper	agobishwin	dametoffel	orquidea	orchidee	ran
Leaf	aniibiish	blad	hoja	feuille	ko no ha

THE ACTIVITIES:

1. Plants in Language.

   Choose a plant. Find or write a legend about your plant. Tell what culture the plant legend is from. List a few plant words in the culture's language. Find out interesting facts about your plant. Illustrate the story. Hint: remember to use basic geometric shapes when sketching. You can add details later.

2. Plants in folk art. Find and label as many real plant parts as you can on Ojibwe beadwork and Scandinavian rosemaling. Or you may choose a design from Africa, Asia or your own culture. Label in English and another language. Color the pictures using real or imaginary colors.

3. Creating Flower Folk Art.

   Make up your own folk art design for beadwork or rosemaling. You can use real or imaginary flowers. Be sure to include ALL plant parts in your design: Root, Stem, Leaves, Flowers, Stamens, Pistil, Petals and Sepals.

Chapter 15

Plant Processes and Reproduction

CONCEPT(S):
Patterns
Cycles
Systems

IDEA (DEFINING CONCEPT):
Plant processes in patterns

TOPIC & THEME:
Plant Processes in reproduction

QUESTION(S):
What stories did the early people tell about Angiosperms (flowering plants) and gymnosperms (cone plants)?

THINKING SKILLS
Observe
Record
Sequence
Compare
Infer
Interpret
Experiment
Collect data
Communicate
Apply knowledge

INTEGRATIONS:
Science
Art
Language arts
Math
Social studies

PLANT PRODUCTION AND REPRODUCTION

THE STORIES: Flowering Plants (from Southeast farming tribes.)

How the People Got Tobacco

In the long-ago time a young man and woman met on a trail of happiness, and they fell in love. In time they married. After many happy years, they returned to the place where they had met. On this very spot grew a lovely flower with musky-smelling leaves.

When they brought the plant home, the elders said. "We will name the plant 'Where We Came Together' in honor of the peaceful and happy young couple. We will dry the leaves. We will smoke them. Whenever we smoke the leaves from this plant it will be to bring peace and friendship among the people." Smoking was used for spiritual purposes only -- not for recreation.

How the People Got Corn

Orphan Boy lived with his Grandmother. Each day he walked in the woods, and came home brimming with questions.

"What is the animal with a fluffy tail and long ears?"

"It is a rabbit," said Grandmother. "You can shoot it with your bow and arrow, because it is good to eat."

"What is the animal with thin legs and antlers?"

"It is a deer, and it is good to eat."

The boy brought home meat, but he didn't know anything about plants. He wondered where the corn and beans came from that Grandmother cooked every night, so one day he spied on his Grandmother. He was astonished as she scratched one leg and corn poured out of the scratch. When she scratched the other leg, beans came tumbling out. That night he was moody, and would not eat. So Grandmother knew it was time for him to take a journey.

She gave him a magic headdress and sent him across the blue mountain to find a wife. But first she told him to go out of the cabin and burn it down. Grandmother stayed inside. The boy was sad, but did as she told him.

After a long journey and many adventures, the boy found a wife. They traveled back to the ashes of Grandmother's cabin, what did they find? A beautiful garden of corn and beans had grown from her ashes. They planted the seeds, and that is how the people got corn and bean plants.

The Facts:

Tobacco grows from a flowering plant (Angiosperm). In traditional cultures it was cultivated in gardens, and its use was restricted by custom and purpose. Europeans had no cultural limits on tobacco, so they used it as a drug.

To get special varieties of corn, Indian farmers pollinated the silk (pistil) of a corn stalk with pollen from the tassel (stamens) of a different plant. In this way they developed sweet corn, popcorn and many others. They carefully selected the monocot seeds to plant. Monocots have long thin leaves with all the veins pointing down to the tip. The monocot seed has just one seed leaf. Beans are dicots, with two seed leaves.

There was good sense in planting corn, beans and squash together. The corn leaves kept the beans from getting sunburned. Tendrils of beans and squash climbed up the corn stalk. Beans provided nutrients for squash and corn, too.

Research shows that growing plants all together like this can produce 50% more food than plants planted in rows. (Navajos, Hopi and Zuni make beautiful silver necklaces using the squash blossom design.)

A CHEROKEE STORY: Gymnosperms: Why Conifers are Evergreen

Creator had finished making all the plants. Now it was time to test them to see which of the plant brothers were truly strong and obedient.

"You will try to stay awake for seven days and seven nights," he said.

At first all of the plants stayed wide awake. They all made it through the first day and night. But on the second night a few plants decided to "just rest their eyes for a minute," and of course they fell fast asleep. The next night a few more plants fell asleep. By the fourth night the trees that were still awake were determined to make it, but again some got too sleepy. The next night some trees were so tired, they just gave up and went to bed.

On the morning after the seventh night only a few trees were still awake to greet the Creator. To these special trees he gave a special gift: they alone would be forever green.

After he woke the sleepyheads up, Creator told them, "Since you like to sleep so much, every fall your beautiful green leaves will turn brown and fall to the ground. With your cold naked branches, you can sleep all winter."

THE FACTS:

Chlorophyll makes plants green. The Ojibwe used spruce and juniper for dyes, medicine, pitch, sewing, and mat making. Sheets of jackpine bark were used to make cabins. Red Pine was used to make toys.

Trees grow in the cambium layer of cells just underneath the bark. It is only one cell thick, so when the cell divides, half becomes bark and half become wood. Porcupines find cambium to be delicious. When the cambium is destroyed, the tree can't grow, and it dies. Porcupines can kill pines trees. Fishers are the only animals who kill and eat porcupines -- *very* carefully!

The Giant Sequoia (a cone-bearing tree) is named for the Cherokee leader who invented a form of Indian writing. Sequoias are among the oldest trees in the world. One of these living trees is nearly 4,000 years old! Its trunk is 30 feet in diameter. (bigger than a school room!) Redwood trunks are not quite so thick, but the trees are even taller. They can grow to be 350 feet tall.

How Plants Produce Oxygen and Energy:

Photosynthesis -- making food with Chlorophyll (the green chemical in plants.)
Wild rice uses chlorophyll and the summer sunlight to make food by using Carbon Dioxide from the air and the water it's growing in. When the plant is done making food, Oxygen is a leftover. Oxygen is released into the air for us to breathe.

Respiration -- making energy for the plant by breaking down food.
The wild rice plant burns oxygen and the food it makes to produce energy. It uses the energy to make more food. Carbon dioxide and water are left over. They are released back into the air. The cycle repeats over and over. Energy and carbon dioxide making food; food and oxygen making energy....

Transpiration -- losing water. If water didn't go out of the plant, fresh water couldn't come in. Wild rice leaves have tiny pores (stomata) like your skin. Water (and gas) go out through the stomata openings in the leaf, so fresh water can come up through the roots.

THE ACTIVITIES:

1. Storytelling: The Vision Quest

Traditional cultures all over the world have encouraged their young people to seek a vision.
Pretend you are a drop of water or molecule of oxygen on a vision quest.
Explain your journey through a plant native to your culture.
What ceremonies do you need to prepare for food-making, energy-making, and transpiration?
What is your place in the universe? What is your vision?
Show the patterns and cycles involved.

2. Illustrate your vision quest with a painting. (Be sure it shows the plant's processes clearly.)

Painting styles to Try:

Style:	Paper	Paint	Pictures
Am. Indian Style:	dry, colored	bright colors	strong designs
European Style:	wet, white	soft colors	real-looking pictures
African Style:	dry, white	strong color	geometric shapes and lines
Asian Style:	wet, white	mostly black	a few strong lines
Australian Style:	dry, black	mostly white	geometric shapes and lines

3. Create your own Sci-Art Experiment. Some ideas:

 * The stomata opening is surrounded by special cells that regulate the opening.

 * Corn seeds (monocots) stay in the ground when the plant starts to grow.
   Bean seeds (dicots) are lifted above ground by the stem when it grows.

 * Try sprinkling the pollen from one plant onto another.

 * True blue and black roses have never been developed

 * Find math, science and art connections of plant spirals and branching patterns.

Chapter 16

Uses of Plants

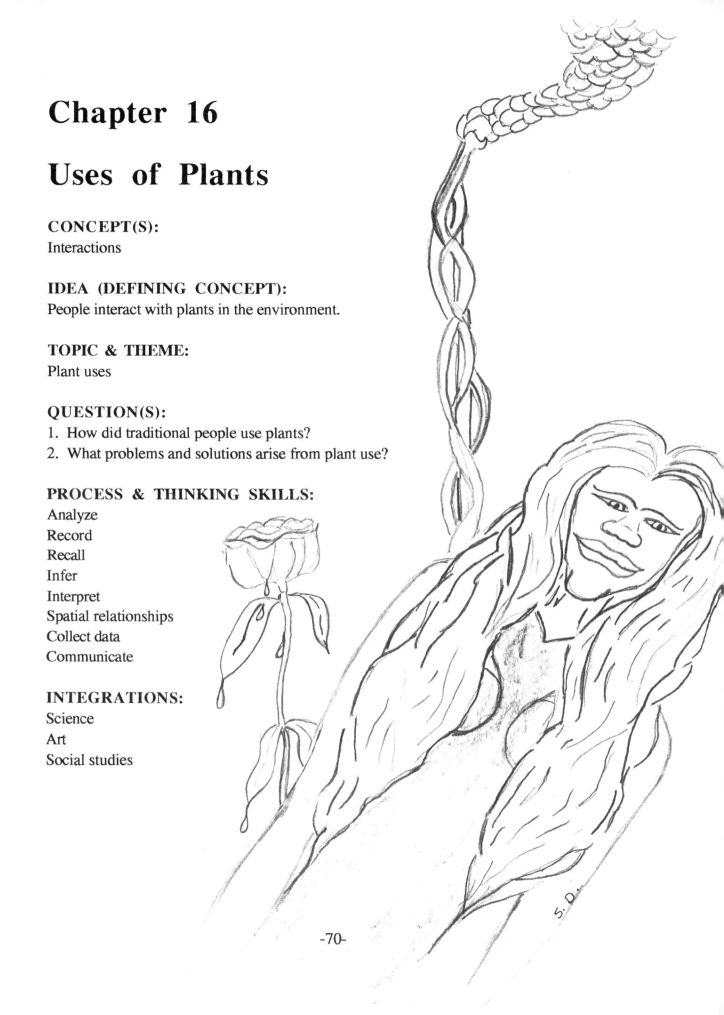

CONCEPT(S):
Interactions

IDEA (DEFINING CONCEPT):
People interact with plants in the environment.

TOPIC & THEME:
Plant uses

QUESTION(S):
1. How did traditional people use plants?
2. What problems and solutions arise from plant use?

PROCESS & THINKING SKILLS:
Analyze
Record
Recall
Infer
Interpret
Spatial relationships
Collect data
Communicate

INTEGRATIONS:
Science
Art
Social studies

USES OF PLANTS

THE STORY: <u>Midewiwin and the Spirit Vine</u>

Earth was young and the Anishinaabe were healthy. Sickness and death were unknown. A beautiful spiral spirit vine connected Earth to the heavens. As people grew old, spirits carried them up the vine to the heavens. No one was allowed to even touch the vine.

Spirits could come and go up and down the vine. One spirit and a boy became friends. The people were very jealous, and they made the boy's life miserable. So one night the spirit and the boy went up the beautiful vine to the heavens, where they could be friends and be happy.

Grandmother was furious. She ran to the vine and began climbing it, to the very top where a thin tendril coiled around the moon and stars. But she was too heavy for the fragile vine. She came crashing back to earth, destroying the plant as she fell. The people were angry with her, but they knew their jealousy had caused the problem too.

With the vine gone, the Anishinaabe began to get sick. They felt pain in their bodies and death in their bones. The spirits were disappointed with the people, but they felt sorry for them too. One night the sky filled with dancing Northern Lights as the spirits came to earth, bringing gifts for the Anishinaabe.

"For every sickness and pain there will be a plant to cure and soothe," they said. "The Grand Medicine Society, the Midewiwin, will seek the cures and keep the knowledge of the plants."

The Facts: The following remedies and dyes are found in Frances Densmore's book, <u>How Indians Use Plants for Food, Medicine and Crafts.</u>

WARNING: DO NOT TRY ANY OF THESE YOURSELF! THE MIDEWIWIN HAD YEARS OF PRACTICE AND WISDOM ABOUT THE PLANTS. VERY FEW PEOPLE HAVE THIS KNOWLEDGE TODAY. USING THE WRONG SPECIES, THE WRONG DOSE, THE WRONG PLANT PART OR THE WRONG PREPARATION COULD BE DEADLY.

Ojibwe Medicine Plants (A Few Examples)

Nervous System:
Roots of the wild peas and snake root were used to treat convulsions.
Yarrow and bearberry leaves were used for headaches.

Circulatory System:
Dogbane and mugwart helped heart patients.
Wild sarsaparilla treated nosebleeds.

Respiratory System:
Goldenrod helped pains in the lungs.
Ironwood and arbor vitae were combined for cough syrup.

Digestive System:
Dried Lady Slipper powder was put on aching teeth.
Chokecherry or Tansy made a gargle for sore throats.
Bluestem and Prairie Smoke were used to treat indigestion.

Excretory System:
The carrion flower root was an old Midewiwin remedy for kidney problems.
Enema tea was made from the inner bark of the white birch.

Skin:
Plantain and wild ginger helped soothe skin inflammations.
Yellow dock and white pine were used to clean out wounds.
Lily was used on snake bites.
Fireweed was used to soothe burns.

Skeletal System:
Sore joints were treated with evergreens.
Wormwood and Balsam Poplar were the treatments for muscle sprains.
Broken bones were splinted with cedar.

General:
Fevers were treated with Catnip or Mountain Mint.
Wild plum was a good disinfectant.
Blazing Star and Prairie Smoke were two veterinary medicines for horses.

Ojibwe Plant Dyes

WARNING: Protect your eyes and clothing. The formulas for good strong dyes can contain poisonous ingredients. Use old pans that you don't use for other cooking.

RED DYE: (The inner bark is used.)
White birch, Red-osier dogwood, Oak, 2 cups of cedar bark ashes, hot water.
Boil everything except the ashes in about 2 gallons of water. Add the sifted ashes.

SCARLET DYE: (Use inner bark)
2 handfuls of bloodroot root, 1 handful wild plum, 1 handful red-osier dogwood, 1 handful alder, 1 quart of water. Boil. Add quills to be dyed.

BLACK DYE: Inner bark of green hazel and butternut. Boil.
The black dye was used to color bulrush mats a deep shiny black.

YELLOW DYE: Goldthread roots and hot water. Boil. (You need lots of roots.)

PURPLE DYE: 2 handfuls of rotten maple wood, 1 handful of grindstone dust. Boil.
Bulrushes, porcupine quills, cotton material and yarn were dyed.
Sometimes items need to be dried and reboiled to get a strong color.

SETTING THE COLOR: The color is "set" by using grindstone dust (silt that contains iron.)
The pioneers set colors by boiling their yarns and dyes in iron kettles.
Copper kettles and tin kettles produced different colors from the same dye.

THE ACTIVITIES: EASY FLOWER PETAL PAINT
Small groups can make several colors with different petals, acid, base and alcohol.
They can compare the *different* colors obtained from the *same* petals when using acid or base.

1. Acid/Base Paint:
Crush 2-4 tablespoons of flower petals. Put them in a zipper lock bag.
Soak them overnight in a little vinegar (an acid) or clear window cleaner (a base).
HINTS: Use strong-colored flowers. Just barely cover the petals with the liquid.
Make a flower painting with your paint.

2. Alcohol Paint:
Crush 2-4 tablespoons of flower petals. Put them in a zipper lock bag.
Soak them overnight in 1-2 tablespoons of alcohol. Use it to make a flower painting.
Decorate your painting with dots and stripes of acid and base (vinegar and window cleaner.)

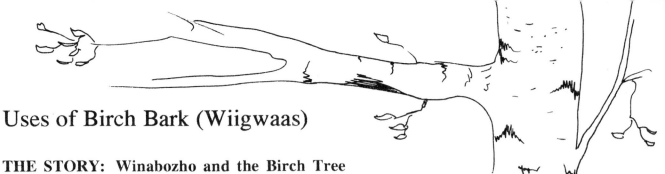

Uses of Birch Bark (Wiigwaas)

THE STORY: Winabozho and the Birch Tree

There are at least two stories of how the birch tree came to be marked, and in both cases Winabozho is responsible. Winabozho was half man, half spirit. He named the animals and the plants. He shared wisdom with the Anishinaabe people. Because he was half human, he made mistakes and learned from them.

WHY GOOD BIRCH BARK IS HARD TO FIND

The Anishinaabe use smooth sheets of birch bark for many things -- canoes, wigwams, boxes, and paper. In these days it's hard to find a good piece of bark that isn't full of cracks and marks, but in the Old Days, all the trees were smooth. The people did not have to go far to find good bark.

"If people can find smooth bark easily, they will not appreciate it," said Winabozho. So he asked Gijigaaneshii (Chickadee) to help him solve the problem. Holding Gijigaaneshii tightly by the tail, Winabozho swung the bird toward the birch tree. With each swing, the little bird's sharp black wings scratched the tree.

Next Winabozho made whips from balsam tree bark and whipped the tree trunk to make it hard and cracked. The people would have to look long and hard to find good smooth birch bark now, and they would appreciate it.

WHY BIRCH BARK HAS BLACK SCRATCHES

Winabozho wanted to catch the biggest fish in the lake, but he needed some special feathers to make the fishing lure. By becoming a rabbit , he tricked the Thunderbirds into taking him to their nest as a pet for their babies. When the Thunderbirds were gone, Winabozho killed the young birds and took their feathers. The adults returned to their nest high in the cliffs, and they were heartbroken and outraged.

"We will get Winabozho for this!" they screeched. Their eyes lit with a yellow fire, and their wings beat like thunder as they streaked out over the forest, looking for Winabozho. He ran like the wind, but soon he felt their breath searing his back. Their sharp beaks snapped beside his head.

Where could he hide? CRASH! He tripped over a hollow birch log. Winabozho slid inside the log and grinned. The Thunderbirds had no power over the beautiful smooth white bark. They flew around it making terrible noises and clawing at the log with their talons, but the birch tree protected Winabozho, and the Thunderbirds knew it was a strong protection. The yellow fire slowly left their eyes, and they flew away.

Winabozho said, "Birch trees will always protect and help people. When people take birch bark, they must offer tobacco to show their thanks." Birch bark is still scarred by the Thunderbird's claws. Some people say the marks look like baby Thunderbirds.

THE FACTS:

Birch trees, like other trees, grow in their cambium layer, just under the bark. Smooth bark stretches and is flexible with the growth of the tree. Trees with very rough bark (like oaks and pines) have rigid bark that cracks as the tree grows.

NOTE: Show respect for this important tree. When taking birch bark, use only the outer layer, so the tree is not killed. Don't be like the porcupine that eats the cambium layer and then leaves the tree to die. Leave something for the tree when you take bark.

Birch bark had many uses, especially for protecting people and storing food.

The Activities:

1. Make Birch Patterns:
   Sometimes thin squares of birch paper were folded smaller in squares, rectangles or triangles. People bit patterns into the folded birch paper with their teeth. The patterns were used for decorations.

2. Make Birch Cut-outs and Toys:
   To make tracing patterns for beadwork, the Ojibwe cut out a birch bark pattern first. Then traced it onto buckskin or velvet to be beaded.
   Paper dolls were also cut out from birch bark or slippery elm.
   Invent a toy or game using birch bark.

3. Make a model Birch Bark Canoe or Wigwam from the following plans.

4. With your class make a full-size canoe or wigwam!

5. Select another plant important to your culture.
   Research all the possible uses of that plant.
   Get samples if you can.
   Create a project with your information to communicate it to others.

6. What environmental issues concern plant use?
   Identify the problems. Analyze them.
   What is the role of government in these problems?
   Use research, solid science information and your own creativity to suggest solutions to these problems. Report your problem and solution clearly in words, pictures, posters or a documentary video.

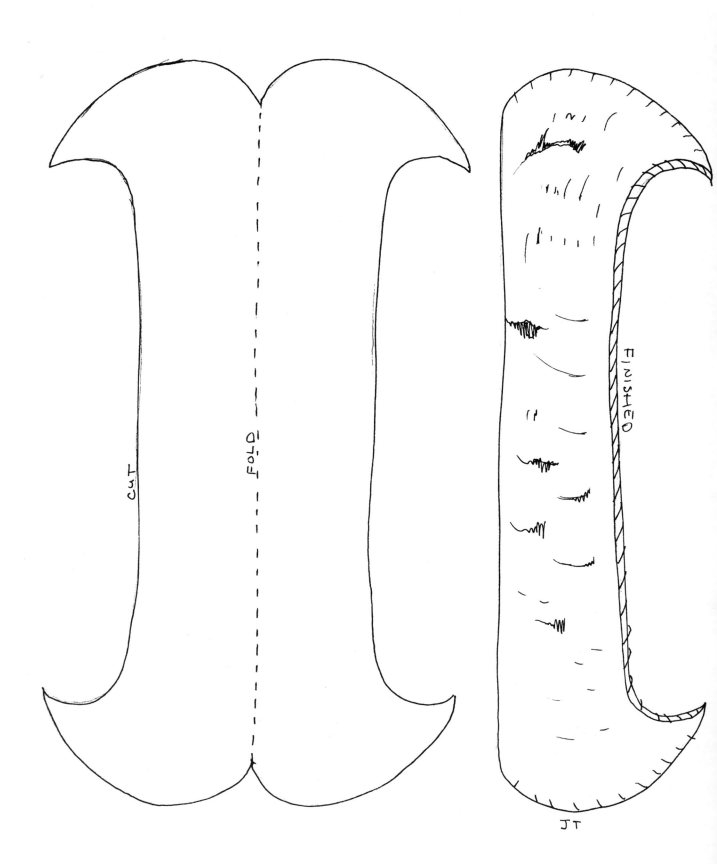

CUT

FOLD

FINISHED

JT

75 A

CUT

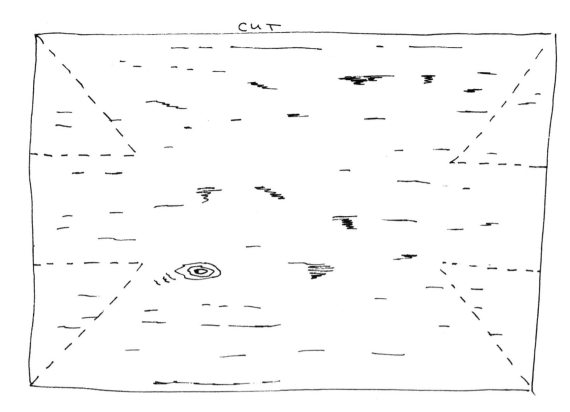

BIRCH BOX

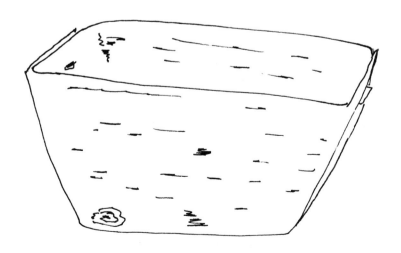

Chapter 17

Plant Responses

CONCEPT(S):
Changes
Systems
Patterns
Structures

IDEA (DEFINING CONCEPT):
Plant systems and structures respond and adapt.

TOPIC & THEME:
Plant responses and changes.

QUESTION(S):
How do Minnesota plants respond to their Northern environment?

PROCESS & THINKING SKILLS:
Observe
Experiment
Collect Data
Recall
Record
Predict
Interpret
Communicate

INTEGRATIONS:
Science
Art
Language Arts
Social Studies

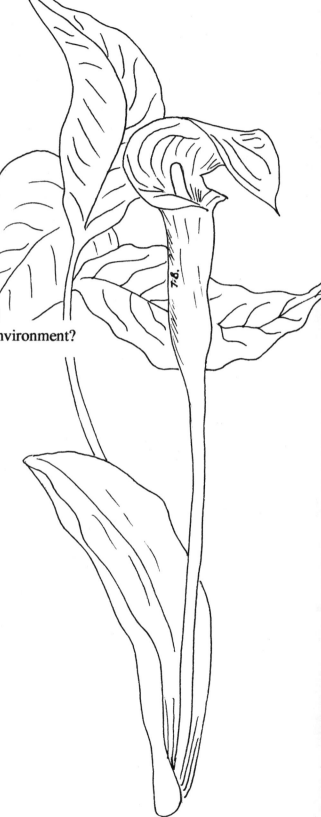

PLANT RESPONSES AND CHANGES

THE STORY: Why The Leaves Turn Red (Micmac)

Late in the spring The People look up at the stars, and they see the Great Bear crawling out of her cave. Seven hunters follow her all summer. Three of the hunters, Robin, Chickadee and Moosebird stay right behind the bear, but the other four fall behind in the autumn.

Late in the fall Robin shoots the Great Bear with his bow and arrow. Bear slowly rolls to her back. Bear's blood spatters Robin's breast. It drips down to earth, coloring all the maples scarlet red. Little Chickadee takes out his pot and cooks a feast for the hunters. They share their food with Moosebird, who always follows the real hunters in Canada.

The Great Bear is dead, but all winter her spirit sleeps in the cave. In the spring a new Great Bear will crawl out of her cave, to be chased all summer by the hunters.

The story of changing leaves, death and birth happens over and over for millions of years.

THE STAR FACTS:

From a star map you can see how the constellations change with the seasons. (It is from the position of the earth). In this story, the Great Bear is the four stars of the Big Dipper.
The three stars in the handle are Robin, Chickadee, and Moosebird. Robin is a reddish star, Chickadee with his cooking pot is a double star. The Micmacs value hunters who share food with people and Moosebird.

Because of the position of the earth in the fall, eastern Canadians see the next four "hunter" stars slowly dip below the horizon. They also see the Big Dipper seem to slowly roll over.

THE PLANT FACTS:

Why do the leaves change colors?
Leaves contain red, gold, and rust pigments all year, but we can't see these colors because there is so much green chlorophyll in the leaves. In the fall, days become darker and colder. The tree stops making chlorophyll, and we can see the other colors.

Why are blueberries found under jackpine trees?
The jackpine needles contain acid that goes into the soil as the needles decompose. Some plants, like blueberries, respond well to the stimulus of acidic soil.

Some plants make a flower, but will not make seeds if they have continuous light.
Think about a rainbow or a prism. Plants respond and grow best with red and blue light. Could

Plants CAN grow in total darkness IF there is enough food. (But they do much better in light, since they need light to make food, through photosynthesis.)

Plants respond to wind. Wind speeds transpiration and shapes the plants.

Some grass tips respond to light by bending toward it. When scientists made tin foil hats for the grass, it didn't bend! When they cut the tips off the grass, it didn't bend. One time they cut the tips off, and "glued" them back on with a dab of gelatin. Guess what happened: The grass bent.

Florists can keep chrysanthemums from blooming by turning on a light for a few minutes every night. The mums need long nights to blossom, and when they get even a little light at night they respond as if it is still summer. When the florists want the chrysanthemums to bloom, they keep the light off all night.

Some trees in the hot dry tropics shed their leaves in the summer, to keep from losing too much water.

Plants respond to gravity. What happened to plants grown in space?

THE ACTIVITIES:

1. Predicting Fall Colors

   In the summer or early fall, collect green leaves.

   Identify them.

   Crush several of each kind, and place them in small jars with lids.

   Cover the leaves with nail polish remover (acetone).

   Cut strips from a coffee filter, and hang a strip in the middle of the jar.

   Cover the jar and let it sit for a day or two.

   Pigments are of different densities, so they will "climb" up the filter to different levels.

   What pigments besides chlorophyll are in your leaves?

   What color will the leaves of that tree turn in the fall?

   In the fall, collect some more leaves.

   Compare your collection with your prediction.

   Collect fall leaves that have not completely turned color.

   Analyze the pigment in the leaves of one tree as it changes from green to mixed green, red, and gold, to a final solid color.

   Save all the dyed strips. Use them in a creative art and science project.

   ### SOME IDEAS:
   * Make a tree! Bring a dead branch to class.

     Cut the dyed filter paper strips into different leaf shapes.

     Draw in the veins with colored pencils.

     (Is the leaf a monocot or dicot?)

     Glue the filter paper leaves to the tree branch.
   * Make a collage of leaf shapes from the dyed filter paper.
   * Make replicas of birch bark toys or patterns by cutting the strips.
   * Think up your own ideas!

2. Experiment with Plant Responses

   Choose a plant stimulus like light, gravity, touch or chemical.

   Ask a question about the stimulus.

   (For example, will a pea vine spiral left or right in different conditions?)

   Design a way to answer the question.

   TRY IT! Communicate the experiment in Language and Art!

   Tell how this knowledge might help mankind.

Chapter 18

Classifying Living Things

CONCEPT(S):
Components
Patterns
Structures

IDEA (DEFINING CONCEPT):
The structure of living things helps us classify them.

TOPIC & THEME:
Classify living things.

PROCESS & THINKING SKILLS:
Classify
Compare
Observe
Experiment
Record
Communicate
Collect Data
Predict
Apply knowledge

INTEGRATIONS:
Science
Art
Language Arts
Social Studies

CLASSIFYING LIVING THINGS

THE STORIES:

Echoes of The Old Wisdom: All cultures use living things for their survival.

Frances Densmore learned about survival from her Anishinaabe friends while living at White Earth, Red Lake, Cass Lake, Mille Lacs, La Court Orielles, and Manitou Rapids. She said of Wounded Knee, "After the song -- the silence." She and her friends, Niskigwun and Mary Warren English, were determined that the old ways would not die with their generation. They set about recording everything they and their friends could remember, for more than twenty years.

Traditional wisdom in many cultures tells us that every sickness has its cure in nature -- that there is a use for every plant. "Health and long life represented the highest good to the mind of the Chippewa, and he who had knowledge conducive to that end was highly esteemed among them," wrote Densmore, in 1918.

Midewiwins, the people of the Grand Medicine Lodge, got their healing knowledge from dreams and experimentation.

A Lakota told Densmore, "In the old days the Indians had few diseases, and so there was not a demand for a large variety of medicines. A medicine man treated one special disease, and treated it successfully." In other words, they were medical specialists.

Densmore lists 265 separate medicines made from plants. Her main sources were three Anishinaabe women from White Earth: Mrs. Martin, Mrs. Burnett, and Mrs. Gagewin. She also got help from: Julia Spears, Albert Littlewolf, Clement Beaulieau, Mrs. Fineday, Mrs. White, Mrs. Defoe and Mrs. Gurneau, Mr. and Mrs. Tom Skinaway, and Mr. and Mrs. William Rogers.

"The strength of the Chippewa in conquering the Sioux and establishing themselves in a new territory indicates that they were well-nourished, that suitable food was available, and that it was prepared in the proper manner. This was the work of the women...." wrote Densmore.

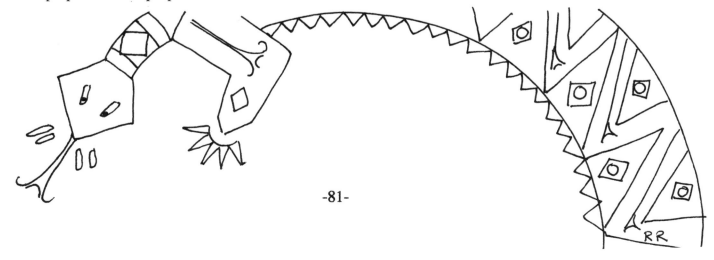

THE FACTS:

Living Things can be classified (so far) into five Kingdoms.
Anishinaabe people had uses for each Kingdom: Here are few examples:

I. Animals

Vertebrates like fish, deer, and beaver were used for food and clothing.
Snake skins were stuffed for ceremonies.
Invertebrates like mollusks and crustaceans were used for food.

II. Plants

Plants with cones: Evergreen twigs were placed on hot stones to make
   a medicinal steam for aching joints.
Plants with seeds:

      Dicots: Basswood was used for twine; maple used for sugar.
      Monocots: Lady slipper was used for treating skin infections.
      Wild rice is a food.
Plants with spores:
    Mosses were used to absorb.
    The root of the rattlesnake fern was used for snake bites.

III. Fungus

The Indian pipe plant is not green. It gets its food from a fungus.
A brown fungus was used to draw infection out of a decayed tooth.

IV. Protists

Algae is an important part of the food chain, providing food for
insects, who become food for fish.

V. Monerans

The Anishinaabe kept harmful bacteria under control by boiling drinking water, careful
washing with a stiff brush, and washing clothes and dishes in a weak lye solution (made by
dripping water through ashes).

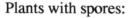

THE ACTIVITIES:

1. Make your own Classification Chart of Cultural Uses.

Research:

What is your culture? Talk to your family. Visit the library. Write
to the Historical Society, a university, the Smithsonian Institution.
How did your people use living things in each category for their survival?

Communicating:

Make a chart to visually explain your research about living things.
Illustrate it.

Write a fiction story about the life of your ancestor, showing how he/she
    might have depended on living things in each category. Try to use some
    words in your native language: German? Ojibwe? Korean?

Keep the chart for your children. Don't let the echoes die.

2. Field Work
   Observing:
   Good observation is always important to good science.
   When you are basically familiar with the types of living things, go
   outdoors and look for examples. Take a partner so you can share ideas.

   Collecting Data:
   Working in small groups, collect samples of each type of living thing.
   Each person should collect at least one sample of each type.
   Keep a notebook or map about where you found each item.

   Classifying:
   Arrange the collection on poster paper, so that each classification has
   its own space.

   Recording: Label each clearly.

   Try to find:
   1). Kingdom 2.) Sub-kingdom 3.) Common name/part 4.) Place/Date found
   For example: 1.) Animal 2.) Invertebrate 3.) crayfish/claw 4.) Lake Bemidji - 9/14/94

3. Experiment -- Design an experiment with some living things you collected.
Ask a Question:
In your group brainstorm a list questions you have about these things.
(First, review Brainstorming Rules in class: All ideas accepted and
recorded, free-wheeling encouraged, no put-downs!)
Narrow down your list and then decide on one question to answer.

Design and Research an Experiment:
(Review ideas of Control and Variable.)
Check with your teacher before starting, and make sure it is safe.

Try out the experiment: Have fun, and work carefully. Think about
what you are doing. You may need to solve problems while you are
working.

Record your results: Make a graph, chart, diagram, or whatever you need.

Generalization: State your findings in one sentence.

Replication: Trade experiments with another group. Do you get the same results?

Communication: Write a short paper about your experiment.
Be sure to tell the Kingdom from which your living thing comes.
Include: * Our Task, We Thought, People in our Group (and their jobs),
We Used, We Did, Results, We Discovered, New Task we might do:
* Based on the Tunnicliffe Shape Sequence (See Resource Notes.)
Think about entering the Science Fair!

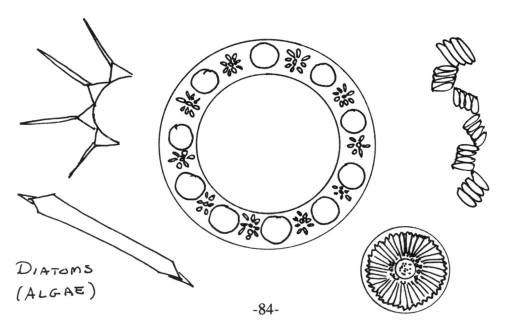

BACTERIA

DIATOMS
(ALGAE)

Chapter 19

Rocks

CONCEPT(S):
Cycles

IDEA (DEFINING CONCEPT):
Exist in cycles

TOPIC & THEME:
Rock Cycles

QUESTION(S):
How is a rock like a circle?
How did traditional people use rocks?

PROCESS & THINKING SKILLS:
Observe
Recall
Record
Classify
Compare
Interpret

INTEGRATIONS:
Science
Art
Language arts
Social studies

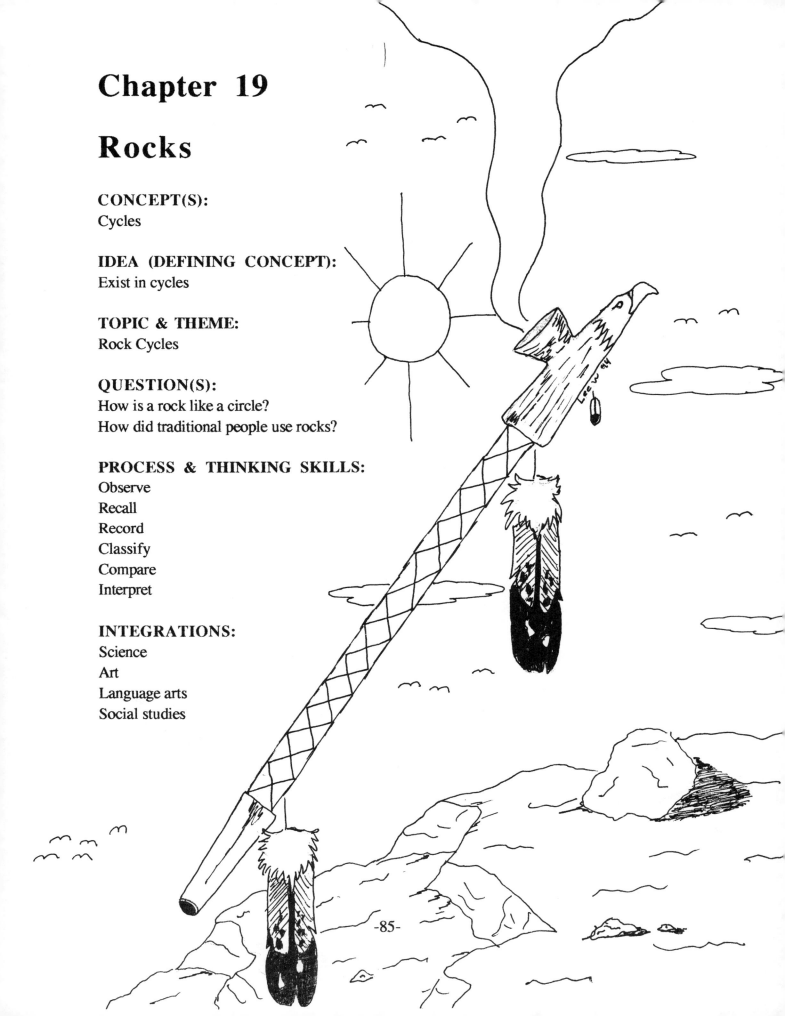

ROCKS

THE STORIES: One hundred and fifty years ago, the Ojibwe elder. Shinvauk, told a story of almost unbelievable skill and courage to Henry Schoolcraft:

> Many years ago, fifty warriors crossed Lake Superior in five birchbark canoes to join our Ojibwe allies in a battle against the Iroquois. They were on the water four days, lead by Kingfisher and Heron. Eagle gave them courage. They were protected by Lynx and the Water Serpents. When the warriors returned home, they told the people they had recorded their journey across this treacherous lake by making rock paintings on the northern cliffs of Lake Superior.

Many people didn't believe that Lake Superior could be crossed by people in canoes, but more than a hundred years later researchers found the warriors' pictographs on the Canadian cliffs of Lake Superior, telling the story just as Shinvauk had reported it.

THE FACTS:

The granite cliffs of the Canadian Shield (where the pictographs were painted) are 3 billion years old. The site of the painting, Agawa Rock, was formed when an ancient fault tore the rock apart. Many generations of Ojibwe used Agawa Rock as a giant canvas for historic and symbolic painting. The red paint was made from crushed Hemitite (a mineral rich in rusty-red iron) probably mixed with fish oil. Hematite was also combined with bear grease and berries.

THE STORY:

Ten men came to vist Winabozho. One man asked for life without end.
  "No Problem!" laughed Winabozho. Twisting the man into a ball, he tossed
the man into a corner where he became a black stone. "You asked for a
long life. Now you will last as long as the world stands!"

THE ROCK CYCLE:

Traditional people and scientists know that all things on Earth change in cycles -- seasons, life, the earth, and even the rocks. Rocks go through the cycle over and over again, taking millions or billions of years.

Clay, a sedimentary rock used for adobe and pottery, comes from the chemical weathering of granite, an igneous rock. Over millions of years, the beds of clay may be heated and pressed into slate, a metamorphic rock (used for making blackboards.) Under more heat and pressure it may be completely remelted and reformed into granite.

This rock cycle was drawn in a traditional style.

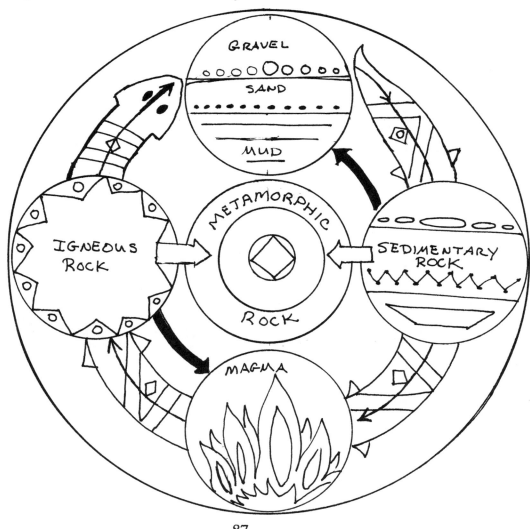

Igneous Rocks are formed in tremendous heat. Rock melted above the earth is lava. Rock melted under the earth's crust is magma. Obsidian is volcanic glass. People used obsidian for scalpels over 2,000 years ago. The granite of the Canadian Shield is igneous, too.

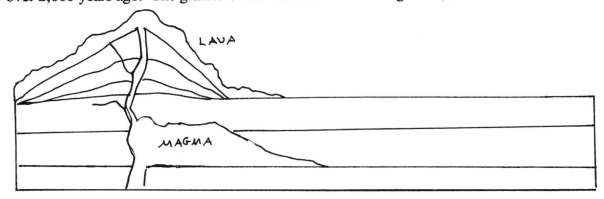

Sedimentary Rocks are formed in layers usually laid down under water. Early cliff-dwelling Indians of the Southwest often built in caves that were naturally carved in limestone cliffs.

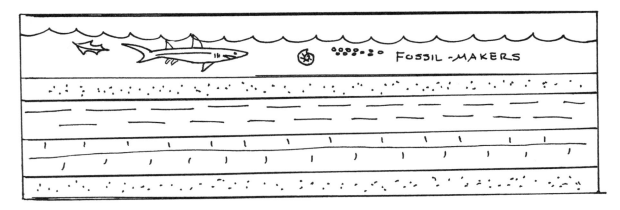

Metamorphic Rocks are formed when rock is changed under great heat and pressure. Limestone under great heat and pressure becomes marble.

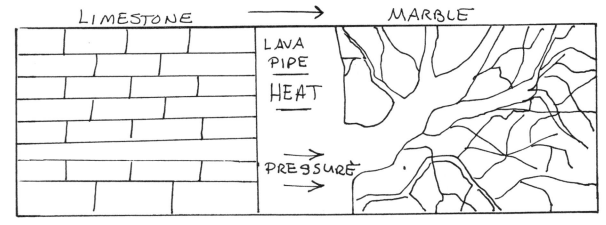

TRADITIONAL USES for Rock(s), Asin(iig), in Ojibwe

Asiniikaa means, "There are rocks there/It is stoney there."

Pigments for paints, Zhizhoobii'igan
(yellow ochre, red ochre, white gypsum, black manganese oxide.)
Crushed rock was mixed with fat to make paint.

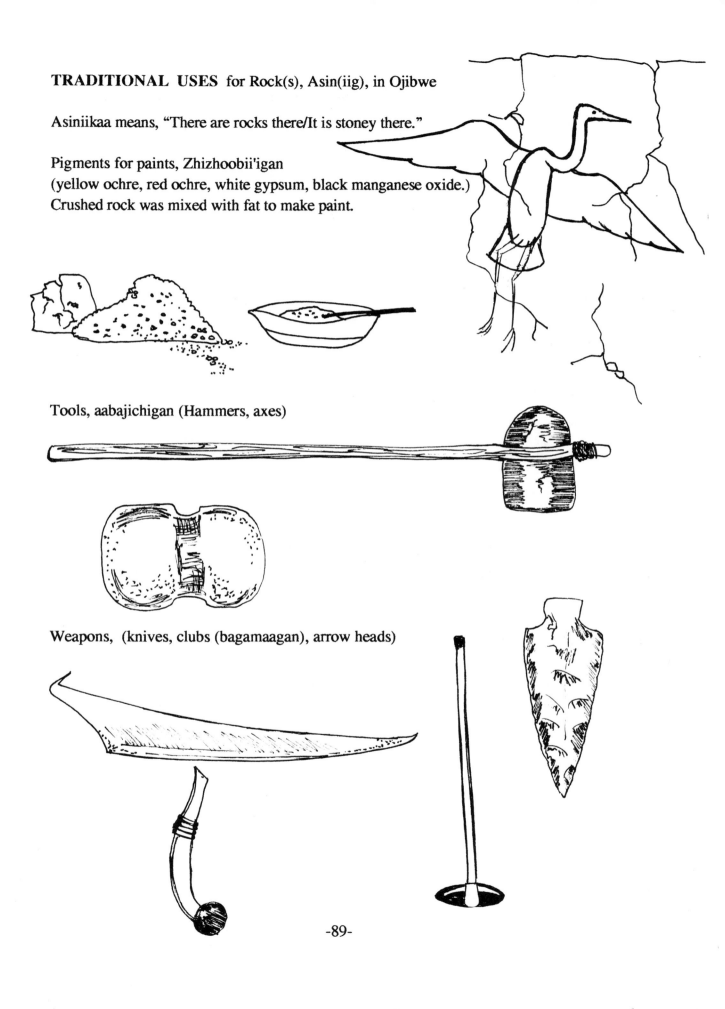

Tools, aabajichigan (Hammers, axes)

Weapons, (knives, clubs (bagamaagan), arrow heads)

Copper, miskwaabik (decoration)

In Michigan the Old Copper Culture People mined nuggets and made them into small cone points, knives, awls, and tools.

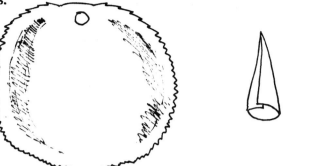

Petroglyphs : Tapping a sharp rock with a hammer-stone, people made rock drawings 5,000 years ago in Minnesota. Many have been detroyed, but more than 2,000 Minnesota carvings can be seen at Jeffers and Nett Lakes.

This Sandstone Arrow Smoother was made about 1,000 years ago. When the arrow shaft was rolled in the sandstone groove, it was straightened and sanded at the same time.

Basalt carving.
This little Zuni bird is carved in basalt and inlaid with turquoise.

Pipes (Catlinite, pipestone opwaaganasin.) Pipestone Quarry was used from about 1600 A.D. Pipestone is a hard clay rich in the red mineral hematite. It is easily carved. All tribes had free and peaceful access to the quarry.

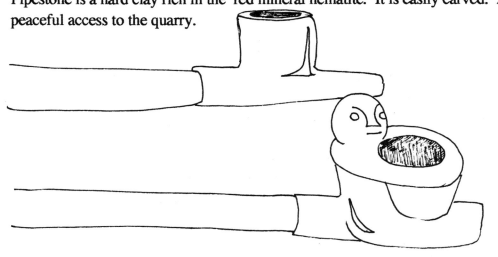

Buildings (clay, adobe, stone)

Pottery (clay) akik (also kettle, pail)
The Mound Builders at Itasca (the headwaters of the Mississippi River) used pulverized granites as temper, and decorated with shapes pressed into clay.

THE ACTIVITIES

1. The Circle (Cycle) of the Rocks
   A. Retell the Rock Cycle as a legend, using elements from your
      culture. Write the story on one half piece of poster board.
   B. Paint a rock cycle on the other half of the poster board.
      Paint in the style of your culture.
      Indian Style -- Flat bright colors and strong designs.
      European Style -- Soft colors, and realistic shading.
      Scandinavian Style -- Rosemaling or Tole Painting.
      African Style -- Bright geometric shapes on white paper.
      Asian Style -- Soft and strong ink shapes. Black on wet or dry paper.
   C. Find examples of the rocks in the cycles, and glue them to the poster board painting.

2. Traditional Uses of Rocks
   Find out how people in many cultures have used rocks.
   Make a picture graph to show the similarities and differences.

ZUNI BEAR

3. Rock Story
   Find an interesting rock. Learn all you can about it.
   Write a fiction story with the rock's origin in the story
   OR Paint a picture of this rock's origin.
   OR Do a beaded pattern to show the rock's origin.
   You can use the rock itself in the item you make. The rock's origin should be as true as possible.

4. Rock Concert!
   Write songs about different types of rocks (igneous, sedimentary and metamorphic.)
   You can also write the tunes, or you can use pop or traditional tunes.
   Give a concert, display your Rock Activities.

5. Clay Critters
   Using self-hardening clay or pottery clay, make pottery or animals for a
   diorama. (Be sure to dry your projects slowly under a layer of plastic
   so they don't crack.) Pottery clay can be fired if your school has a kiln. Write a Title,
   explaining your diorama setting as part of the rock cycle.

6. Micro Rocks
   Draw your rock using basic geometric shapes. Look at the rock through a magnifier. Draw it
   as slowly and realistically as you can. Try to find more math shapes as you draw.

Chapter 20

Minerals

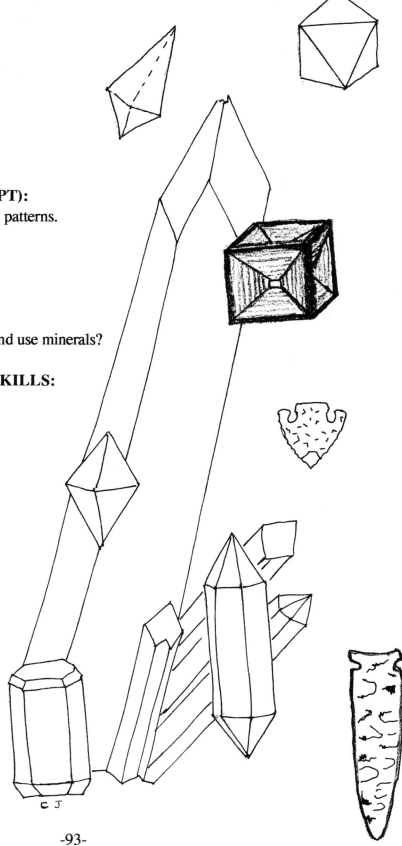

CONCEPT(S):
Properties
Process

IDEA (DEFINING CONCEPT):
The structures of minerals follow patterns.

TOPIC & THEME:
 Mineral patterns

QUESTION(S):
How did traditional people find and use minerals?

PROCESS & THINKING SKILLS:
Recall
Observe
Record
Collect and Organize Data

INTEGRATIONS:
Science
Art
Language arts
Math
Social Studies

MINERALS

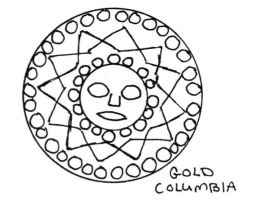

GOLD
COLUMBIA

The Traditions of Precious Minerals

New World Minerals

In the high mountains, where thin oxygen makes fires burn cool, the **Incas** invented special wind-oven smelters to remove pure copper from ore. Then they made bronze alloys of copper and tin. Bronze, a stronger metal than either copper or tin, was important to the technology of farming and war.

A **Mixtec** tomb in Mexico contained 500 beautiful ornaments of gold, jade, copper, turquoise and silver. Copper gives turquoise its blue color.

Champlain was given a sheet of copper a foot long when he went up the St. Lawrence River 400 years ago. **Michigan Indians** melted lumps of copper together, poured it out in sheets, and beat it with stones. Copper ornaments were found in burial mounds in **Itasca State Park** at the headwaters of the Mississippi River.

Spaniards were given 500 pounds of exquisite gold ornaments by native people in Central America.

When the great artist Albrecht Durer saw the work of **Aztec** goldsmiths he said, "I have seen nothing in all my livelong days which so filled my heart with joy." (Durer was the famous German artist who painted the "Praying Hands." Durer's father was a goldsmith.)

Old World Minerals

Two **African** cities became immensely wealthy trading salt and gold. A camel caravan, loaded with salt from Sahara desert mines, would leave with camping supplies for six months. When they finally reached Ghana, they sold their salt for gold, loaded up the camels, and returned home.

Africans invented their own mining technology, digging shafts through rock along gold veins 100 feet deep. Gold was also panned and washed through troughs, leading a visitor to write in amazement, "They grow gold in rows on the desert -- like carrots!"

Egyptians relied on bronze weapons and tools.

The African people of Meroe, a city on the Nile, smelted iron from ore.
Sultans of Kilwa, a city on the southeast coast of Africa, became rich selling gold, copper and iron. They minted coins and lived in beautiful four-story houses.

Ancient **Chinese** made gunpowder from the mineral sulfur (with charcoal and chemicals.)
For 400 years they only used it for beautiful fireworks displays.

Even earlier, they smelted bronze and invented the potter's wheel.

Three thousand years ago the Chinese made iron into swords and plows.

In China, iron and salt supported the emperors' budgets for a thousand years. Salt miners drilled holes two thousand feet deep into salt beds.

Chinese (and Ancient Americans) carved jade into beautiful objects.
Jade is usually green. Jade is a hard mineral gem formed under extreme pressure.

Viking, Franks, Celts, Saxons
Many European tribes honored the eagle, and made beautiful eagles from minerals of gold, silver and bronze, set with rubies or colored glass.

Silver good luck charms were made by Vikings.

Viking goldsmiths made filigree work of golden wires and golden beads.

Have you seen water bead on a hot frying pan? That's how the Vikings made golden beads. When they dropped tiny pieces of gold wire onto a hot charcoal fire, the wire instantly formed a tiny golden sphere.

Both the Vikings and Central Americans made splendid axe heads. The Central American Indians carved jade into a dramatic and useful axe. The Vikings pressed silver wire into complicated groove patterns in their iron axe heads.

Norwegian sea adventurers used calcite to observe polarized light. This allowed them to navigate on cloudy days, before the compass had been invented.

THE FACTS

- There are more than 3,000 minerals. Only 20 are found in a pure form.
- Igneous rocks are made from melted minerals. Each mineral cools at a different temperature. Water carries metals to cracks in the cooling rocks where they form veins of copper, silver and gold. Turquoise is found in narrow veins and patches in lava.
- In Upper Michigan, Indians cracked the rocks from around veins of copper with fire and water.
- Native peoples in Arizona mined salt and precious metals long before the Spanish arrived.
- Salt and agates are sedimentary minerals. Salt was dug out of beds where the mineral was deposited by water from the chemical weathering of quartz type rocks. Lake Superior banded agates come from chemically weathered quartz. Slowly, water drips around the granite carrying silica into cracks where it turns into a thick gel. As the water weathers different rocks, it makes colored bands in the forming agate. Agates have microscopic crystals. In petrified wood, the wood is replaced by agate minerals!
- Garnets, rubies, sapphires, diamonds, and staurolites form when certain minerals are heated under great pressure.
- Metamorphic minerals are often banded, as the crystals get squeezed into bands when they are heated and pressed.
- Staurolite crystals are often twinned in a cross shape.
- Jet, a glossy black mineral, is a very hard form of soft coal. People used it for buttons and beads.

Shapes of Some Crystals:

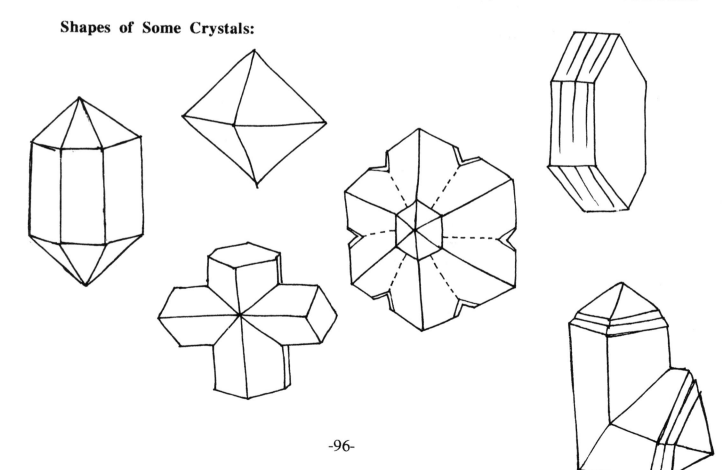

Crystals Grow in Interesting Patterns:

Needles

columns or fibres

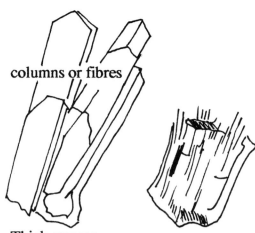

Thin sheets

Thick masses

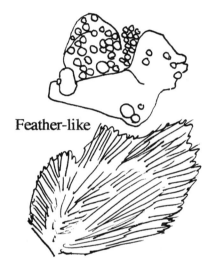

Folded

Feather-like

Stars

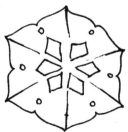

Branches

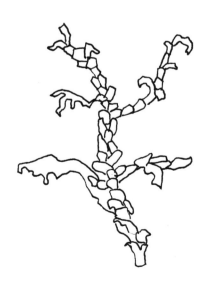

Twinned

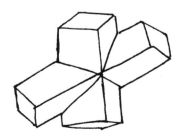

THE ACTIVITIES

1. Native peoples from every corner of Earth have used, minerals, metals and gems.
   A. Find out how your culture used them.
   B. Create a new art form using aluminum or copper foil.
   Hint: You might base the design of something in nature.
   It might be a cutout (like the Ojibwe did on birch bark).
   Or it might be a neckpiece from the Old Copper Culture.
   Or you might make a Viking good luck charm.
   Or -- Come up with your own idea!

COPPER
NORTH AMERICA

2. Look in a rock book to find your favorite mineral.
   Write a few sentences to describe its traits and uses.
   Write a fact or fiction story about how it might have come to be.

3. Write songs about your favorite minerals for your Rock Concert.
   (Can you make them both true and fun?)

4. Crystals
   Draw some crystals as seen through a microscope or in a rock book.
   Make three-dimensional crystals from clay.
   Find similar shapes in nature. (You can use the actual item, a drawing,
   or a magazine picture of the object.) Label the geometric shapes.
   A. Make posters or a diorama using the shapes
   B. Design beadwork or birchbark cutout designs based on these shapes.
   C. Try big abstract drawing or painting based on these shapes.
   You might include elements of your culture in the painting.

5. Try growing some crystals. (Be very patient.)
   What shape and pattern do they have?

6. Cut paper designs. Many cultures use cut paper to make strong designs.
   Cut crystal patterns from colored construction paper.
   Arrange them on a sheet of black construction paper in a fascinating
   pattern or shape.
   OR you can make something imaginary like a "crystal animal."
   OR use the shapes to make a mask design from your culture.

Chapter 21

The Changing Earth

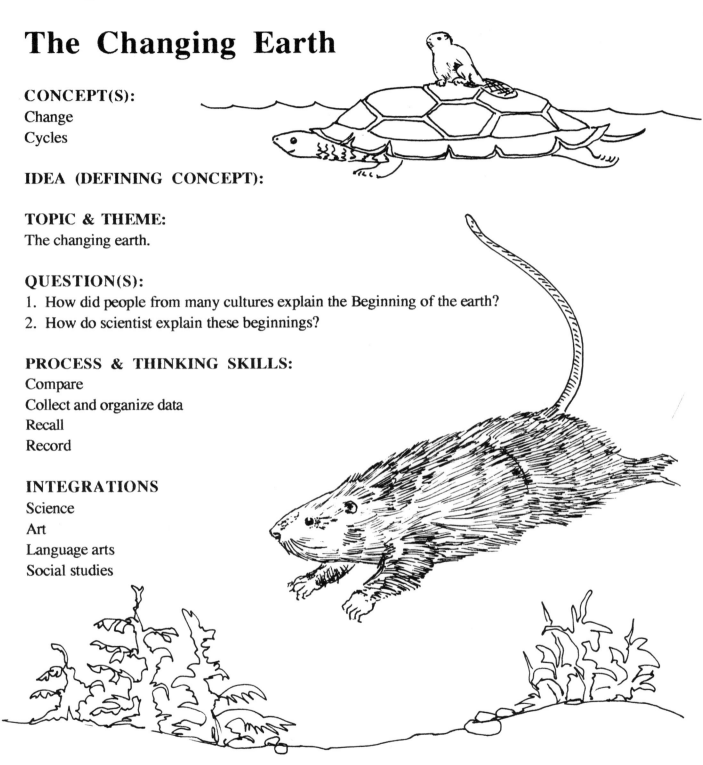

CONCEPT(S):
Change
Cycles

IDEA (DEFINING CONCEPT):

TOPIC & THEME:
The changing earth.

QUESTION(S):
1. How did people from many cultures explain the Beginning of the earth?
2. How do scientist explain these beginnings?

PROCESS & THINKING SKILLS:
Compare
Collect and organize data
Recall
Record

INTEGRATIONS
Science
Art
Language arts
Social studies

THE CHANGING EARTH

THE STORIES: From earliest times people have attempted to discover the Beginnings of the Universe and Life on Earth. Since these early people had no scientific methods to test their ideas, they simply imagined The Beginning as it could have been. Through time the stories became an important part of every culture. These beautiful stories create a vast and important literature that connects all peoples of this earth. To a scientist, one culture's stories are no more "true" than any other culture's stories. Each story has its own special beauty.

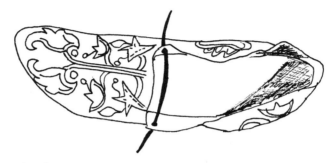

OJIBWE

In The Beginning the first Earth was called Ca'Ca. It was dark. People had no wisdom, no clothes, no fire. They were cold and hungry. Gichi Manidoo sent Winabozho to teach them. He gave them fire and showed them how to cook meat. He gave them dreams for knowledge. He told them to keep their minds clear, not to drink alcohol, and to use tobacco only for ceremony.

Winabozho taught The Anishinaabe to use plants, disguises and other tricks (adaptations) for survival. One time Winabozho made Lake Spirit very angry, and He sent a flood to punish Winabozho. But Winabozho, Muskrat and Beaver escaped in a canoe to the top of a tall tree. Beaver dove down to the bottom of the endless lake, but could not find any land. Muskrat tried too. Finally little Muskrat brought up some mud on his paw. As Winabozho blew his breath on the mud, it became land, and grew so big that the waters collect in the lakes and oceans.

CHINESE (From several versions)

In The Beginning there was Chaos in the form of a huge yellow bird with a body like a bag and no face at all. It had six feet and four wings, and sometimes its body glowed fiery red. The bird danced and sang from its home of jade in the Sky Mountains.   His name was Phan-Ku.

There was no heaven or earth. The egg of chaos divided into two parts as heavy elements sank to the bottom, and airy elements drifted upwards. This separation is the yin and yang. Phan-ku was born from the egg. Every day the sky lifts ten feet higher from the earth with Phan-ku filling all the space in between. When Phan-ku died his eyes became the sun and moon; his voice became thunder.   The hairs on his head became the stars and planets. His tears became rivers. His teeth were transformed into white stones. His bones became precious metals, with marrow of jade. The tiny fleas on his body became ancestors of The People.

GREEK

In The Beginning, there were Emptiness and Confusion. The first children were Darkness and Death. But their child was Love. And Love created Light and Day. Heaven and Earth were the First Mother and First Father. Their children were the forces of earthquakes and volcanoes, the 12 giants: Titans. Saturn was the king of the Titans. When his son, Zeus, took over, Saturn created a land of peace and harmony in Italy.

Pandora disobeyed the gods, and opened a beautiful forbidden box. Out of the box flew all the seeds for death and disease in the world. But down in the corner of the box Pandora also found Hope. This, too, is a gift to people.

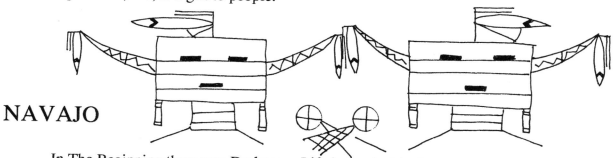

NAVAJO

In The Beginning there was Darkness. Life began inside the earth in the First World. People, animals and rocks all developed there. The people were not human then. First Man, First Woman and Coyote came up to the Second World through hollow reeds, where a hazy light was made from the Sun and Moon. The Third World was a beautiful place with good soil and blue skies. The people would be happy and safe -- as long as they didn't hurt the Water Giant.

One day Coyote was out playing and he saw the children of the Water Giant. He decided to take them home to be his own children. The Water Giant was outraged when he found that his children were missing, and he suspected the people. As the Water Giant chased the people he created a huge flood. Badger tried digging a way up to the Fourth World, but the Flood came too fast. Locust found a way up to the Fourth World, and asked four swans to help them. The swans opened the way for the people to escape; the children of the Water Giant returned to their father.

When the people emerged into the Fourth World, they found themselves in the middle of a marshy swamp with no solid ground. The God of Darkness cut the mountains to make the water drain away. The God of Winds swirled around to dry out the earth. Then the people piled up the earth into four mountains that can still be seen in the desert today.

The people had many more adventures, quarrels and wars with giants before First Man and First Woman led they way to the Fifth (present) world. Their daughter, White Shell Maiden held an ear of corn, and a corn tassel. She wore a rainbow necklace. White Shell Woman came to the people and said, " We want you to be more like us. Bring me two perfect ears of corn-- one white and one yellow." The people brought the ears of corn and wrapped them in buckskin. White and yellow winds blew and blew. When the dust cleared, and the buckskin was unwrapped two human people sat up, a man and a woman. "Dineh" is like "Anishinaabe". It means, "The People."

VIKING

In The Beginning there was Nothing. Not sand or sea or waves or earth or heaven. There was only a huge chasm with ice on one side and fire on the other. Where the fire and ice met, the water droplets formed Ymir (the First Giant) and the Frost Maidens. Odin, the Sky Father, was their son. He and his brothers killed their wicked father, creating stars, sun, earth, sun and sea from his body.

They created First Man and First Woman from trees in their garden. They also created Dwarfs, who were wonderful craftsmen, and Elves, who cared for streams and flowers.

The Universe was held up by a beautiful tree. But an evil snake was constantly eating away at the root of the tree, and the tree was doomed to die. When the tree died, it would crash downward destroying the Earth. Odin's job was to postpone The End of the World as long as possible. The only way to do this was through courage and heroism. His responsibility was so great that he was always deep in thought. He didn't even eat. At feasts he gave his food to his two pet wolves, Thought and Memory. He paid with one of his eyes to drink from the Well of Wisdom, and he passed this Wisdom on to Humans. To make life better for Humans, Odin risked his own life to steal a precious drink from the Giants. When Humans drank it, they became poets. Odin's maidens, the Valkyries, took the spirts of brave warriors to a beautiful paradise. The story finally has a happy ending. After the End of the Earth, a new and more beautiful Universe will be born.

FON AND YORUBA (AFRICAN)

In The Beginning there was only Nana Buluku, First Mother. She created the universe and the world. Her twin children were Mawu the Moon Woman, and Lisa the Sun Man. They had no children until they came together in an eclipse. Then they had seven sets of twins. Storm Twins ruled the sky. Iron Twins gave people tools for farming and hunting. Each pair had a special job. Many gods were responsible for listening to The People, who were created by first mother molding them from clay as a woman molds pottery.

In The Beginning the world was a misty marsh. The Creator lived in the sky with other gods, and sometimes they would climb down spider webs to play in the swamp. One day the Creator told Great God, "I want you to make some solid ground in the world. Take this snail shell to the swamp for me. "

Inside the shell was earth, a pigeon and a hen. First, Great God sprinkled the earth on the swamp, then set the birds on it. Of course, when they started scratching, they sent the earth scattering. Wherever it landed, more earth was formed. Creator sent Chameleon to earth, and he reported that the earth was wide and dry. Then Creator sent Great God to make animals, plants, and rain. People were molded from clay. The Rainbow is the hunting bow of the Great God, so the people can hope to never be hungry.

JUDEO-CHRISTIAN

In The Beginning there was Darkness. The Creator made Heaven and Earth, Light and Darkness. He made Land and Oceans. On the land he made grass and plants. In the sky he made sun, moon and stars. Then he made animals. The Creator picked up some clay and made the First Man. He made First Woman from a rib of the Man. They lived in perfect garden of plenty and happiness.

But First Man and Woman disobeyed the Creator, by eating the fruit of a forbidden tree. So he sent them out of the garden into a place where there was pain, disease and hunger. So the years passed and the world filled with people. But the people were wicked, and The Creator decided to wash them away in a huge flood. He told a man named Noah to build a big boat in order to save his family and two of every animal. They floated for a long time without seeing any land. Noah sent out two birds, and when the Dove brought back a twig, he knew the waters were going away. The Creator gave Humans the Rainbow as a sign of hope.

HINDU (INDIA)

The Song of Creation
In The Beginning...there was no realm of air,
No sky beyond it. What covered and where?
What gave shelter? Was there water?
There was no day or night.
All that existed was the great power of warmth.
And the first seed arose.
Who knows the truth of where life came from,
Or the truth of the coming of Creation?

TREE OF LIFE

SCIENTISTS -- The Big Bang Theory

In The Beginning there was One Force, and everything was simple, elegant and beautiful. Gravity, Electro-magnetic, Weak and Strong forces, were all part of the One Force. 15 billion years ago a tremendous explosion released the forces. Atoms formed. This is called the Big Bang. Some atoms formed into elements. Atoms, molecules and elements formed for billions of years.

More than four billion years ago the Earth solidified from Cosmic materials. First Life evolved on Earth three billion years ago from elements and energy on our planet. The First Life had single cell. It divided into two Daughter Cells. These divided over and over for more than 2 billion years. Cells joined with cells to create new life forms:

The seas were full of mollusks, snails and plants 500 Million years ago.

Insects crawled around nearly 400 Million years ago.

Primitive fish and sharks swam in the seas 350 Million years ago.

Dinosaurs and other reptiles thrived 150 million years ago.

Birds evolved from flying dinosaurs 150 million years ago.

Flowers dotted the Earth 120 Million years ago.

65 Million years ago, the dinosaurs became extinct. Early Mammals were small rodents.

A giant giraffe-rhinocerous lived 30 Million years ago.

Ancient beavers, 3-toed horses, wolves, apes and humans all lived 20 Million years ago.

1-toed horses, mastodons, bear-dogs and giant camels roamed Texas six million years ago.

And Humankind? The Modern Human Family evolved just 40,000 years ago.

THE SCIENCE:

When scientists make a statement anyone can try to prove or disprove it.

What real proof do scientists have for their theories?

1. Because rocks give off radiation, scientists can determine their age.
2. The universe is still expanding from the Big Bang.
3. Scientists can repeat Mini "Big Bangs" in labs. The elements and amounts of elements formed are identical to predictions based on Big Bang ideas.
4. Scientists can create the conditions for early life in a lab.

THE ACTIVITIES

1. Chose two creation stories. Compare them with words and pictures.
   Which stories are your favorite? Why?
   Write a new creation story using your favorite elements of several.
   You may find many more in the library.
2. Write and illustrate a science-based creation story.
   Make it just as interesting and delightful as the mythological stories.
   You may want to illustrate it and use it as a poster, book, or even a play.
3. Write a science-based creation story for your "Rock Concert."

Chapter 22

Surfaces of the Earth

CONCEPT(S):
Structures
Components

TOPIC & THEME:
Surfaces of the earth.

QUESTION(S):
1. What are the traditional stories about the earth's surface?
2. Why does Minnesota have so many lakes?
3. Why doesn't it have mountains?
4. What was Minnesota like in the past?

PROCESS & THINKING SKILLS:
Record
Experiment
Predict

INTEGRATIONS:
Science
Art
Geology
Social Studies

SURFACE OF THE EARTH

THE STORIES AND THE GEOLOGY:

Lake Superior (Ojibwe)

Winabozho, the messenger/creator of the Ojibwe people, was born on an island. He grew up almost overnight, and was so big that he could walk over any lake with one big step. To catch beavers he dammed up the rivers until Lake Superior was created. The Apostle Islands are piles of dirt that Winabozho dug up while damming the lake. Winabozho was a world-traveler. Wherever he walked, his footprints made mountains and lakes.

To make the world safe for the Anishinaabe, he had to kill the monsters that lived on the earth first. The fossil bones we find today are the remains of those monsters.

The Great Lakes (Loggers)

According to the lumberjacks, the Great Lakes were dug by Paul Bunyan.
The lakes, they say, were big watering troughs for Babe, Paul's giant blue ox. Babe was in the habit of drinking the rivers dry, which was very bad for logging since the logs were floated down the rivers to the mill towns. Paul dug the lakes near the huge forests so Babe could drink whenever he wanted. While Paul was digging the lakes he lost his mitten, and it became the lower part of Michigan.

Paul wanted a way to ship logs from Minnesota, so he dug the Mississippi River too. Dirt that he flung over his right shoulder made the Rocky Mountains. Dirt that he flung over his left shoulder made the Appalachians. After he was done, he threw the shovel away. It became Florida.

Geologists tell us that The Superior Basin was formed by an enormous crack (rift) a billion years ago. The crack went from Minnesota to Kansas. During the Ice Age the northern part filled with a glacier that cut it deeper and wider. The cut was 360 miles long, 160 miles wide and 1300 feet deep. If you used the Grand Canyon for a scoop, it would take seven Grand Canyons to scoop out all the material from the Superior Basin!

Sea reptiles and ancient sharks swam in the sea that covered Minnesota during the Age of Reptiles (70 million years ago). Since Minnesota was under water then, we don't find fossils from land dinosaurs here.

Gigantic beavers weighing 500 lbs roamed Minnesota during the warm times between the Glaciers 200,000 years ago. Mastodons may have been hunted by the earliest Minnesotans, 10,000 years ago.

Three Maidens (Ojibwe-Lakota)
The three giant boulders at Pipestone Quarry are the eggs of the war eagle.
Some people call them the Three Maidens who guard the quarry.

The Geology: The Three Maidens were once one huge granite rock that was brought by the glacier from Millstone, South Dakota, more than 100 miles away! Frost action split the giant rock into three parts. Big out-of-place boulders are called "erratics."

Mountains and Rivers (German)
When the world was new it was wet, smooth and glossy. Giants lived on the earth then, and the Men Giants became impatient for the world to harden. They began clomping around the world. Wherever they went, their big boots sunk into the smooth surface, making a lake or sea. And when they picked up their big feet, enormous clumps of earth and rocks fell off their boots, making mountains and hills. When the Lady Giants saw the mess their husbands made they began to cry. Their huge tears rolled down the mountains and across the land, making rivers and filling the lakes with water. These German giants could only move around after dark. One morning a ray of sun caught them. The giants turned to stone. Today we call them the Sudaten Mountains.

Scientists tell us that the German Sudaten Mountains are blocks of folded gneiss (granite that has been heated, pressed, lifted and weathered).

Horseshoe Valley (Norse-Viking)
Iceland has a giant horseshoe-shaped valley. The Norse said it was the hoof print of Odin's magical 8-legged horse.

The Iceland horseshoe was formed by an ancient river and waterfall. A volcano underneath a glacier probably made the river of flooding meltwater.

The Giant's Love Story (Norse-Viking)
Once upon a time a barbaric Norwegian giant fell in love with a lovely lady giant. She didn't like him at all because he was a churlish clod. Besides, she had already fallen in love with a very nice giant, Torge, who loved her and treated her respectfully.

The Barbarian became furious with her refusals. He chased her and shot an arrow at her. Quick-thinking Torge was nearby, throwing his hat at the arrow to stop it. The Barbarian tried to flee on horseback, but was turned to stone by the first ray of the sun.

Torge and the lovely lady giant lived happily ever after. Today you can still see Torge's giant hat with the hole in it, and the stone island that remains of the Barbarian.

What made the hole in the hat? Geologists say "Torghatten" (Torge's Hat) is a high hill on a Norwegian Island.   Hundreds of thousands of years ago, between the glaciers, the climate was warmer, and the water level was higher than it is today. Heavy waves pounded smaller rocks into the "hat" until a natural tunnel was carved through it, at a spot where a crack had weakened the big rock. A nearby rocky island is barbaric giant turned to stone.

The Blue Mountains (Nez Pierce)

Every year seven giant brothers came east to devour children. Every year the People tried to stop them, but nothing worked. Then Coyote had an idea. Calling all the digging animals together, he asked them to dig seven very deep holes. When this was done, Coyote filled the holes with steaming hot red-yellow liquid. When the giants marched toward the camp of the the people, they fell into the holes, splashing the liquid on themselves. Coyote quickly changed the giants into seven mountains. The splashes became copper deposits.

Scientists tell us that the Blue Mountains are huge blocks of basalt with a granite core. Copper was deposited as the molten rock cooled.

Devil's Tower (Kiowa)

One day while out berry-picking, seven little girls were chased by giant bears. They scrambled up on a low rock and prayed to the spirit of the rock to save them. Suddenly the rock soared upward. When it reached the sky, the little girls became the seven dancing sister stars, Pleiades. The giant bears tried to chase them up the rock, but it was too steep and too tall. Today you can see the long gouges that the bears' claws made on the rocks.

The Geology:

Devil's Tower is the neck of an extinct volcano! The rocks around it were softer and have weathered away, leaving a plug of hard basalt exposed.

The columns (bear claw scratches) form naturally in some lavas. As they cool, shrink and crack the lava forms hexagonal shapes.

The hexagon is an important math shape in nature. Honey bees build honey-combs with hexagonal cells. This shape gives the largest inside area with the least amount of outside perimeter. To a bee this means that they use less wax to store more honey!

Northern Minnesota's Surface

Billions of years ago there were mountains and volcanoes in Minnesota. They have mostly weathered away, but you can see remains of these ancient rocks along the North Shore. Look for different rock formations, faults, folding, dikes and sills. Ice Age Glaciers determined how much of Minnesota looks today. See "Climate" for more about Minnesota's glaciers.

Billions of Years in Minnesota is an interesting book by Edmund C. Bray. County by county, you can learn about Minnesota's rocks and history as you drive through the state. For example:

NORTHWESTERN MINNESOTA

Beltrami & Lake of the Woods Counties
* Beltrami County was the bed of immense Glacial Lake Agassiz, which covered parts of Minnesota, North Dakota, much of Manitoba and Ontario.
* Today all that is left of Lake Agassiz in Minnesota is Red Lake and Lake of the Woods. MN Highway 1 runs along the south shore of the ancient lake.
* A mighty river drained this lake through Southern Minnesota.
* St. Paul had a waterfall twice as tall and twice as wide as Niagara!
* Lake Bemidji was formed when an enormous block of ice melted.
* Beltrami County's hills are moraines (piles of rock and sand left as the glacier melted).
* In the spring, look for tiny "moraines" at the edges of snow drifts.

Cass County
* In Cass County, the hill from Walker to Pillager is a long moraine.
* Most of the lakes were formed by huge melting ice blocks.
* Boy Lake was an ice block in the moraine.
* Cass Lake and Lake Winnibigoshish were ice blocks in the outwash till (rocks and sand that were carried out of glacier by streams.)
* Leech Lake was formed when water was trapped behind two moraines.
* You can see an outcrop of ancient granite West-Northwest of Pillager and South of Boy River.
* The point in Pine Mt. Lake at Backus is probably an esker. (Eskers are long, winding ridges formed from the sand and gravel in a river running under a glacier!)
* At Remer, the west side of Laura Lake is an esker.

Clearwater County
* Itasca State Park is in the outwash plain of a glacier.
* Lake Itasca is the Headwaters of the Mississippi River.
* An Esker 50-60 feet high runs north and south on the east side of
    Lake Itasca.
* The marker at Peace Pipe Springs tells visitors the geology of the park.
* The Mississippi River formed from overflowing glacial lakes as they melted.
* Indian people may have seen the last glaciers leave Minnesota 10,000 years ago.
* The Bison Kill site in Itasca State Park proves that people lived and depended on the
    river 9,000 years ago.
    The oldest dog skeleton in Minnesota was found at this site.
* About 1,500 years ago people lived near the Mississippi River, eating
    wild rice, building burial mounds and making clay pottery and copper ornaments.
    Villages had 600-800 people.

Hubbard County
* Drumlins are long, low mounds of sand and gravel shaped by glaciers.
    You can see drumlin hills in the Badoura State Forest.
* All the lakes are basins that contained huge melting ice blocks.
* The chains of lakes near Akeley and east of Park Rapids are ice block
    lakes in outwash in valleys that existed before the glaciers.
* The big Itasca Moraine is crossed by U.S. 71 North of Park Rapids and by MN 64
    north of Akeley.

Mahnomen County
* Mahnomen County is covered with glacial deposits.
* Lake Beaulieau, like most of the county's lakes, is a ice block lake.
* The chains of lakes are in valleys that existed before the glaciers.
* Little Elbow Lake (16 miles East of Waubun) is a lake in a moraine.

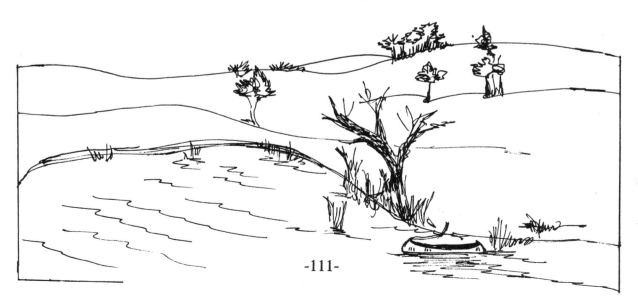

NORTH CENTRAL MINNESOTA

Iron Range Area
* Behind the Gilbert Elementary School you can find Ely Greenstone, lava that bubbled up in pillows under water. Then it was heated and pressed into a hard green rock. Some greenstone is 5-6 miles thick!
* Driving along MN 135 between Virginia and Gilbert, you can see slate.
* Fossil shark teeth and fish bones from 100 million years ago are found in the mine dumps west of Hibbing.
* The steep hills north of Hibbing are moraines.

Itasca County
* Lake Winnibigoshish and Ball Club Lake, like most of the area lakes, are ice block basins in the glacial drift. (Drift is all the rock material carried by the glacier.)
* Lake Pokegama and the Mississippi River cut through a moraine near Grand Rapids.
* Fossils of sharks, fish and   long-nosed crocodiles are found near Calumet. These swam in the seas long before the glaciers.
* An esker 60-70 feet high can be seen in Scenic State Park.
* The park also has many erratics, big boulders left there by glaciers.
* North of Nashwauk look for volcanic ash, granite and greenstone.

St. Louis County (Glacial)
* A moraine crosses St. Louis County.
* Glacial Lake Upham covered much of the county during the Ice Age.
* Most lakes were caused by ice blocks that gouged out the bedrock. (This is different than lakes to the west, which are found in glacial till. The bedrock doesn't have much calcium, so it can't buffer the effects of acid rain as well as western lakes. This is why some lakes suffer acid rain damage and some do not.)
* Pelican and Vermil ion Lakes were formed by water being trapped by a moraine in a bedrock basin. You can see this north of Orr on US 53.
* Graywacke is a coarse gray sandstone. Near Cook you can see it changed (metamorphosed) into slate.

Tower-Soudan Area
* Two and half billion years ago, volcanic lava and enormous oceans drifted over this area.
* Cracked Sedimentary rocks with magma pushed into the cracks can be seen on MN 169, 2 miles west of MN 135.
* Water seeped through the rocks and carried the iron minerals into deposits that are mined today. Gold was even mined here.
* A marker on MN 169 tells about mining.

NORTHEASTERN MINNESOTA

Cook County
* On the Gunflint Trail, lakes formed in long broken ridges of bedrock. Some lakes, like Gunflint Lake, were dammed by glacial till. At the Gunflint Lake Overlook, you can see nickel-copper minerals and iron formations in the roadcuts. At the Laurentian Divide, water flows into Hudson Bay or the St. Lawrence River.
* In the town park at Tofte, you will see lava pipes formed by gas bubbles.
* At Cascade Falls water churns over a 15,000 foot thick layer of lava. Because the lava hardness varies, the water weathers it at different rates. That's why the falls "cascade" at different levels.
* Remember the hexagons at Devils Tower? Rock has cooled into hexagonal columns at Grand Marais too.
* Isle Royal is a sandstone layer over lava.

Lake County
* 19 different lava flows can be found in Gooseberry Falls State Park.
* Split Rock State Park has cliffs of feldspar formed billions of years ago.
* The red lava flows of Baptism River State Park contain dikes and sills.
* Two glacial moraines meet at Isabella.
* The rough Tetaguche country around Illgen City is hard granite that hasn't weathered as fast as the surrounding material.

St. Louis County (Duluth)
* Dark hardened magma (gabbro), sometimes 5 miles thick, can be seen along the North Shore drive from Duluth.
* Look for ancient lava flows over older sandstones along Interstate 35.
* Skyline Drive on the shore of Glacial Lake Duluth is 500 feet above the level of Lake Superior.
* Glacial Lake Duluth was formed about 10,000 years ago.
* Duluth Harbor was formed when the glacier melted, drowning the mouth of the river, and making the Harbor.

THE ACTIVITIES:

1. Petroglyphs Stories

    Small groups of two or three children.

    Choose an area of Minnesota from the list in this chapter.

    Design petroglyphs (simple pictures) to describe the surface of the area.

    (Use scratch paper first).

    -- Redraw your designs with paint or chalk on rock-colored paper.

    -- Write the story of the rocks in your own words.

    -- Write a myth to explain the formation as traditional people from
       your culture might have explained it.

2. Write a Minnesota Rock Song for your "Rock Concert!"

3. Find an interesting rock (any size). Try to identify it.

    Most surface rock in northern Minnesota was deposited by the glaciers.

    Tell the story about where the rock might have come from, and how it got
    to your home. Illustrate your story with a picture or a diorama "home"
    for your rock.

4. Invent a Game!

    Use all the earth's surface vocabulary words in your science book.

    Use any of the stories or facts you need. Look up more if you can.

    Invent cards, pebbles for markers, dice....whatever you need.

    Make the game as silly, as competitive, or as cooperative as you wish.

    (Just make sure you can LEARN with it!)

Chapter 23

Layers of the Earth

CONCEPT(S):
Components
Structures

TOPIC & THEME:
Layers of the earth

QUESTION(S):
1. How is the earth like maple sugar cake?
2. What can layers of rock tell us about Minnesota during the last 4 billion years?

PROCESS & THINKING SKILLS:
Observe
Collect and organize data

INTEGRATIONS:
Science
Art
Geology
Math

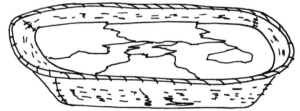

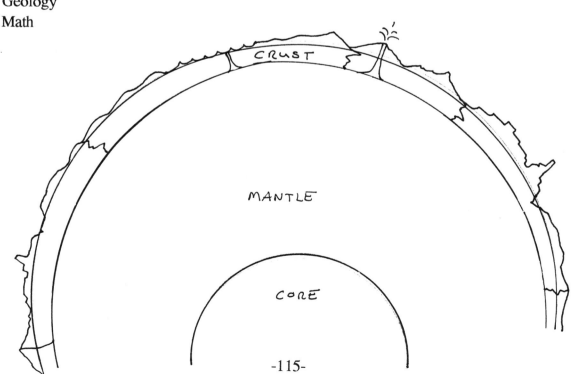

LAYERS OF THE EARTH

THE FACTS:
Think about making maple sugar from boiled sap.
What happens when the boiling sap is poured into a mold?
If the mold is metal, the bottom of the pan is hot and solid metal.
As it cools, the outside becomes a thin crust.
The sugary syrup under the crust is a hot thick liquid.

This is a good model for our earth's layers.
The outside crust of hard rock and ocean is only 25 miles thick.
The mantle is made of hot, thick melted rocks. It's about 1800 miles thick, and surrounds the core like a mantle (an old Latin word for "big coat.")
The core is made of heavy metals like nickel and iron, 2100 miles across.

If you shake the maple sugar before it's completely cool the crust will crack.
Some of the hot sugar-syrup might leak out of the crack on the cooled crust.
This is how the land crust builds up.
Some of the crust might sink down into the hotter sugar-syrup and get remelted.
Rain, wind, (or a hungry person!), could affect the cooled sugar too.
This is how the land crust gets worn away.
Scientists now have evidence that the Earth's crust is cracked into big plates. Some plates are spreading apart, and others are squeezing together.
This is how the continents have moved.
This is what causes major earthquakes and volcanoes.

Earth	maple sugar cake	zhiiga' igan
crust	maple sugar	ziinzibaakwad
mantle	maple taffy/syrup	bigiwizigan/ zhiiwaagamizigan
core	metal	biiwaabik

Pretend your Grandma invents a new layer cake that has a topping of maple syrup, cornmeal pudding in the middle, and a wild rice crust on the bottom.

How can you tell which layer she had put in the pan first, second and last?
Rock layers of the Earth are like a layer cake.
The first (oldest) layers are on the bottom.

ROCK STORY CHART: Photocopy the following pages and tape them together to make a long vertical chart.

MINNESOTA ROCK STORY CHART

YEARS AGO: ACTIVITY:

Today

The Earth's crust continues to build and wear down.
The Continental Plates continue to slowly shift.
The climate is getting warmer, just like after the other
glaciers. People and other mammals dominate the Earth.

10,000

The last glacier melted. Minnesota was full of lakes
and rivers. The Mississippi River was born.
The very first Minnesotans, early Indian people, may have
seen the glacier as it melted north.
They hunted bison in the grasslands.

**100,000-
10,000**

The "Wisconsin" Glacier formed, making Minnesota's
landscape of low hills and lakes.
It ground rock to powder, which weathered into good
farming soil in Southern Minnesota.
Cold-weather animals like Ice Age elephants lived here.

**100,000-
120,000**

In this warm time between the glaciers, the oceans were
25 feet higher than they are today.

**120,000-
150,000**

The "Illinois" Glacier formed, almost completely covering
Minnesota. It went as far south as St. Louis, Missouri!

**150,000-
400,000**

The "Kansan" Glacier grew and retreated as the climate
became colder and warmer. In the warm periods Minnesota was home to giant sloths, beavers, musk ox and
elephants.

---

2 million -

400,000

The Ice Age Begins!
The first big glacier (called the "Nebraskan" Glacier)
covered Minnesota. Colder climate caused some snow
not to melt over the summer. This made the air even
colder, so less melted the next year. The white snow
reflected the sun's energy back to space, making Earth
even colder. That's how the glaciers grew.

45 Million	The North American Continent separated from Europe as the Continental Plates moved apart.
70 Million	The Age of Mammals began. Minnesota's land slowly weathered. There were no big seas or volcanos at this time.
136 Million - 70 Million	The Age of Reptiles booms but Minnesota is under a huge sea, so we did not get any land dinosaurs. Minnesota did have sea-going reptiles and sharks!
200 Million - 136 Million	An enormous sea covered Minnesota. The sea is shaped like Leech Lake, except it stretched from Canada to Texas. The One Huge Continent began to break apart, drifting on the separate Continental Plates.
225 Million- 200 Million	No new rocks formed. The surface of Minnesota slowly weathered. Pine trees and reptiles evolve.
350 Million- 200 Million	Minnesota was a swampy wet land of primeval trees and ferns.
350 Million- 400 Million	In the seas that covered Minnesota fish and coral evolved.
435 Million- 400 Million	Minnesota was a dry land of gentle weathering.
500 Million- 435 Million	Seas covered most of North America including Minnesota. The sand became a soft pale yellow sandstone layer from Minnesota to Arkansas and Detroit. The sandstone is 99% quartz, great for glass-making. Underneath Minneapolis the earth is full of tunnels where people mined the sand- stone. The seas also created limestone and shale full of Interesting invertebrate fossils.

| 500 Million | The Age of Invertebrates. Life forms began, evolved, and flourished in the quiet seas that covered Minnesota. |

| 1 Billion | A huge rift (crack) formed from Minnesota to Kansas. Magma pushed through the crack. You can see this magma along the shores of Lake Superior. When the magma was squeezed out of the crack, it left a huge hole in the earth. A billion years later, this is the bed of Lake Superior. Weathering of earlier igneous rocks produced sand that drifted to the bottom of the great sea. The sand hardened into pink quartzite (hard sandstone). |

Lake Superior Agates were formed by colored minerals slowly seeping into round holes in the rift magma. The holes were formed by gas bubbles in the liquid rock.

| 2 Billion | New volcanoes in Minnesota and Wisconsin created granites.
These were folded and heated and pressed into gneiss. |

| 2 1/2 Billion | Volcanic activity slows down, and erosion takes over. Seas covered Minnesota twice, laying down thick layers of clay, shale, slate (metamorphosed shale) along the North Shore, Gunflint and Mesabi Ranges. Mesabi taconite is formed. |

| 3 Billion | Giant masses of lava poured from cracks in the earth in Northern Minnesota.   Since much of Minnesota was under an ancient sea, the lava became "pillowed".
Water seeped through the lava and carried iron into veins.
Erosion and weathering broke down some of the granites into sand and other sedimentary rocks.
Magma pillows were heated and pressed into Ely Greenstone, a metamorphic rock. |

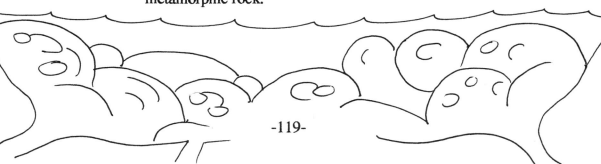

4 Billion	Minnesota bedrock granite was formed from magma in the earth. Sedimentary bedrock came from even OLDER granites. For the next billion years, folding, heat and pressure continued to change the "oldest rocks in the world."
4 and Half Billion	The Universe was formed from cosmic materials.

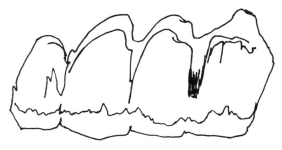

MASTODON AND MASTODON TOOTH

THE ACTIVITIES

1. Make a model (like the maple sugar cake) of the earth's layers using
   some natural or native object or plant from your culture.
   Make a card explaining your model.

2. Research the Minnesota Rock Story Chart
   Tape it together to make a long, vertical time chart.
   Research other plants and animals that could have lived in Minnesota's past.
   Draw small pictures to represent the events, rocks, plants and animals
   at each stage in Minnesota's rock history.
   Attach them to the side of the Chart.

3. "Incredible Time Graph" (A Math integration)
   Students (in groups or as individuals) will select a geologic time.
   They will make an appropriate prop. (Mastodon bone, volcano....)
   (The props can be drawn and cut out of big poster board.)
   Students can assign a measurement-value to a time value in years.
   (For example, one inch could equal a million years.
   Let students come up with their own values!)
   Students can interpret this span of time by placing a person (holding a
   prop) in each stage in Minnesota's rock story.

HINTS:
   If one inch equals a million years, you will need about 4,000 inches to
   make a 4 billion year time chart.
   4,000 inches is 333 feet, or 100 yards.
   You can use a football field to make a giant graph!
   Kids can really get a feel for how long ago things took place.
   (Students can graph this out on big paper with "yard lines" to help guide
   them outside.)

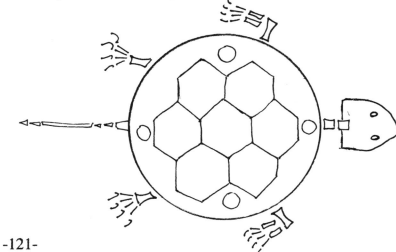

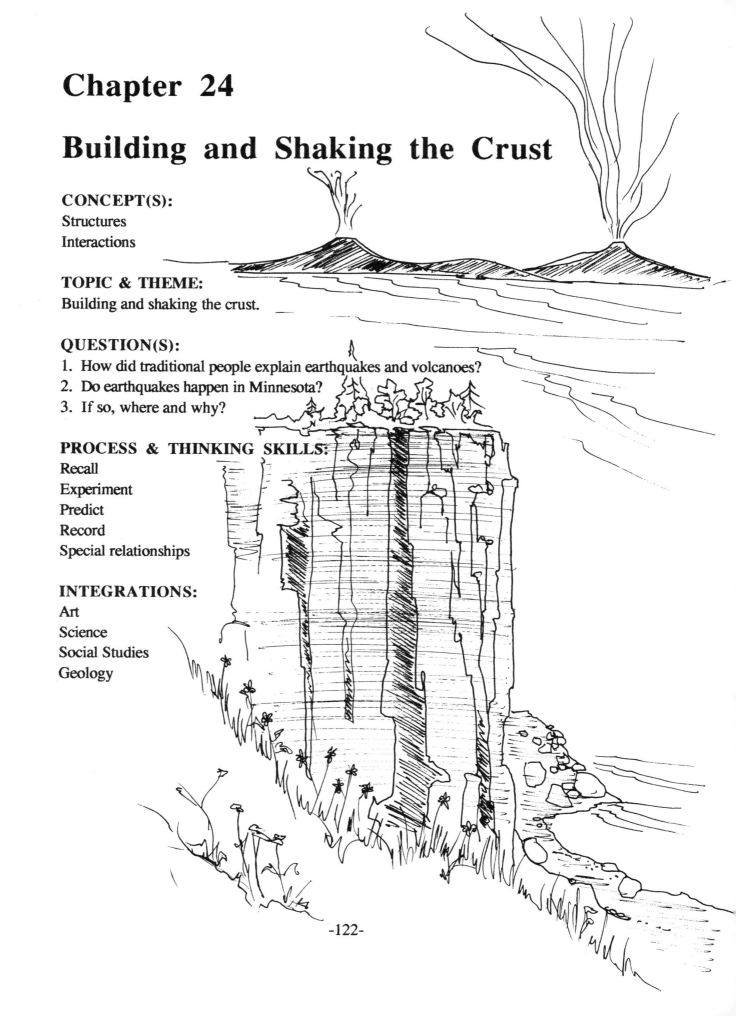

Chapter 24

Building and Shaking the Crust

CONCEPT(S):
Structures
Interactions

TOPIC & THEME:
Building and shaking the crust.

QUESTION(S):
1. How did traditional people explain earthquakes and volcanoes?
2. Do earthquakes happen in Minnesota?
3. If so, where and why?

PROCESS & THINKING SKILLS:
Recall
Experiment
Predict
Record
Special relationships

INTEGRATIONS:
Art
Science
Social Studies
Geology

BUILDING AND SHAKING THE CRUST

EARTHQUAKE STORIES:
Many cultures have invented stories about earthquakes and volcanoes to
explain these happenings with the best knowledge they had available at the time. While no story is
more true or real than any other story, they all are creative and often beautiful or terrifying.

Japan, a country of many earthquakes, developed this tale:
The Earth is balanced on the back of a great catfish. The fish is usually
held steady by the god, Kashima, who holds a large "pivot stone" on the
fish's head. However, if the people are not good, the god goes away for a
while and lets the catfish shake his head and swish his tail. That's what
makes the earth shake.

In East Africa, the Masawahilis believed that the a giant fish swam in
the Universe Ocean. A huge stone rested on the fish's back. A cow stood
on top of the stone. The cow had two horns. The Earth rested on the tip of
one horn, and after a while the cow's neck got tired.   Earthquakes
happened when the cow shifts her head, rolling the Earth to her other horn.

 People shake with "chills" when they have a fever. Shakespeare wrote
that an earthquake was caused by a "fever in the Earth".
 "...some say the earth with feverous did shake,"   -- Macbeth

The Greek thinker Aristotle said that earthquakes resulted from winds
trying to escape from underground caves.

Like the Japanese, the Judeo-Christians told that earthquakes were
sent by divine anger to punish humans. In the 1700's a Belgium chemist
declared: Earthquakes happen when an angel (angry with the wrongs of
people) hits the air so hard that the vibrations cause music and shock
waves on earth.

Indians of Peru had a happier explanation:
The earth goes dancing and kicks up its heels.

EARTHQUAKE FACTS:
Earthquakes are caused by rocks lurching past each other along a fault (crack) in the earth.

MORE STORIES:

Sodom and Gomorrah

People of Bible times explained the famous burning of Sodom and Gomorrah as God's punishment of the wicked people. King Lot and his family escaped, but God warned them not to look back. Lot's wife couldn't stand it. She had to see her city one last time. She instantly became a pillar of salt, for her disobedience.

Scientists, doing some geology detective work, believe that the firey destruction of Sodom and Gomorrah was caused by an earthquake in the Dead Sea fault 4,000 years ago. They found that natural asphalt, oil, and rocks containing coal were often squeezed out of the fault in Bible times. The awful Dead Sea smell was probably sulfur gas. People used the coal rocks and asphalt to build their houses. Since these materials are easily ignited, all it took was one bolt of lightning, or even a kitchen fire, to start the whole city burning.

The Pillar of Salt was eroded by rain water and separated from the huge salt dome, which rises more than 700 feet above the shore of the Dead Sea. There have been many pillars of salt in the valley.

Reelfoot Lake, Tennessee

This Chickasaw Indian story tells about Reelfoot, a young chief with a lame foot,who fell in love with a beautiful Choctaw maiden. Because of his disability her father would not let them marry, so the young people eloped. This angered her father, members of both tribes, and even the Great Spirit. Reelfoot and his bride were enjoying a celebration party with their friends when they were all punished for their disobediance. Great Spirit shook the earth, forcing the Father of Waters (Mississippi River) to flow backwards, flooding the campground. Reelfoot, his bride, and all their friends perished under the waters of the new lake.

Geologists have learned that a series of earthquakes in 1811 caused a low land next to the Mississippi River to sink. After the earthquake, the waters of the Mississippi temporarily reversed, probably because land-slides blocked the channel. Water from the flood and streams drained into the sunken land, making a lake. The Reelfoot earthquake was as strong as the famous San Francisco Earthquake of 1906.

Shock waves from this 1812 earthquake were probably felt in Minnesota by Indian people and immigrants.

VOLCANO STORIES AND FACTS:

People of all cultures who lived near the terrifying forces of volcanoes needed to explain and pacify this life-destroying power. Nearly all cultures believed the violence came from spiteful gods or demons that demanded human sacrifice.

Pele, Goddess of Volcanoes

Pele, the Hawaiian goddess of volcanoes, is said to have come from the south after a stormy fight with her older sister. Wherever Pele dug with her magic stick, a firey crater opened in the earth. The dirt she threw out became the hills and islands of Hawaii.

Pele's sister saw the smoke rising from the volcanoes, and she knew Pele was alive. She chased Pele and killed her. But Pele's spirit rose in the smokey fire from the volcanoes. The sister surrendered and fled. Pele invited her relatives to live with her in the volcanoes where they play games, dance to the music of the crackling, bubbling lava, and surf on waves of magma. Pele's bad moods explained eruptions.

Pele often disguised herself as a beautiful human lady, visited a human village, played their sports and games, and fell in love. One of her favorite games was holua sliding. (It's like snow-sledding on a steep grassy hill. The holua boards are fourteen feet long, but only 5 inches wide, so it takes a lot of skill to balance one.) When Pele's handsome boyfriend beat her in a holua race, she stamped around until she caused an eruption. The lava turned the young man and his friends to stone.

Geologists tell us that the "stone people" are really tree molds, caused by lava cooling around tree trunks. When the tree trunk burns or rots away, the mold is left standing upright, like a big hollow pipe.

The Fighting Volcanoes

Klamath Indians of the Northwest explain eruptions of two volcanoes as a battle between the gods of the Above World and the Below World. Skell, chief of the Above World, threw rocks and fire from his home at Mt. Shasta. Llao, chief of the Below World, spewed firey lava from his home at Mt. Mazama. He thrashed around so much that the volcano's peak caved in under him. All that's left of the mountain today is Crater Lake.

Geologists say that this is really a very good description of what really happened at Crater Lake! The mountain top at Mazama did in fact collapse during a violent eruption 6,500 years ago. The lake that was formed is a beautiful caldera, a round lake in the top of a volcano.

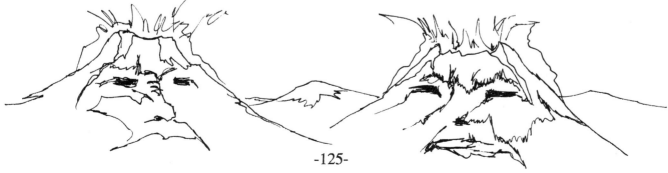

The Hopis of Sunset Crater
(From the book, *Earthfire*, by Malotki and Lomatuway'ma, Northland Press, Flagstaff, AZ.)

Long ago a good Hopi maid fell in love with a kind and intelligent young stranger, who was really a Kachina, a spirit. They decided to marry.

"It's too far to walk to my village," he told her. So they climbed onto the rainbow, and it sped them to his village, where his family welcomed her. The maid had to go through a dangerous test to see if she was good enough to be the wife of a Kachina. She had to grind ice and hail stones into water while she sat in a freezing blizzard. Spider Woman, who knew she was a good woman, gave her turkey feathers to keep her warm.

"You have passed the test!" the Kachinas said. "The water you produced will go to your people for their crops. They will never be hungry again."

The Hopi maid and Kana Kachina were married in a beautiful ceremony. The Kachinas brought gifts of food to her village. The maid's family built a home for the young couple, and they were very happy. Kachinas protected the Hopi. Kana Kachina and his wife were generous. The rains came, the crops thrived, and the Hopi people were prosperous.

But every village has its troublemakers. Some jealous people hated the young couple and tricked them into destroying their own happiness. Kana Kachina was furious when he discovered the evil, but it was too late.

"I will punish them!" he exclaimed.

That night he rode the rainbow to his home, and asked the elders what he should do.

"We know you are very angry," they said. "But don't destroy all the Hopi because of a few bad ones. Just shake them up a little. Dig a small hole in the mound near Hopi village. Light a fire in the hole. Wind will made the fire grow until the Hopi get scared."

That's what Kana Kachina did, but he was so angry that made the hole a little bigger.

Once the fire started it blazed and blasted down into the earth. There it met the fire from the Underworld. Sparks, cinders, and red hot lava shot everywhere. The mound grew into a tall mountain of black and red cinders. Kana Kachina withdrew his protection from the people, and the Hopis had no crops for four years. He gave his wife and her family an ear of sacred corn that kept their supply room always full of food. When the evil, jealous troublemakers had all died of starvation, Kana Kachina and his relatives came back to the village, bringing gifts of every crop -- corn, squash, beans, watermelon. Everyone had a gift. The Hopis finally regained their good way of life.

Geologists tell us that about a thousand years ago lava forced its way into a crack in floor of the Arizona desert. First steam and gas escaped. Then lava foam was blasted out of the crack high into the sky. As it cooled, it fell back to earth as cinders. Big bubbles of lava, only cooled on the outside, and hit the earth like molten cannonballs. Lightning and high winds shot around the eruption, which continued for 25 years! The cinders piled up around the opening 1000 feet high.

Some of the cinders contained iron oxides which give the cinder cone a red and yellow sunset color. Sometimes it almost looks like it's still on fire! Sunset Crater has the same symmetrically sloping sides as Mt. Fuji.

Mt. Fuji and the Giant

A very ambitious giant decided to fill the Pacific Ocean with dirt. There was a lot of dirt in Siberia, so he took his bag and began to fill the ocean. All night long he worked in the cold wet darkness, stretching his body to Siberia, filling the bag with dirt and rock, and emptying it into the water. All night he wondered, "How much ocean will be left? I wonder how much land I'll see when the sun rises." Well, when morning came the ocean looked just the same. The giant's work didn't change a thing.

"BaaaH!" shouted the giant, as he flung the last bag of dirt at Japan. It became Mt. Fuji.

Geologists tell us that Mt. Fuji is a composite volcano made of layers of lava and volcanic ash. Cinder cones in Arizona near the homelands of the Hopi look just like Mt. Fuji. Look for an Activity that will help you find out why volcanoes have a unique shape.

SUNSET CRATER

HOPI KACHINA

MINNESOTA'S EARTHQUAKES

Although Minnesota hasn't had major earthquake activity for a billion years, several faults run through Northern Minnesota. Sixteen earthquakes have been reported in Minnesota since the Civil War times -- 130 years ago. One major fault has greenstone pillow lava (2 billion years old) on one side of it, and metamorphic gneiss (3.5 billion years old) on the other side.

Geologists evaluate an earthquake's strength and damage:

*The Richter Scale measures the strength of an earthquake from 1 to 10.
1 is a little tremor. 10 is a tremendous earthquake.
Every number is ten times stronger than the one before.
The earthquake at Lake Reelfoot (measuring over 8.0) was probably 10,000 times stronger than the Minnesota earthquake at Long Prairie in 1860 (measuring 5.0).

* The Mercalli Scale measures the damage of an earthquake from I to XII.
I nobody even feels.
XII destroys everything: bridges, dams, railroad tracks, pipelines.

Red Lake had an earthquake on Feb. 6, 1917. People said it rumbled loudly and lasted one minute. Seven months later a strong quake that lasted only 20-seconds shook the Staples/ Motley area, breaking windows, cracking walls, and knocking down chimneys. Reports said it even knocked down houses in Bemidji.

People in Alexandria were wakened by a loud low boom at 4:00 a.m. on Feb. 15, 1950. They said their beds shook!

Thousands of people in four states felt the Morris earthquake on July 9, 1975. Seismographs from Newfoundland to Mexico reported the waves. The quake produced cracked walls, windows and chimneys. 200 people reported a loud rumbling sound, like heavy equipment on the move.
Most of Minnesota's Earthquakes have been about 4 .0 - 5.0 in strength and IV - VII in damage.

At IV dishes, windows and doors rattle.
At V sleepers wake up.
At VI people have a hard time walking. Windows and dishes break.
At VII it is hard to even stand up. Plaster cracks and bricks fall.
Big bells even start ringing.

THE ACTIVITIES:

1. The Elders and the Earthquakes

   Ask the old people you know if they remember any earthquakes in your state.

   Try to find stories in your library or at the newspaper office about old earthquakes.

   From the damage reports, assign a number from the damage scale.

   Make a class book for your school library containing your information.

2. Build a Seismograph.

   Use materials like straws, clay, string, twist-ties and a marker.

   (Ojibwe made frames like these of reeds to dry small hides.)

   Hold the frame steady while pulling a sheet of paper under it.

   Pull the paper straight through and the mark is straight (no shocks).

   Move the paper from side to side, and shock waves are recorded.

   Use graph paper to measure the intensity.

   Use the pattern as a beadwork design.

3. Why are cinder cone volcanos always shaped the same?

   Try slowly pouring sand into a little pile. What shape does it take?

   Pour the sand into three or four different size piles.

   Measure the angle of the sand with protractor.

   Why does the sand always stack up this way?

   Geologists tell us that the sand crystals have tiny sides that hold

   together at this angle. (Physics calls this the Angle of Repose.)

4. Make two illustrated maps of your own imaginary volcano or earthquake.

   Use ideas and labels from your science book.

   Show how this event happened both as a Story Illustrator and as a Geologist.

5. For the "Rock Concert," create a modern or traditional dance that would

   explain the processes of building and shaking the earth. Include the circle of life:

   A. The forces that create the event.

   B. The effect on people, plants and animals.

   C. The renewal of life after time has passed.

6. Research New World buildings in Central and South America.

   How have they withstood earthquakes for thousands of years?

   In small groups make earthquake-proof buildings of various materials.

   Put the buildings one by one in the center of a table and shake the table to test which

   building is the most earthquake proof.

Chapter 25

Earth's Oceans

CONCEPT(S):
Change
Structures

TOPIC & THEME:
Earth's oceans

QUESTION(S):
1. What ocean stories did traditional people use?
2. I wonder why the water is blue...?

PROCESS & THINKING SKILLS:
Experiment
Predict
Collect and organize data
Record
Observe

INTEGRATIONS:
Art
Science
Social Studies
Language arts

F. G.

EARTH'S OCEANS

THE STORIES AND THE FACTS:
Many cultures have stories about a huge flood or ocean that covers the land.
In most cases the flood is caused by the gods as punishment to bad humans.
In all the stories, everyone is destroyed except for a handful of good people who climb to high place or float on the ocean.

The Ancient Ocean (Canadian Ojibwe)

Gichi Manidoo (The Great Spirit) had a vision of an Earth full of trees, sunshine, moonlight, starlight, rocks, animals, flowers and people. He made a beautiful world and it followed the laws and cycles of nature.

Then the beautiful creation was destroyed by a flood. All was covered with water.

A lonely spirit woman lived in the sky, and the water animals of earth decided to help her. They invited her to sit on Turtle's back as he swam in the ocean. Soon, she asked the water animals to bring her some mud from the bottom of the sea. Beaver, fisher and marten all tried to reach the bottom, but came up empty-handed, ashamed, and gasping for air.

"I could try," suggested little muskrat.

"You?" the other animals laughed. "You're too little! If the big animals couldn't find the mud, what makes you think you can?"

Spirit woman smiled encouragingly. "You try," she said.

Muskrat swam down and down. He was gone so long that the others thought he had drowned. Finally, half dead, little muskrat rose to the surface -- with a tiny bit of mud on his paw.

Spirit Woman placed the mud on the turtle's back and blew her warm breath on it. As turtle swam away, an island formed from the mud. This island is Mackinac Island today. The animals brought twigs and seeds. She breathed on them and they became trees and flowers.

Most of the North American Indian flood stories probably come from the huge floods that must have occured as the last glacier was melting. As ice dams melted and broke apart, the water behind them plunged across the land, racing across the thawing land, and flooding everything for miles.

Ocean Children (Ute)

Because the people were wicked, the gods destroyed everything except for the rocks, gold, silver, rich soil, corn, and two children.   To rebuild the land on the vast ocean, the Creator dropped rocks, gold, silver and rich soil to make mountains and flat land for crops and animals. A thirsty lizard was sent by the Creator to lick up the extra water. The two children survived the flood by making a raft of corn stalks. Creator was pleased with them.

"They are good at solving their problems," he said.

Creator dropped corn kernels to the children, who planted them in the rich soil. When we see falling stars, we are seeing corn kernels dropped by the Creator.

Noah and the Ocean (Judeo-Christian)

Noah's ocean story is based on earlier stories from ancient cultures. One story tells about 40 days of rain, and the two birds that Noah sent out to find land. The other story tells about the size of the boat and the rainbow. Two of each animal were saved on Noah's boat. The stories were blended together. The people who told these early stories lived in a very small part of the world. They only knew about 300 animal species. By 1750 more than 15,000 species had been identified. Today we know about more than 30 million different species! Three hundred species might fit on a boat. Thirty million would not.

Giant Sea Waves (Araucanian Indians)

The Indians of Chile did not believe that disasters were punishments. They said that during an earthquake the underground serpents shook the earth, just to prove their powers. The people saved themselves from the Tsunamis (huge sea waves) that followed the earthquake by climbing a mountain that floated near the sky. They carried bowls on their heads to protect themselves from the blazing sunlight. Today they still carry bowls on their heads.

Tsunamis (seismic sea waves) are usually caused by underwater earthquakes. Out in the ocean these powerful waves are less than 2 feet tall, but more than 100 miles long from crest to crest. They travel about 450 miles per hour -- as fast as a jet airplane! (The deeper the water, the faster they travel.)

When the wave gets close to shore, the bottom of the wave drags on the coast while the top keeps moving. Water ahead of the wave gets sucked back into the wave, making it grow taller. Waves from behind pile into the first, making it even higher. Seismic sea waves hit the shore as a wall 60-100 feet high. (That's about as tall as four houses stacked on top of each other!)

Seismic sea waves can do tremendous damage. One of the worst was caused by the eruption of the volcano on Krakatoa a hundred years ago. The wave killed more than 36,000 people, and it went completely around the world.

THE LANGUAGE:

Many cultures live near big bodies of water. What words do they use?

ENGLISH	OJIBWE	SPANISH
ocean	zaaga'igan (lake)	oceano
water	nibi	agua
along the shore	jiigibiig	orilla
waves (roaring)	mamaadweyaashkaa	ondas bramidos
big waves	mamaangaashkaa	ondas grandes
blue/green	ozhaawashkaa	azul/verde
motion	animibide (it moves)	movimiento
shelf	desaabaan	estante
floor	michisag	piso
it is deep	dimii	hondo

I WONDER:

* HOW BIG ARE THE OCEANS?
  Oceans cover 3/4 of our planet. 97% of Earth's water is in the oceans.

* WHERE DID THE WATER COME FROM?
  Scientists think that the planet was hot and dry for millions of years after it formed from cosmic dust. Water vapor and other gasses escaped from the surface, and formed clouds and rain.
  As more vapor escaped more rain fell until there were oceans.

* WHY ARE THE OCEANS SALTY?

Rivers take salts and other minerals from the rocks and soil into the oceans. When the water evaporates, the salt gets left behind.

*WHY IS THE OCEAN BLUE?

Think about a prism breaking up light into rainbow colors.
Some colors have longer light waves than others.
Blue light scatters more easily than the other colors.
So when light hits the water, the blue light waves are scattered back
    to your eyes.
The other colors are absorbed by the water.
Sometimes the ocean looks green.
That's because particles in the water reflect the green light waves.
The more clear the water, the bluer it looks.

* WHAT ARE WAVES?

A wave is pattern of movement on the surface of the water.
The water does not move.
Only the energy of the motion moves.
The energy comes from wind.
The water moves in a circle.
When the wave gets close to shore, the bottom drags on the sand.
This friction slows down the bottom of the wave, so the top spills over.

* WHY ARE THERE RIVERS IN THE OCEAN?

Warm water and cold water don't mix very easily.
The cold water is denser and saltier than the warm water.

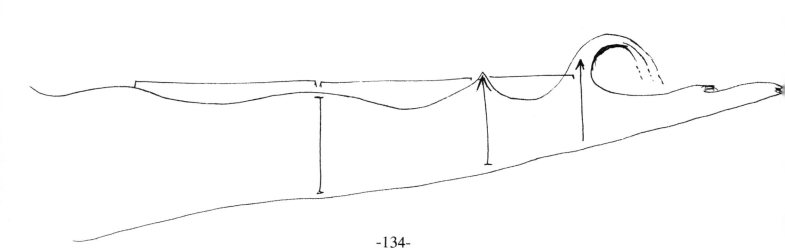

THE ACTIVITIES:

1. The Ocean and Lake Floors.

    Get topography maps of lakes in your area. What do the contours mean?

    Lay a ruler in a straight line across the map.

    If you were a fish, swimming along that line, what would you see?

    Where does the land go up? Where does it go down? How steep is it?

    People of many cultures make and decorate baskets with water or fish designs.

    A. Draw a basket (from the side) on a big sheet of paper.

        Make a design on the side of the basket to show the fish's journey across your lake.

    B. Try a design for the ocean floor.

        Include the trench, ridges, basin, slope, shelf and land.

    C. Draw a basket (from the top) with a little opening.

        (It will look like a small circle on a big circle).

        Make a design showing ocean currents.

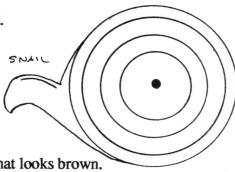

SNAIL

2. Water Colors!

    Collect a pint of water from each of three sources --

    a lake that looks blue, a pond that looks green, a swamp that looks brown.

    Keep them in separate, labeled dishes until they evaporate.

    Which had the most particles? Which had the fewest?

    What can you infer about the color and particles in a body of water?

    Interpret your results with a graph or bead design.

3. Tides

                                 HARPOON

    A. Make a tide model.

        Invent a game or simple 3-D model to show how tides work.

    B. How did traditional people use and depend on tides?

        Research different people in many countries.

        Make a colorful classroom graph to show similarities and differences in uses.

5. Make a wave machine to study wave action in slow motion.

    (These are beautiful, but the liquids are dangerous. Use Care!)

    Use a clear plastic bottle with lid. (liquid dish detergent or cooking oil.)

    Fill 1/3 of the bottle with rubbing alcohol. Add blue food coloring.

    Fill the rest of the bottle with paint thinner, so no air is in the bottle.

    Screw on the lid tightly! Rock the bottle on its side using two hands. Watch the waves!

    Write unrhymed poetry about waves using science ideas in your poems.

Chapter 26

Ocean Life and Use

CONCEPT(S):
Relationships
Structures
Components

TOPIC & THEME:
Ocean life and its uses

QUESTION(S):
1. How did life begin in the oceans?
2. What life is in the oceans today?
3. How did Native peoples depend on the ocean?

PROCESS & THINKING SKILLS:
Record
Analyze
Recall

INTEGRATIONS:
Language arts
Art
Science (Biology)

OCEAN LIFE AND USE

THE STORY: How the Salmon came to the Squamish

    Long ago the Sqaumish people had no salmon to eat, and they were hungry. Four brothers went around the world helping people, and they decided to help bring salmon to the Squamish. The brothers were magical. Three of the brothers traveled in a beautiful canoe that was really the youngest brother in another form.

    "The Sun will know where the salmon live. We must trick him into coming to earth and telling us," the brothers decided. So they made a plan. The youngest brother took the form of a salmon, tied to the shore with a string. The Sun wanted that salmon, but he was afraid of tricks, and disguised himself as an eagle. When he flew to earth, he grabbed the salmon in his talons and flew off, breaking the string.

    "Could you be a bigger sea animal next time?" asked his brothers. The young man became a whale, tied to the shore with a big strong rope. When Sun glided to earth to pick up the whale, his claws got stuck in the thick hide. When he tried to fly away, the strong rope held fast.

    "Give up, Sun-eagle!" the boys called, "You can't escape unless you help us."

    So the Sun-eagle told the brothers where to find the salmon, and they freed him to go back to the sky where he could watch over the earth and keep it warm. The brothers found the salmon and showed the Squamish where to find them so they would never be hungry.

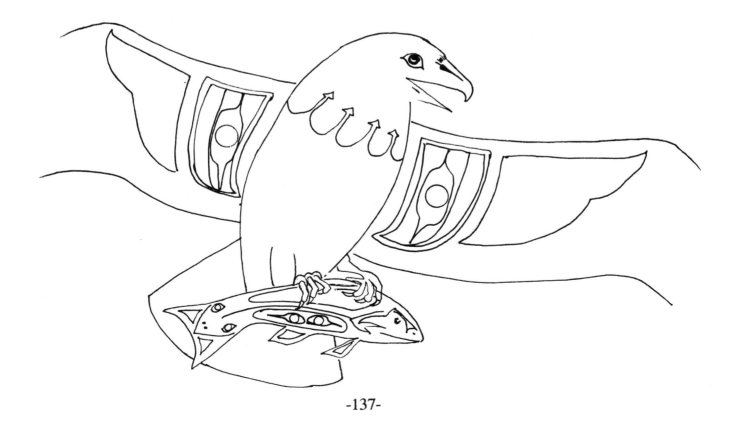

THE FACTS:

Many traditional stories and modern scientists explain that all life began in the sea. In the traditional stories a powerful being or god creates life from water, air, earth, or fire -- things ancient people could see and touch without a microscope.

Today scientists use evidence from dating rocks and fossils to determine that life began as the ocean's chemicals reacted with energy from the sun nearly 3 billion years ago. Simple bacteria came first, then more complex single and multi-celled forms evolved.

Life stayed in the sea until 400 million years ago when insects and amphibians adapted to live on land.

More than 500 million years ago, 140 species of invertebrate sea animals lived in a bed of mud. When the mud hardened into a rock it became Burgess shale, known for its special fossils. Two fossils look like this:

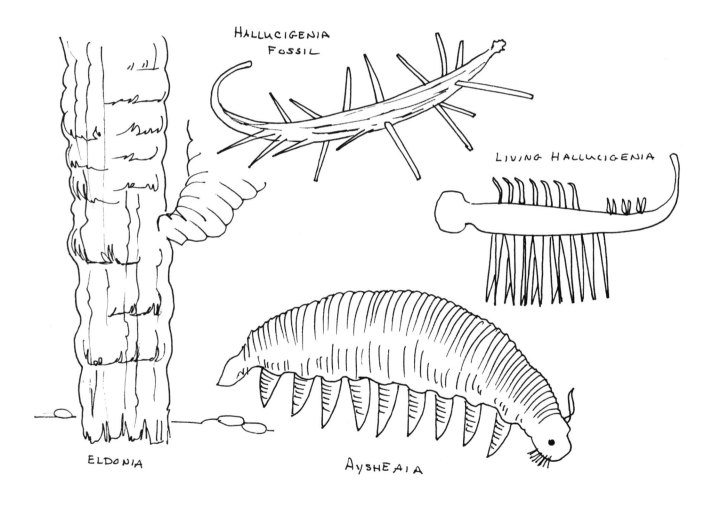

THE EXPLORATION:

If you were a marine biologist, you would use dive tanks and dive ships to explore the ocean depths. You would find plants and animals like these. These are drawn with basic math shapes, so you can try them too.

Invertebrates (without backbones) Many are used for human food.
CRABS • How does a Hermit Crab find a house?

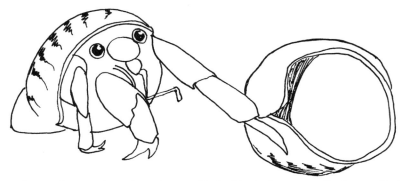

Hermit crabs go house-hunting for snail shells (whose snails have died.) When they outgrow their present shell, they "try on" new ones till they find one that fits just right.

SAND DOLLARS

* How does a sand dollar eat?
    It collects food with its tube feet.
    The food is passed along the "legs"
    to the mouth.

SEA SHELLS:
* How does a mollusk make a sea shell?
    When a mollusk hatches from its egg, it already wears a miniature shell.
    New shell material (mostly calcium) is squeezed out along the lip of the shell. Then it
    hardens. Many shells have a spiral shape.

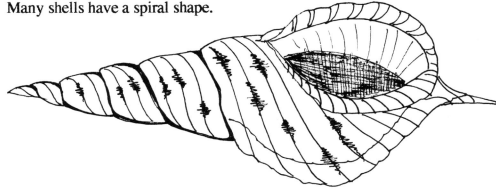

Delicate denitalium shells were used as money by many Indians, but the Nootka had the most, living near the sea. They cleaned, sorted and packaged them by size in boxes -- like sorting $ 1, $ 5, $ 10 dollar bills!

Water changes in tidal pools twice a day. The pools are very salty. In a tidal pool you might find sea stars, sponges, anemones, shrimp.

SEA STARS AND STAR FISH

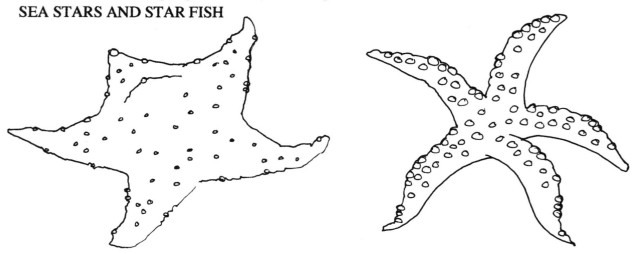

SPONGES (Sponges are found in tidal pools, and also in deep ocean trenches.)

So far we know about 5000 species of sponges. They live in all the oceans, but the biggest ones come from Antarctica and the Caribbean. Sponge names can be colorful: Red Finger Sponge, Blue Cloud Sponge, Purple Tube Sponge.

Sponges feed on bacteria collected by filtering the water through tiny pores.

Some sponges produce antibiotic substances to help people. The Greeks used bathing sponges in early times.

Red Fingered sponge (actual size)

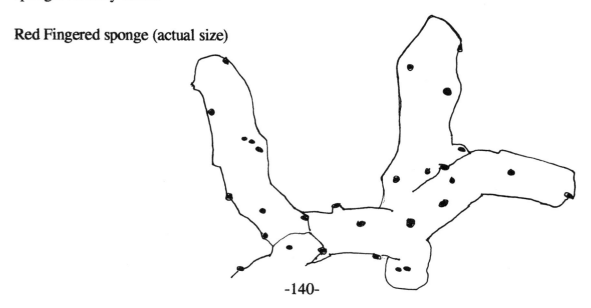

CORALS

Usually we only see the coral's calcium skeleton that becomes limestone. The actual animal is usually shaped like a bubble, only a quarter inch in size. Since Minnesota was under the sea for millions of years, many fossil corals are found here.

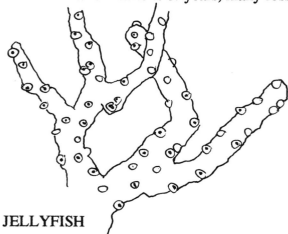

JELLYFISH

Jellyfish have no skeletons at all.
A ring of tentacle feeds the mouth.
Pulsing muscles make jellyfish swim.
Jellyfish stingers are like harpoons
on triggers.

SEA ANEMONES

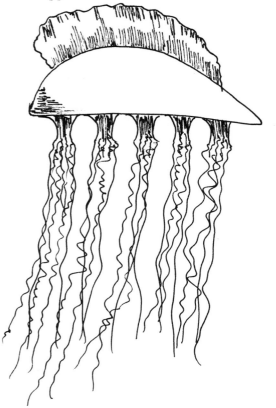

Sea Anemone species are related to jellyfish and corals. The skeleton (when they have one) is calcium or horn.
It can be inside or outside the animal.
Colorful clown fish and anemones protect each other.

Fish:

CHINOOK SALMON
A baby Chinook Salmon drifts down the Columbia River from the creek where it hatched, out into the Pacific Ocean -- 700 miles away. At first it eats plankton. Growing larger, it eats small fish. Bigger fish, sea lions, birds and people eat the salmon. Survivors swim back up the Columbia to their original home to spawn and die.

Salmon is an important food to coastal Indian peoples of the Pacific Northwest, Canada and Alaska.

Little Candlefish were so full of oil that they were lit for candles by the Tlingit. They also saved the oil for cooking.

LUNGFISH
Lungfish evolved almost 400 Million years ago when many seas dried up. They have lungs and gills. They have strong fins which they can use for crawling (to find more water.) And they can stay out of water for four years. This is how evolution occurs. Animals simply adapt to their changing environment.

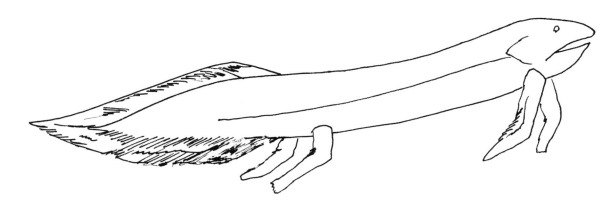

FLYINGFISH

The flyingfish swishes its tail for speed to escape enemies. When it hits the surface of the water, its side fins act like glider wings -- at 35 mph!

SHARKS:

Sharks are very ancient fish. 100 million years ago prehistoric sharks swam in the vast sea that covered the whole middle of the continent, including Minnesota. Fossil shark teeth are found today in Minnesota.

    *Sharks still have some of their ancient traits:

      The skeleton is made of cartilage (like your nose) instead of bones.

      They have 10-14 gill openings instead of two.

    *Sharks can smell one drop of blood in 100 million drops of water.

     (100 Million drops would fill 1,000 gallons full of water!)

    * One species of shark is just 4 inches long. The whale shark is 50 feet long.

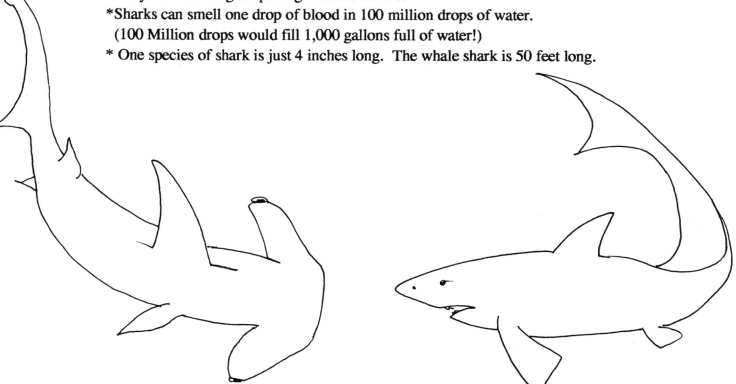

Reptiles:

SEA SNAKES live in the waters around the equator.

The tail is shaped like an oar! Their front fangs are fixed, not hinged.
Their eggs hatch inside their bodies. Most sea snakes are 3 to 5 feet long.

SEA TURTLES

The front feet have evolved into flippers.
Sea turtles use the front feet for swimming
and back feet as rudders.
Leatherback sea turtles eat jellyfish!
They lay more than 100 round white eggs
at a time. Both turtles and eggs are eaten
by people. Shells are used for rattles by traditional
people in many cultures.

Birds: PENGUINS
Penguins can't fly in the air. They used their
wings like flippers to swim in the water. The
motion they make is like flying in water.

Mammals: WHALES

Baleen whales eat tiny animal plankton (krill). The baleen is made of plates like your finger nail. Huge amounts of water are filtered through the baleen. Plankton sticks to the plates. The whale sucks the plankton off the plates.

Toothed whales eat other animals and fish.

Dolphins are just small toothed whales.

The narwhal's long spiraled horn is really his left front tooth!

Inuits (Eskimos) hunted huge whales in fragile boats covered with walrus skin (umiaks). Sometimes, after the whale was harpooned, it dragged the boat for three or four dangerous days. After the meat and blubber were stored, everything else from the whale was used. Skin of the liver and lungs was used to make drum heads. The ribs were used for clubs. Whale bone was used for knives. Muktuk, dried whale fat, was chewed as a snack. This snack of high fat and calories helped keep the people warm in the arctic climate.

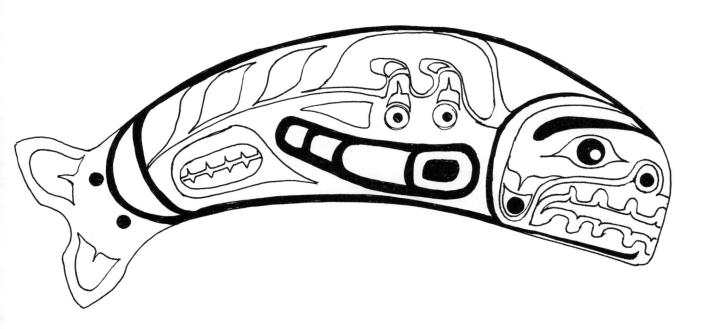

SEA OTTERS grow to be six feet long.
The back feet are shaped like flippers. Sea otters are the only mammals
besides primates (like apes and humans) who use tools. Lying on its back,
it strikes clam shells on a stone to break them open. Native people hunted them for warm
furs. Later, immigrants hunted them almost to extinction, but now they are making a good
come back in protected areas. Otters are related to mink, badgers and other weasels.

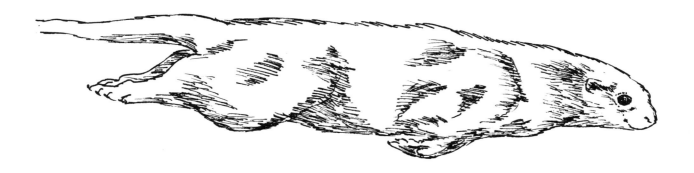

POLAR BEARS have a triangle shaped body to glide easily through the water.
The front feet are webbed like a duck. Each hair is a transparent tube that catches sunlight,
and carries the warmth down to be absorbed by the black skin. They prey mostly on seals.
If an Inuit hunter killed a mother polar bear, he sometimes brought the cub home for a pet.

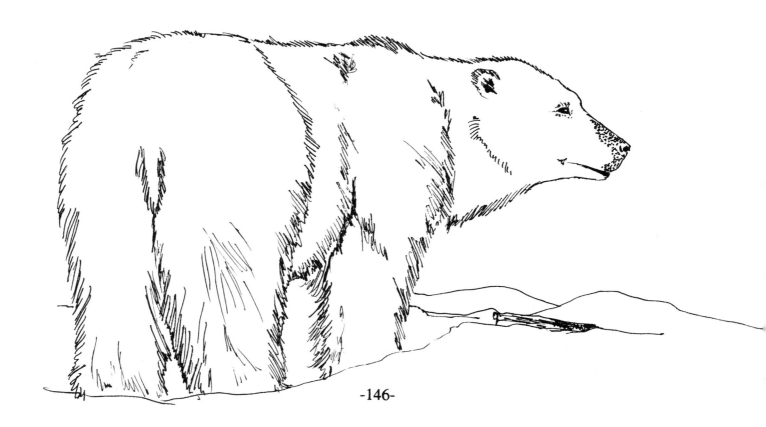

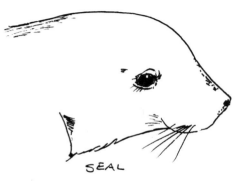

SEAL

SEALS, SEA LIONS, and WALRUSES

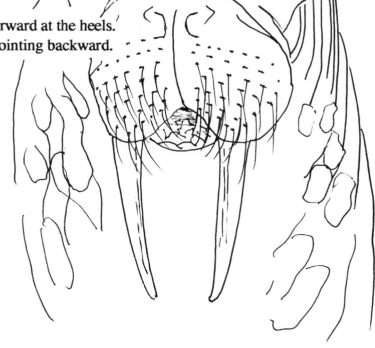

SEA LION

How can you tell a seal from a sea lion?
Ears: Sea lions and fur seals have tiny ears.
Seals have no external ear flaps.

Motion in Water:
Sea lions flap their front flippers.
Seals propel themselves with their tail.

Motion on Land:
Sea lions "walk" with their back legs bent forward at the heels.
Seals drags their back legs along with toes pointing backward.

The walrus tusks are two very long teeth.
Sea Lion teeth were used are decorations
Elephant seals can weigh 8,000 kg.

Inuit people used all parts of these animals.
Walrus stomach was used for drum heads.
The meat, fat and oil were used for food.

The gut was translucent and waterproof.
After it was washed and dried, it made a
good window or skylight.
It was used for rain coats, sailboat sails,
and small tents too.

Have you ever seen an apple peeled in one long peeling? Inuit hunters cut seal skin around
and around to make a long thin rope -- good harpoon rope.
The seal's stomach made a good pouch for carrying fresh water while hunting on the ocean.
Walrus ivory was carved into beautiful shapes.

PLANTS:

Plenty of light reaches the surface of the ocean, but 300 feet down the
ocean is dark. We find plants (which have chlorophyll, and need sunshine to make food)
at the surface of the ocean and near the shore where they can get enough light.

Algae and plant plankton live at the ocean's surface.
 Ocean algae gives off more oxygen than all the land plants put together.
 Diatoms are tiny one-celled algae. When they float to the ocean floor, after a long time,
 they become like rock.

Tlingit women harvested seaweed, drying it for winter food.
They also traded salt to tribes living away from the salty ocean.

How did the Aleutians fool the killer whale? Aleut whale hunters ingeniously used kelp
stems to keep killer whales from stealing their catch -- a great gray whale. Sound carries in
water. The hunters found kelp stems that had broken off of their holdfasts. They laid the
30 foot long kelp stems around their whale. When the killer whales came, the hunters
roared through the stems, sending loud, confusing sounds through the water. The killer
whales swam away in panic!

DIATOMS -- One Celled Algae

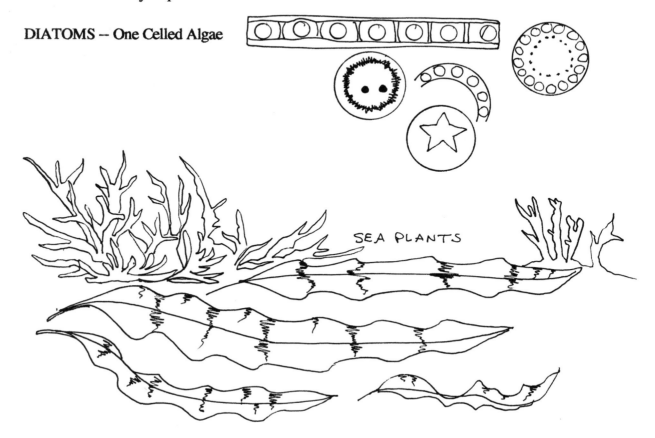

SEA PLANTS

THE ACTIVITIES:

1. Webbing
   With a partner make a web to show how all life forms are related.
   How do they depend on each other?
   How does the web change when you add traditional and modern humans?
   Make your web in the style of a dream catcher.
   What dream would you like to catch?
   What kind of ocean job would you find interesting?
   (It can be a modern or traditional job.)
   In this job, who depends on you? Who do you depend on?

2. Designing an ocean totem pole.
   Northwest Art uses special designs.
   The surface is usually covered with smooth curves
   showing animal or human forms.
   Totem pole carvers often include the clan symbol.
   The carvings might represent important events.
   On flat surfaces, like blankets and boxes, elements
   of an animal's face might be used creatively in the
   design.

3. Think about your life.
   Design a totem pole about yourself and the ocean.
   Here are some ideas:
   You might include your favorite ocean animals,
   -- Or ocean animals and plants you depend on.
   -- Your totem pole might honor all the things you
       need and enjoy from the ocean.
   -- Your pole might show ocean life at different
       depths.
   -- Come up with your very own idea!

   (HINT: Do some research to find out more things
   that we get from the sea.)

Chapter 27

Earth, Sun, and Moon

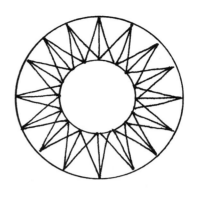

CONCEPT(S):
Structures
Components
Systems
Cycles

TOPIC & THEME:
Earth, sun, and moon.

QUESTION(S):
How did traditional people use legends and science
to explain the sun, moon, and earth?

PROCESS & THINKING SKILLS:
Special relationships
Analyze
Experiment
Predict
Record

INTEGRATIONS:
Social studies
Art
Science
Language arts

EARTH, SUN AND MOON

THE STORIES: Many cultures see a face in the moon. Sometimes we call it the Man in the Moon. The Ojibwe see a Grandmother or a Woman in the Moon. This is one Ojibwe story.

Gichi Manidoo had a vision of a sky filled with sun, moon and stars. He created rock, fire, water and wind. With these he made the earth, sun, moon and stars. Sun had the power of light and warmth. Earth had the power of growth and cures. Moon fell in love.

Many years ago Lone Bird, a beautiful girl, lived happily in the lodge of her parents. Many young men came to court her, but she turned them away coldly. "My mother loves me, and my father takes care of me. I do not need to marry," she told them. Her mother and father loved her very much. They encouraged her to visit with the young men, but she would not listen. Finally, her father held a great contest. "Whoever wins the race can marry Lone Bird," he announced. Race day arrived. Young men from many bands came to race for Lone Bird. Gichi Manidoo heard Lone Bird weeping, and fixed the race so all the young men tied at the finish line.

One night, walking home from maple sugar camp, she saw the beautiful full moon rising and shimmering over the lake. "Oh Moon!" she cried. "I have always loved *you*. I would be happy to be your wife." Gichi Manidoo heard her voice, and carried her to the moon. At first her parents were sad and lonely, but then they looked up at the moon they saw her face smiling happily down on them. When the moon is full we can see Lone Bird's face in the moon, and we are not lonely.

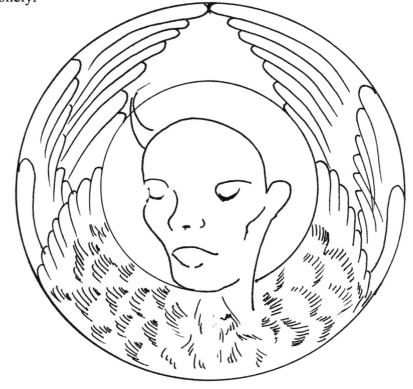

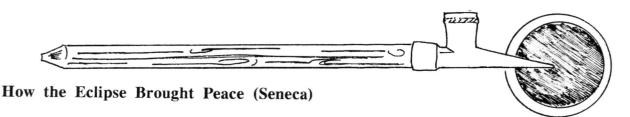

How the Eclipse Brought Peace (Seneca)

For a long time the Seneca had been at peace with their neighbors, but after a while some young men became bored and went on the warpath against the Mohawks. They took many captives. The Mohawks sent a war party to fight the Seneca and bring home the prisoners, but the Seneca decided to kill the prisoners first. Suddenly a young woman screamed,"Look! the Great Spirit hides his face and will not watch his children at war!" It was true. The sun was slowly covered until the forest was as black as night. The chiefs, warriors, captors and prisoners of both tribes were in a panic.

Then the oldest and wisest Seneca said in a grave and firm voice, "The Good Brother Sun is angry with us. We must live as brothers and smoke the pipe of peace together again." As the pipe was smoked, the sun shone brighter and brighter. The Seneca continued to live in friendship and joined the Iroquois League.

THE FACTS:
* Scientists tell us that the Moon's face is made of three big craters on the surface of the moon.

* When the sun, moon and earth happen to line up in a straight line we see an eclipse. The sun is eclipsed when the moon comes between it and the earth. The moon is eclipsed when the earth comes between it and the sun.

* The science of astronomy is more than 5,000 years old.
   Old World Astronomers lived in Babylon, China, Great Britain, India....
   Most famous of the the New World Astronomers were the Maya and Aztec of Mexico, the Mound Builders of Cahocia, and the Anasazi (early Hopi) of the American Southwest.

Anasazi Sun Watchers
* A thousand years ago 30,000 Anasazi may have lived in large, productive cities east of the Grand Canyon. One city had 120 kivas (places of worship). The circular kivas were built partly below ground, and 10 to 60 feet across. The walls represented the sky and the roof was the Milky Way.

* Kiva Wall supports were put up at the four directions.
   How did they figure out exactly where the four directions were? They may have used a gnomon, like many other prehistoric astronomers. The true directions can be found from a stick stuck straight up in the ground. **See the activities to make one yourself.**

* We have seasons because the earth is tilted. Only on the first days of spring and autumn do we have equal time of daylight and darkness. On the those days the sun rises exactly in the east and sets exactly in the west. Those were important days in farming societies, like the Anasazi, so they wanted to predict when those days would be.

The Solar Calendar:

First Day of Spring (March 21) There are equal hours of day and dark.
Every day from Spring to Summer the sun rises a bit farther north along
the horizon. At noon the sun is a little higher in the sky.

First Day of Summer (June 21) This day has the longest day and shortest night.
This is as far north as the sun rises. It seems to pause for a few days.
Every day from summer to fall the sun rises a bit farther south along the
horizon. At noon, the sun is a bit lower in the sky.

First day of Autumn (Sept. 21) Day and night are again the same length.
From Autumn to Winter the sun continues to rise a little farther south
every day. At noon it continues to be a little lower in the sky than the
day before.

First Day of Winter (Dec. 21) This is the shortest day and longest night of the
year. The sun rises as far to the south as it will go. Again it seems to
hover or pause at this point for several days.

From Winter to Spring the sun will rise a little farther north every day,
until the day and night are again the same length. On the first day of
spring the cycle starts all over again.

* If you lived in a flat, treeless place, surrounded by mesas, mountains and buttes, you could
    see the sun rising at different places around the horizon as it moves north and south with
    the seasons. Every year the sun would rise over a certain mountain on a certain day, and
    cast a ray of light in a certain place at sunrise.

* The Indian astronomers carved pictures on rocks to "catch" the first ray of sun on these
    important days. It was the same year after year. At Pueblo Benito, special windows were
    cut in houses to throw rays of light into certain places or corners on certain days of the
    year.

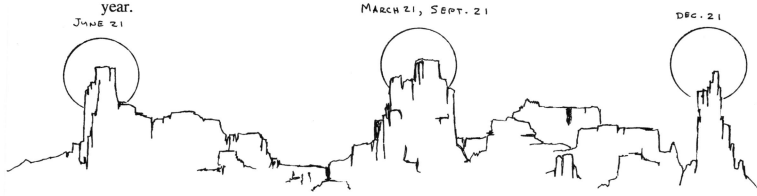

-153-

* Sun Dagger.   As a ray of sun moves across a rock face, these two simple spirals still predict and record sun and moon events a thousand years after they were carved on Fajada Butte.

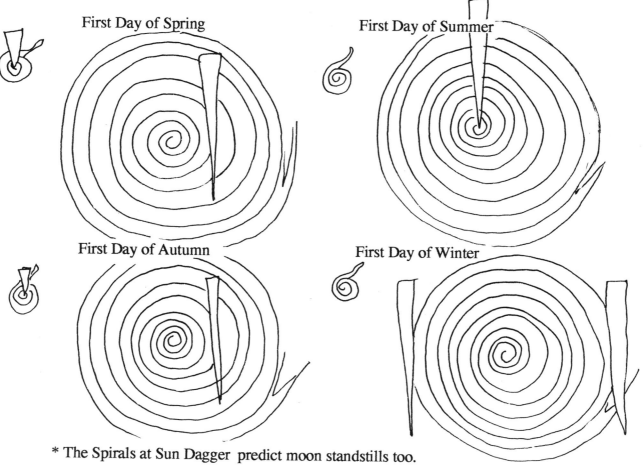

First Day of Spring

First Day of Summer

First Day of Autumn

First Day of Winter

* The Spirals at Sun Dagger predict moon standstills too.
Every 19 years, the shadow of the moon just touches the edge of the
big spiral (which has 19 grooves cut in it.) Along the edge of the shadow a groove has
been cut into the rock. Scientists think it is exceptional for a culture without writing to be
able to predict moon standstills.

* In March 1057, a full moon rose between twin chimney of rock. It took 19
years for the full moon to rise there again on that same date. Astronomers
call this a "standstill".
This was a time of other unusual events:
   -- an exploding Super Nova blazed in the sky during the day for three
       weeks in 1054. People could see it at night for two years.
   -- 1066 Halley's Comet made an appearance.
   -- 1076 there was a total solar eclipse.
   -- 1077 was the beginning of sunspots that lasted for 200 years.
   -- 1097 marked another total eclipse.

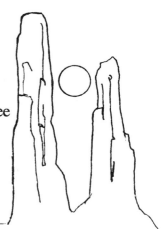

*   Chimney Rock is not a very pleasant place to build a city.
    Of all the ancient pueblos, it is the highest, most remote, and farthest
    from a good water source. Almost all the building rocks and the water
    had to be hauled up the cliffs. Why did the Anasazi build here? Some scientists
    think they built this city to be an observatory of these solar events.

* The Maya of Mexico could predict the date so accurately, they even knew about leap year!
    Their civilization discovered the idea of "zero" along with only two other ancient cultures.
    (Europeans learned about "zero" from the Chinese.) The Maya held conferences about
    their calendar and mathematics.

* Legends from the Greeks and Indians of North and Central America tell of the careless son
    of the Sun. In all three legends, the son begs for a chance to carry the sun across the sky.
    In all three, the boy comes too close to earth, nearly setting it on fire.

These stories may reflect a colossal ancient volcanic eruption whose dust made fiery sunsets
for several years around the world. When Krakatoa erupted a hundred years ago, fire
departments in at least two U.S. cities were commanded to fight a flaming inferno that people
were sure was blazing west of their city.

* Spiral patterns, like the Spiral at Sun Dagger, are common in the universe and in nature. Our
    own galaxy is a spiral.

ROCK CARVING

The Language:

English	Ojibwe	Pictograph
Sunrise	waaban	
Moon	dibik-giizis	
Earth	aki	
Circle (It is round)	waawyeyaa	
(Nine) Days	(zhaangaswi) giizhig	
Noon	naawakwe	

SOLAR
ECLIPSE

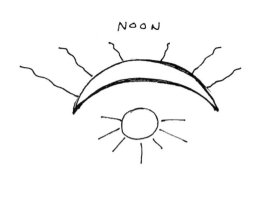

NOON

Ojibwe Moon Calendar

Dec./January	manidoo giizis	Moon of the Spirit
February	namebini giizis	Moon of the Sucker Fish
March	onaabani giizis	Moon of Crust on the Snow
April	iskigamizige giizis	Moon of the Sugar Camp
May	waabigwani giizis	Moon of the Flower
June	ode'imini giizis	Moon of the Strawberry
July	baapaashkizige giizis	Moon of the White Ash
August	miini giizis	Moon of the Blueberry
September	manooninike giizis	Moon of Wild Rice Harvest
October	binaakwii giizis	Moon of Raking
November	gashkadino giizis	Moon of Freezing
December/Jan.	manidoo giizis	Moon of the Spirit
Spring	ziigwan	
Summer	niibin	
Fall	dagwaagi	
Winter	biboon	
day	giizhig	
night	dibikad	
month	giizis	
year	biboon	

WINTER

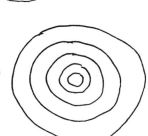

THE ACTIVITIES:

1. Circle of the Sun Models

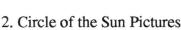

   With a partner make a working model of the sun, earth and moon.
   Practice showing some ideas in your science book with your model:
   tides, eclipses, seasons, day and night.
   You can decorate your model with artwork from your culture.
   Take your model to a classroom in a lower grade to teach these ideas to
   a team of younger children.

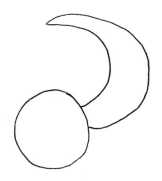

2. Circle of the Sun Pictures

   Which idea is the hardest for you to understand or teach?
   Work the model until you understand it.
   Then make a picture of that idea.
   Use art or symbols from any culture you wish. (You can mix them.)
   Label the parts of your picture using English words and the words of
   another language.

3. Make and use a natural calendar, equinox predictor, or gnomon.
   Remember, the gnomon helps you find the four directions.

   The gnomon works like this:
   1. Put a stick in the ground.
   2. All day, mark the shadow at end of the post using small stones. (You can do it every
      hour or every half hour.)
   3. Tie a string to the bottom of the post. Use it like a compass to mark
      out a circle that cuts across the shadow stones.
   4. Where the compass circle touches the shadow stones, put small sticks
      in the ground.
   5. Connect the sticks with a piece of string
      or a mark scratched on the ground.   THIS IS EAST/WEST.
      West is where the sun goes down.

   6. Scratch a line perpendicular to the east/west line. This is
      north/south. Where is north?

4. Recording
   Leave a record of your work for future archeologists.
   Use a picture, words and symbols to tell how to make and use a gnomon.
   * (Note: "Gnomon" comes from a Greek word that means "To Know"
   When you use a gnomon, you KNOW where the directions are.

Chapter 28

Traveling the Solar System

CONCEPT(S):
Systems
Change
Interaction
Cycles

TOPIC & THEME:
Traveling within the solar system.

QUESTION(S):
How are traditional patterns related to the solar system?

PROCESS & THINKING SKILLS:
Experiment
Predict
Record
Special relationships
Recall

INTEGRATIONS:
Language arts
Science
Art

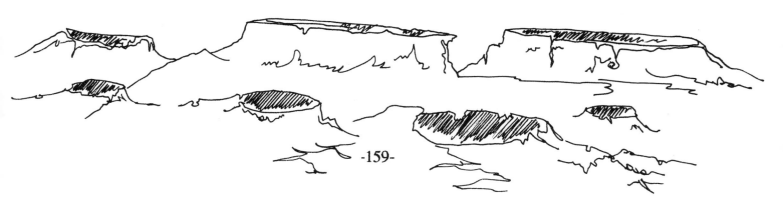

TRAVELING THE SOLAR SYSTEM

THE LANGUAGE:
An Ojibwe-English way to remember the order of the planets:

Planet	English Phrase	Ojibwe -English	
Mercury	My	Makade	Black
Venus	Very	Very	Velvet
Earth	Elderly	Esiban(ag)	Raccoon(s)
Mars	Mother	Madwengwaam	Snore,
Jupiter	Just	Jachaam	Sneeze,
Saturn	Served	Sh	And
Uranus	Us	Unbend	Unbend
Neptune	Nine	Newe	Bullsnakes
Pluto	Pizzas	Pane	Continuously

THE FACTS: The Solar System contains planet-spheres that orbit around the sun.

Karen Good is science teacher at Red Lake. She is also an enrolled tribal member. She says,

> "Our people have always known the earth is round. We didn't have to
> wait for Columbus to tell us this. We looked at the circles, cycles
> and spheres all around us: The Moon and Sun, Life, the Seasons,
> rain and clouds.... Ojibwe people observed all these circles, and knew
> the Earth was also round."

OJIBWE SIGN   "MAN WHO SITS ON THE GLOBE"

How Far Apart are the Planets?

Scientists measure the solar system with Astronomical Units (AU).

1 AU is the distance from the Sun to the Earth.

Mercury and Venus are closer to the sun, so their AU's are smaller than 1.

This makes it easy to make a model of the solar system. 1 AU can be an inch, ten centimeters, or a meter, depending on how big you make your model.

Planet	Astronomical Units from Sun
Mercury	.4 AU (almost halfway between the Sun and the Earth)
Venus	.7 AU (almost 3/4 of the way between the Sun and Earth.)
Earth	1.0 (93 million miles or 150 kilometers)
Mars	1.5
Jupiter	2.3
Saturn	9.6
Uranus	19.4
Neptune	30.1
Pluto	39.8 (Pluto's orbits varies a lot. Sometimes it is even inside of Neptune's orbit.)

SATURN 9.0

How Big are the Planets?

Scientists measure the size of planets in Earth Diameters. It is an easy way to tell how big the planets are compared to our home planet. The Sun is 109 ED across! (It could contain a million earths!) Mercury is only about .4 ED (about half as big as Earth.)

Planet	Earth Diameter Size
Sun	109.0
Mercury	.4
Venus	.9 (almost as big as Earth)
Earth	1.0 (of course)
Mars	.5 (half as big as Earth)
Jupiter	11.0
Saturn	9.0
Uranus	3.7
Neptune	3.5
Pluto	.2

JUPITER 11.0

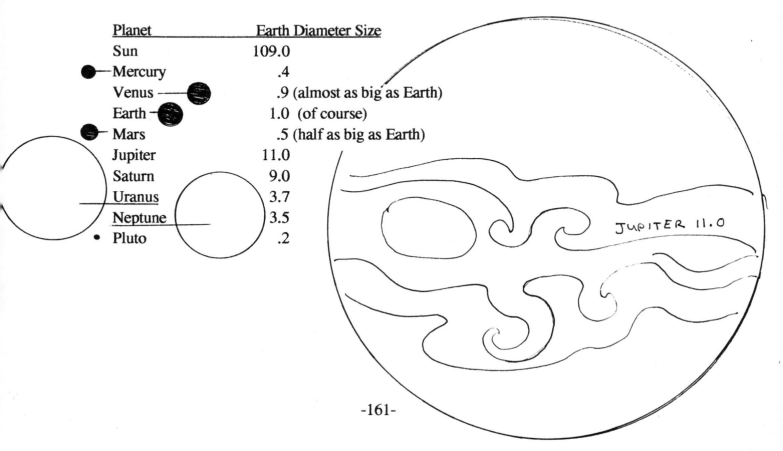

THE ACTIVITIES:

1. Science/Math/Art Model
   First research the solar system. Find out the relative sizes of the planets and their distance from each other. First try mapping the Solar System to scale on the playground. Then try it on a smaller scale (10 cm = 1 AU) on adding machine tape. You will need 4 meters of adding machine tape for each project. Make the planets to scale. Try using Traditional items when possible. For example, Earth could be a dried cranberry and Saturn an acorn.

2. Abstract Symbols
   Invent a creative symbol for each planet. Make sure it relates to the science facts about the planet. (For example, if a planet is small, rocky, hot and red you would need a different symbol than if it were a large planet made of poisonous gas. Design a traditional bead pattern or petroglyph story using these symbols.

3. Traditional Painting
   Using colored paper, opaque paint, and strong designs, paint your interpretation of the the solar system. It should contain real science information, but it can contain your favorite Ojibwe signs or solar designs too.

4. European Painting
   Tape a piece of white drawing paper to the desk or cardboard. Dampen the paper with water. Paint over the whole thing with a dark color to make the sky. While it is still wet, sprinkle it with LITTLE salt. (When the salt dries it will look like stars!) When the paper is completely dry, use opaque paint to show the planets.

5. Multicultural Painting
   Combine both styles as many creative artists do now.

6. Write factual paragraphs about your solar system paintings. Write fictional legends or stories about your planets. Underline any real science facts (like Earth having oceans, mountains and volcanoes.)

Chapter 29

Star Patterns

CONCEPT(S):
Patterns
Cycles
Change

TOPIC & THEME:
Star Patterns

QUESTION(S):
How did ancient cultures explain and use the stars?

PROCESS & THINKING SKILLS:
Collect and organize data
Recall
Infer
Special relationships
Observe

INTEGRATIONS:
Language arts
Science
Art
Social studies
Math

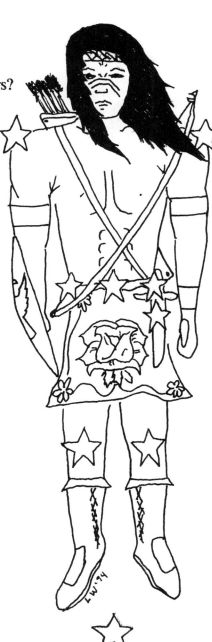

STARS /PATTERNS

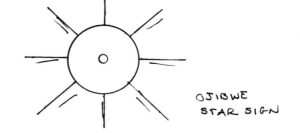

OJIBWE
STAR SIGN

THE STORIES: The Brave Fisher

Long ago the People of the Sky kept the sun's warmth to themselves. People of the Earth needed the sun's warmth and energy. Without it, they were always cold and often hungry. Little Fisher and his friends went on a quest for the sun. Wolverine tried to jump up high enough to penetrate the heavens, making a hole big enough for plenty of sun to shine through. But he failed. Fisher was lean and strong from climbing up and down tall trees and fighting porcupines. He concentrated on his jump, visualizing himself gathering his muscles and propelling his long furry body successfully toward the sky. When he was ready, he gave a cry and hurdled upward like a meteor, cracking hard against the sky.

As the Sky People became alert to the intruder, Fisher shook his stunned head. The Sky People shouted and ran toward Fisher. "Stop! We want ALL the sun!" With a quick look over his shoulder, Fisher began to bite at the hard edges of the sky. As the hole opened, bright sunbeams poured through the opening to warm the earth. Closer came the Sky People, now shooting arrows as they came. Fisher bit faster at the opening, refusing to leave until he knew the Earth People would have enough sunlight. As one deadly arrow struck Fisher, he tumbled through the hole, happy that he had opened the hole enough for at least half of the year to be sunny and warm.

Gichi Manidoo, the Great Spirit, was touched by Fisher's steadfast efforts to help the tribes of the earth, so he gently caught the brave little animal and placed him in the night sky. The Spirit used bright stars to show the people where he had placed Fisher. In this way Fisher is still honored for bringing sunlight to The Earth People.

THE FACTS:

The Fisher Constellation (The Big Dipper) was known as the Great Bear by many cultures around the world: Greek, French, Italians, Spanish, Onadaga, Cherokee, Blackfoot, Zuni, and Eskimo. The Germans saw a Great Wagon in the same constellation. A circle of stars above the Great Bear is often called the Great Bear's Den. To the Anishinaabe, the circle of stars may have been the hole that Fisher bit in the sky.

The Anishinaabe understood the importance of the sun (a star) as the giver of life to the energy cycle. The lodge door faced East, the direction of the dawn. The first person awake in the lodge would greet the dawn and say:

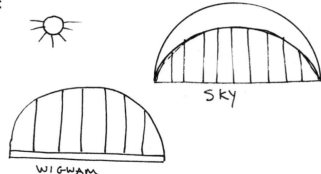

By you, Father, through the sun,
You work your powers to dispel the night.
Bring day anew -- a new life, a new time.
To you, Father, through the sun,
We give thanks, for your light,
For your warmth that gives light to all.

Traditional Navajo hogans are also placed so that the door opens to the east.

People of the Southwest, living in a harsh and dry climate, relied on star positions to accurately predict weather patterns and crop planting times.

The Maya of Mexico were farmers too, and they depended on the study of the stars (astronomy) to determine their farming activities during the year. They were so accurate that they produced extra food. This meant they could take life a little easier. They had time and energy to develop beautiful pieces of art, wonderfully designed buildings, books, higher math, and more science.

The Mayan star observatory was a designed as a tower within a tower. The base was 37 feet across. Priests climbed a spiral staircase to a small room at the top of the tower where they predicted and observed patterns in the sky through slits in the heavy walls: eclipses, the equinox, movements of Venus and other planets.

The Patterns of the Universe:
Star Patterns like The Fisher are called constellations.
Our galaxy is a spiral pattern. Spiral patterns are all around us.
Some galaxies are elliptical.
Stars follow patterns of movement. Comets follow elliptical patterns.
The timing and number of sunspots follow a pattern too.

METEORS

Patterns of color and light:
* Auroras occur when solar flare radiation reaches earth. Their light comes from colliding electrons. (See the Chapter on Magnetism for details.)
*Starlight moving away from us is shifted to the red end of the color spectrum. Starlight moving toward us is shifted to blue.

* Look into a fire. See the different colors?
When we say that something is "red hot" we mean REALLY hot.
White and blue flames are even hotter than red.

The Life and Death of a Star
(Birth) Stars are born from clouds of gas and dust (Nebula).
Gravity and heat cause fusion of hydrogen.

(Life) Big bright stars only live about a million years because they use up their energy.
Stars of average and small size can shine for 10 billion years.
Our sun is one of these. Most stars look white. Many stars are twins, orbiting around
each other. Sometimes three stars orbit together.
Some stars, like our Sun, are solo.

(Middle Age) The star uses up its hydrogen gas. It starts to collapse.
The star gets so hot that fusion starts in other elements.
The star grows and cools. These huge, cooler stars look red. They are called Red Giants.

(Old Age) The Red Giant collapses , forming a hot blue star called a White Dwarf ("Blue
Dwarf" might be a better name.)
If the old star gets energy from its twin it's called a Nova or Supernova.

(Death of a Star.) Small and average stars can just drift and burn away.
The death of massive stars is explosive. Supernovas become tiny, dense stars (neutron
stars) or black holes, with so much gravity that light cannot escape.   Pulsars are neutron
stars that give off regular radio waves.

THE ACTIVITIES:

1. Patterns of stars
   What time of year is it?
   Learn the constellations for this time of year by going outside and
   looking at the sky. Use a star map for a guide.
   What are other constellation stories from your culture?

   Many traditional homes are dome shapes, like the dome of the sky.
   Make a model of a dome home. Place the constellations on the inside,
   so people inside the home could see the constellations as they would
   appear outside.

2. Adopt a constellation. Observe and report its movement once a week for
   a whole season. How does it move in relation to other constellations?
   Write and illustrate legend-style stories about your constellation.
   To illustrate, you can use charts, star maps, and/or traditional art from
   your culture. This might be rock painting designs, bead and quill work,
   watercolor painting or silver jewelry.

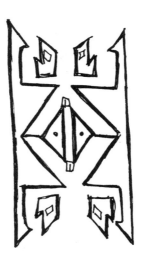

3. Retell the Life of Star story using patterns of poetry and/or art.

4. In a small group, design a dance to demonstrate the beauty and power involved in the
   life and death of stars. The dance can be from any culture. Turn your design plan into a
   notebook, a bulletin board, or an actual dance. What costumes, outfits, and stage
   designs will you need? Draw or describe them.

5. Design a board game or card game to help teach star patterns to your classmates and
   younger children. Your game should connect the pattern with astronomy and culture facts.

6. Spirals!
   The galaxy is a giant spiral.
   Observe, collect and record spirals:
   Do they wind clockwise or counterclockwise?
   Were they made by humans or nature?
   Are they tight or loose?
   Design spiral patterns on circular graph paper.
   Create a story or poem about your spiral design.

Chapter 30

Weather Elements and Patterns

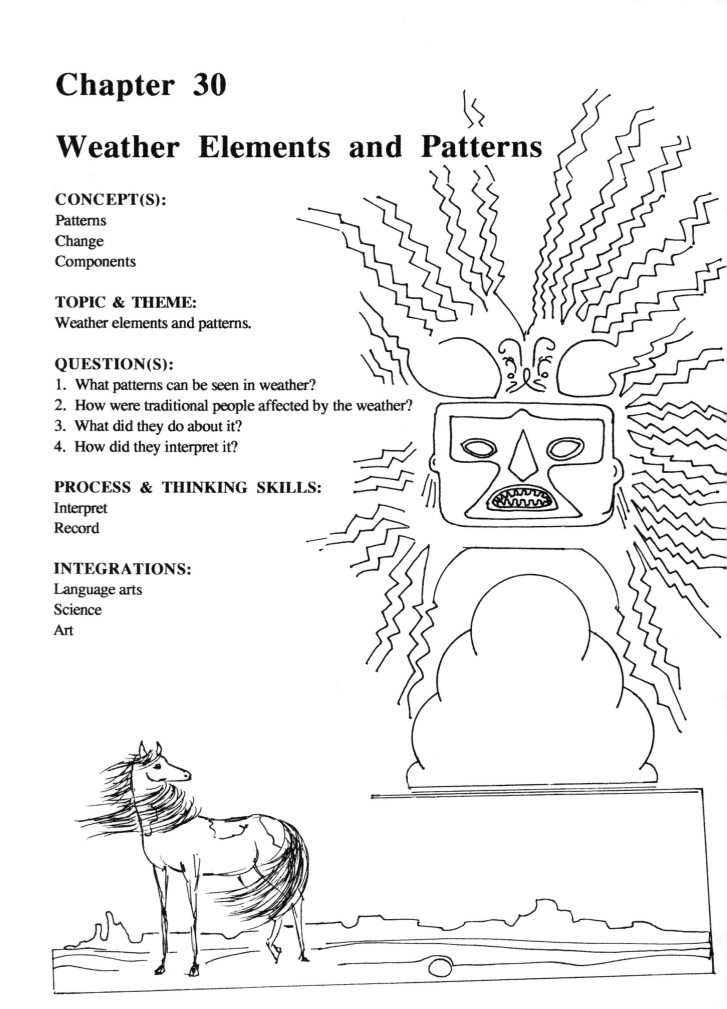

CONCEPT(S):
Patterns
Change
Components

TOPIC & THEME:
Weather elements and patterns.

QUESTION(S):
1. What patterns can be seen in weather?
2. How were traditional people affected by the weather?
3. What did they do about it?
4. How did they interpret it?

PROCESS & THINKING SKILLS:
Interpret
Record

INTEGRATIONS:
Language arts
Science
Art

WEATHER ELEMENTS AND PATTERNS

A STORY-TELLER: O Shaw Gus Co Day Way Qua, Woman of the Green Prairie
(Susan Johnston)   1772-1843.

O Shaw Gus Co Day Way Qua was the youngest daughter and favorite child of a famous Ojibwe chief, Waub-o-jeeg. The family lived on the South shore of Lake Superior at a time when life was changing for the Ojibwe. When O Shaw Gus Co Day Way Qua married John Johnston, a respected Irish trader, she took the name Susan Johnston. The Johnstons were respected in both worlds. Susan helped preserve peace between the Americans, the English and the Ojibwe.

The Johnstons' eight children learned both Ojibwe and British ways. They could speak both languages fluently. Their daughter Jane became the wife of Henry Schoolcraft, who was the first white person to identify Lake Itasca as the Headwaters of the Mississippi River. Schoolcraft learned many things from his Indian friends and relatives.

This story, Shin-ge-bis Fools the North Wind, was told to Henry Schoolcraft by his wife Jane, who learned it from her mother. You can find more of O Shaw Gus Do Day Way Qua's stories in your library or government publications.

A STORY:

Long ago around the Great Lakes, the great Ka-bib-on-okka ruled the wintertime just as he does today. He was the fierce North Wind. All summer long, kindly Sha-won-dasee, blew his warm breath over the land. He was the great South Wind from the land of the Sunflower. His breath warmed the forest. Birch trees sprouted green leaves and lady slippers bloomed in the warm rain and sunshine. The people worked hard during the long warm summer days to gather enough food for long winter. They caught fish and picked berries. In the cool days of fall, Sha-won-dasee filled the valleys with misty water vapor from his pipe, and the people harvested wild rice.

When winter came, they all moved to a warmer place. Every fall the people had plenty of warning about the coming cold. Smoking his pipe in the sunshine, Sha-won-dasee grew sleepy. As his eyes closed for longer and long times, Ka-bib-on-okka, the North Wind, blew closer to camp. Days became shorter, and woven mats flapped against wigwam doorways in gusts of icy wind. Feathery snowflakes drifted to earth from low gray clouds. Ice skimmed the lakes.

"Ka-bib-on-okka is coming!" the people shouted. "It's time to leave!"

"Not me!" laughed Shin-ge-bis. "I'm tired of moving around every year. Ka-bib-on-okka doesn't scare me! I'll stay right here."

The people liked Shin-ge-bis. He laughed all the time. He was brave. He could even change himself into a duck. But the people didn't think these skills were enough to save him from the icy anger of Ka-bib-on-okka.

"Please come with us," they pleaded. "You would have to become a fish or a bear to survive Ka-bib-on-okka."

But Shin-ge-bis laughed again. "Brother Beaver lent me his fur coat. Brother Muskrat lent me his fur mittens. I have food and firewood. I'm not afraid of the Old North Wind!"

So the villagers sadly packed and left, never expecting to see their friend alive again.

Shin-ge-bis cheerfully set about his work. Every day he gathered extra firewood for emergencies. He fished through holes in the ice. At night, while trudging home with his long string of fish, he would make up silly songs about the cold weather and the North Wind.

One night Ka-bib-on-okka heard him. The idea of a human daring to stay all winter made him angry. The cozy wigwam and food made him mad. The cheerful song poking fun at the Great North Wind made him furious!

"When night comes, I'll show that arrogant Shin-ge-bis who he's dealing with!" fumed the freezing storm-maker. That night Ka-bib-on-okka blew up the biggest snow storm he had produced in more than a hundred winters.

What happened to Shin-ge-bis? Absolutely nothing! He had a huge log on the fire. He was grilling a delicious fish -- and singing ANOTHER silly song about the old North Wind. He was so warm and happy he didn't realize there was a storm blowing at all. In fact, the snow piled up in gigantic soft drifts around the cozy little wigwam, insulating it and keeping it safe from the icy wind.

When Ka-bib-on-okka realized his mistake, he screamed down the chimney to frighten the human. But Shin-ge-bis laughed again. "The forest is so silent in winter, your noise is a welcome change!"

North Wind rattled the thick hide over the door. He shook the whole wigwam. "Come in you old fool," called Shin-ge-bis. You must be very cold out there."

Ka-bib-on-okka couldn't resist this dare. He stormed inside. It was freezing cold! It was so cold the frost immediately turned to water vapor, filling the wigwam with fog. Shin-ge-bis pretended he didn't notice. He put another log on the fire and sat down to see what would happen.

Before long he wanted to laugh. The North Wind was melting like a snowman in the spring. His eyes, nose and ears were dripping with long melting icicles. His hair became a little waterfall. He was turning into a puddle.

"Oh, come a little closer to the fire," teased Shin-ge-bis. Suddenly North Wind fled in a shower of raindrops.

Once outside, the freezing air renewed him. He felt fiercely angry.

"Come out and fight fair!" he shouted into the wigwam.

Shin-ge-bis thought about it. "Old North Wind sounds strong, but I think he's still weak from the heat of my fire. I think I can beat this cool fool," he laughed.

As soon as he stepped outside, Ka-bib-on-okka grabbed him with long freezing fingers, but Shin-ge-bis fought back confidently. All night long they fought, and in the morning when the sky turned from black to peach, the blizzard was gone. Mist hung over the lake. A bird sang.

The North Wind was beaten by cheerfulness and courage.

The people, who now live in the Northern Forest all year long, tell stories in the winter. It helps us stay cheerful and courageous when the North Wind blows.

THE PATTERNS AND ACTIVITIES

Rhyming Patterns: Be like Shin-ge-bis. Make up a silly song or poem about the weather. Write down your rhyming pattern.

Water Patterns Activity:
Illustrate the story. How many kinds of water are mentioned?
What does water look like in these forms? Find more snow and ice shapes.

Ice Crystal   Snowflake   Water Molecule   Water Vapor

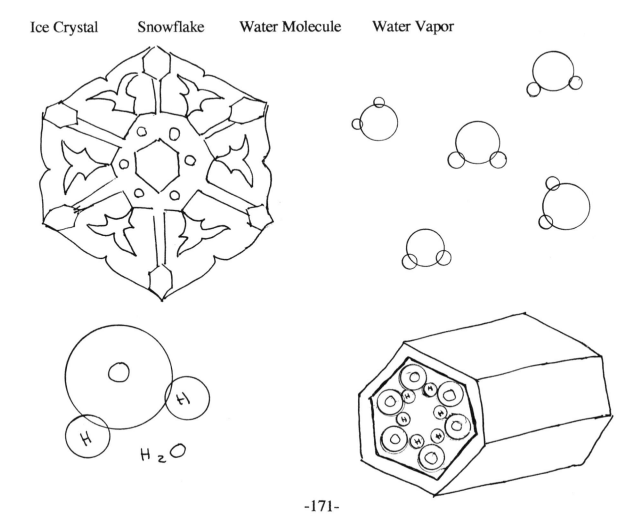

Temperature Patterns

Temperature is a measurement of hotness or coldness.
It is measured with a thermometer.

THE FACTS: Temperature determines how fast wild rice ripens.

It is important to put unripe rice beds off limits to harvesters so the rice isn't hurt.
Different beds will be off-limits every year depending on how fast it happens to ripen. A
good Rice Chief is also a good weather observer.

Winter temperatures can kill plants, animals, fish, and people.
Temperatures determine when the sap starts running in the maple trees.

THE ACTIVITIES:

Temperature Graph Activity: Bead design Pattern
Make a bead design of temperature patterns on graph paper.

1. Put the temperatures along the left side of the paper.
You can decide if you will record in Fahrenheit or Celsius.
You can decide how much temperature change you will record.
For Example:
If you record temperatures from -30 to 110 degrees f at ten degree/space, this would be
15 spaces. Using 1/4 inch graph paper your graph will be 3 3/4 inches high.

2. Record months and days along the bottom of the graph.
You can decided how many days to record.
The longer you record, the more interesting the pattern will be.
If you recorded all 365 days your design will be 91 1/4 inches long
(using 1/4 inch graph paper).
Try it! Make a bigger graph that would go around the cafeteria or gym!

3. Choose colors that represent the seasons for recording your pattern.
Use Primary and Secondary Colors (Red, Yellow, Blue, Orange, Green,
Purple) and Black and White. Color the graph. How is this like a cycle?

4. Make this into an actual piece of bead work by choosing the temperature on every
fifth day. This will give you six beads/month.
Your beadwork will be 1 1/2 inches high and about six inches long.
You could use it for a bracelet, barrette or arm band.

Air Pressure and Humidity Patterns

Air pressure tells us how many molecules of oxygen are packed into a certain space.
It is measured with a barometer.
If the air is warm, the molecules float farther apart.
Fewer molecules are in the space. Pressure is low.
If the air is cold, the molecules pack closely together.
Pressure is high.

Humidity is the amount of moisture in the air.
It is measured with a hygrometer.

High pressure can carry fewer water molecules because the space is already packed with oxygen molecules. (High pressure air is drier.)

Low pressure can carry more water molecules because the space isn't so packed with oxygen molecules. (The air is more moist--humid.)

What is Wind? High pressure air pushes low pressure air out of the way.
High pressure weather is fair since the wind pushes out, and clouds can't form.

THE FACTS: Drums and Toys

Q. How is a drum head affected by air pressure and humidity?

A. The air space inside the drum contains more oxygen molecules on high pressure days. The drum head is pushed up (made tighter) by the air inside.
On high humidity days, the air inside the drum contains less oxygen, so the drum head may sag. Drumheads are designed to be tightened or loosened.

Indian and pioneer parents were creative. They made toys for their children from things that were available in nature. Sometimes they made balls from the cleaned bladders of animals. When the bladder was not blown up enough it was limp. It would not roll or bounce. There were not enough molecules of air inside the bladder. The air pressure inside was too low. When the bladder was blown up more, it contained more molecules of air. The air pressure was higher. Children could then toss and play with the ball.

AIR PRESSURE AND HUMIDITY ACTIVITIES

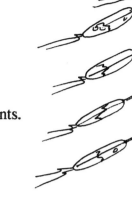

1. Predicting with patterns

Observe the weather every day.
Is it fair or rainy? How does it "feel?" Wet or Dry?
Check with a weather station or your own weather instruments.
What is the humidity?
What is the barometric pressure?
What is the wind direction and speed.

Record your observations and the weather reports using the Temperature graph as a model (p. 171). Can you find a pattern?

Interpret the pattern on a graph using numbers and pictures.

Use symbols, signs, and language from your culture to forecast the weather.

2. Write a story about weather cycles or patterns.
Use weather symbols and cultural symbols in place of some words. This can be a "realistic" story or a legend.

3. Make a drum barometer with a coffee can, balloon, rubber band, straw, glue, paper, tape, clay and ruler. Find ways to record the air pressure inside the drum.
Use your creativity to interpret the results.

4. Draw the water cycle. It can be "real" or done in symbols.
   Explain how the water cycle works.
   You can use "weather report" words.
   You can write a traditional story or poem.

Cloud Patterns

Make cloud paintings showing different kinds of clouds.
You may make a European or traditional American Indian painting.
Describe your clouds in European or Ojibwe words. (p. 176)

This will help you with style:

	European	Indian
paper	white	colored
paper surface	wet	dry
paint	transparent	opaque
	(watercolor)	(tempera)
style	realistic	imaginary
symmetry (balance)	asymmetric	symmetric
colors	soft	bright
shading	round	flat

You might enjoy mixing styles too.

Cirrus

Stratus

Cumulous

Cumulo-nimbus

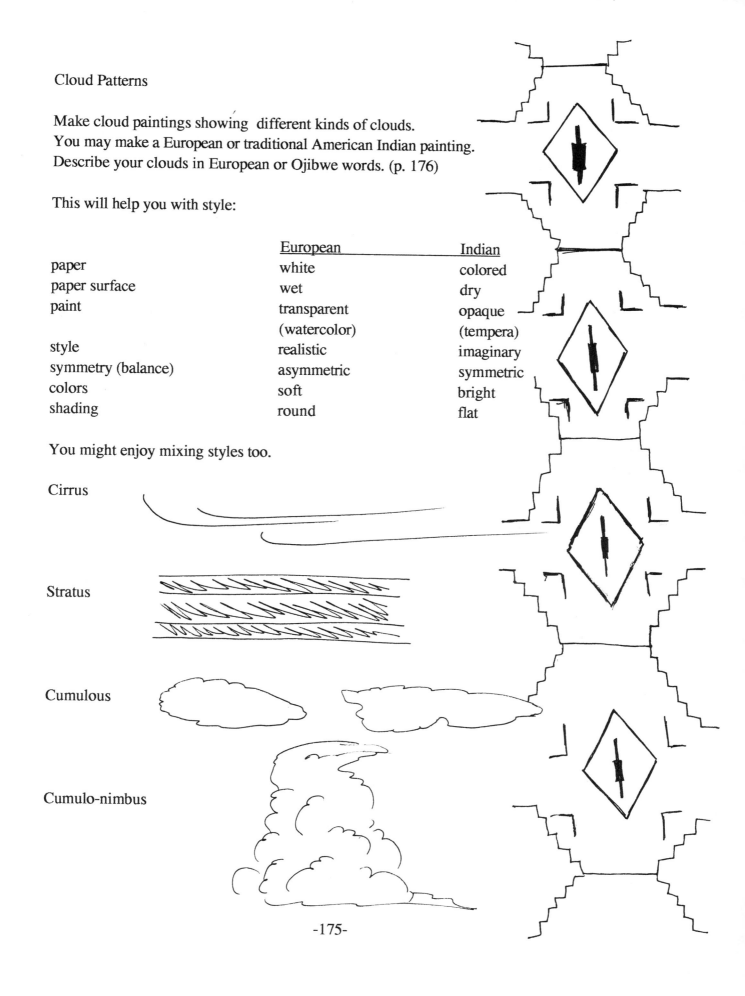

-175-

THE LANGUAGE:

High Pressure (and low humidity)

It is a nice day	Minogiishigad
It is clear	Mizhakwad
It is windy	Noodin

Low Pressure (and High humidity)

It is nasty	Niiskaadad
It is cloudy	Ningwaanakwad
There's a blizzard	Biiwan
It is snowing	Zoogipo
It is foggy	Awan
It's raining	Gimiwan
It is thundering	Animikikaa

Temperature

It is hot	Gizhaate
It is warm	Aabawaa
It is cold	Gisinaa
It is cool	Dakaayaa

Use these words to tell a story or lable a card under your painting of weather.

Chapter 31

Storm Patterns

CONCEPT(S):
Patterns
Components
Change

IDEA (DEFINING CONCEPT):

TOPIC & THEME:
Storm Patterns

QUESTION(S):
1. What patterns can we see in wind and storms?
2. What traditional wisdom can we learn about wind and storms?

PROCESS & THINKING SKILLS:
Record
Interpret
Recall

INTEGRATIONS:
Science
Art
Social studies

AIR MASSES AND STORMS

THE STORIES: Iroquois

Thunder Boy lived with his father in the sky. With no children around for friends, he was a lonely child. His major fun was shooting his toy arrows of lightning into big thunderclouds made by his father.   The toy arrows seemed small in the sky, but on earth they could knock over trees. So he was very careful not to aim at earth.

He was lonely for friends, and he was lonely for his mother, who was an Iroquois lady and could not live in the sky. Finally, Thundercloud let him go to earth for a visit. "Be very careful not to shoot anything. And NEVER aim at people!" he warned his little son.

Thunder Boy had a wonderful time on earth. He was happy to be with his mother and new friends. But whenever the other boys wanted to go shoot their arrows, Thunder Boy had to say "No, I can't." After a while the boys teased him. And the teasing got worse. Finally Thunder Boy couldn't stand it. He grabbed an arrow and shot toward the boys.

The white-hot arrow split the air. Thunder boomed and vibrated around the forest. Trees fell under the path of the arrow. A forest fire ignited as the arrow struck a tree. The boys shook with fear and amazement. Thunder Boy had disobeyed his father.   A huge Thundercloud rose in the sky and rushed through the forest, sweeping the child up to the sky in a blanket of wind. He lives there today, shooting arrows of lightning and remembering his happy time on earth.

Scandinavian & Greek

The ancient Scandinavians called their Thunder god, Thor. Thursday is named for him. Zeus was the powerful Thunder god of the ancient Greeks. Both of these gods hurled lightning bolts, like Thunder Boy in the story. Stories of many traditional cultures link thunder with lightning -- as they are linked in nature.

Ojibwe

Ojibwe stories tell that when First Man reached the prairies on a vision quest, the Little Thunders tried to keep him from crossing the plains. The mountains and eastern prairies have about fifty thunderstorms every year.

As First Man was returning home from his quest, a little whirlwind puffed in his face and danced away. No matter how fast he ran or how hard he tried to trick the whirlwind, it always stayed tantalizingly close, but far way enough not to get caught.

"Who are you?" called First Man, nearly out of breath.

" I am Bay Bee Mi Say Si. I am little brother of Tornado and Hurricane. My purpose in life is to be foolish, to tease, and to play with those who are too serious. Remember there is a time to laugh as well as to cry."

As the whirlwind skipped away, First Man thought about his life. Soon he would return to his people. He decided to show them foolishness and humor as well as greatness and generosity. This is how the people would learn. His new name was Winabozho, the Trickster.

ATMOSPHERE PATTERN ACTIVITIES:

1. Atmosphere art

Choose an art style you enjoy -- American Indian painting, European Painting, colored pencil sketching, charcoal pencil drawing, ink, collage . . . .

Draw a small planet Earth on a sheet of paper.

(You may cut the paper into a circle if you wish.)

Choose four colors to represent the four layers of the atmosphere.

Be able to tell why you chose each color. Color the layers lightly.

Hint: There are no "right or wrong" colors.

You might use colors that represent heat or distance from the Earth.

Draw pictures of what you might find at each layer.

OR make a collage in each layer from magazine pictures.

Or invent symbols that represent the objects found in the atmosphere.

DISCOVERED IN THE LAYERS: Think of the atmosphere as layers inside a ball.

Near the Earth we may find eagles. Mt. Everest is ten miles above the earth.

UP TO 10 MILES AROUND THE EARTH: Troposphere means "changing."

Most cloud activity and most aircraft are found here.

Temperatures drop as you climb upward.

10-30 MILES AROUND THE EARTH: Stratosphere means "spread out."

Manned balloons can be 20 miles out. Weather balloons are found at 30 miles. Temperature gets warmer as you rise in the Stratosphere because the ozone layer is absorbing heat energy from the sun.

30-60 MILES AROUND THE EARTH: Mesosphere means "middle."

Air here becomes coldest in the atmosphere -- down to $-95^{\circ}C$ ($-139^{\circ}F$)

About 60 miles out from Earth you might find meteor trails and even an X-15 aircraft.

60 to 500 MILES AROUND THE EARTH: Thermosphere means "hot."

The temperature is around $50^{\circ}C$ ($122^{\circ}F$). In the Thermosphere you might find: rockets at 200 miles out, Aurora at 200-400 miles, and weather satellites at 400 miles.

2. A story -- Out of this World!

Pretend you are riding a Thunderbird or a Rocket. Describe what you see and feel as you fly farther from earth. Illustrate your story if you wish.

Chapter 32

Climates

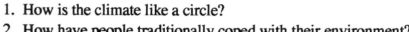

CONCEPT(S):
Change
Cycles

TOPIC & THEME:
Climates

QUESTION(S):
1. How is the climate like a circle?
2. How have people traditionally coped with their environment?
3. How and why is the climate changing today?

PROCESS & THINKING SKILLS:
Record
Analyze
Experiment
Predict
Special relationships

INTEGRATIONS:
Science
Art
Math

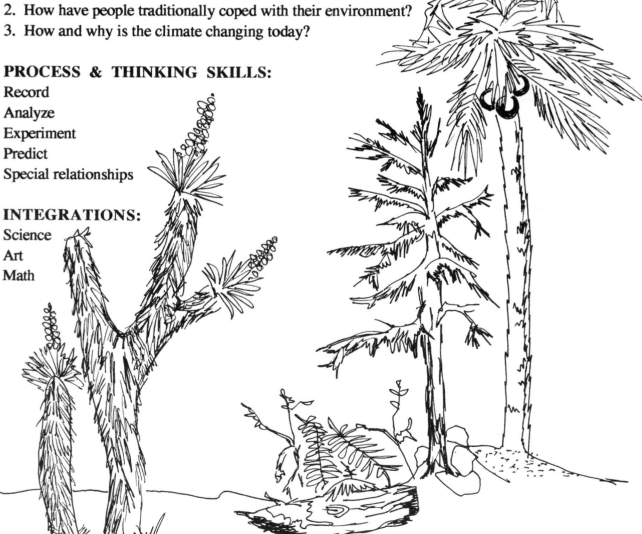

CLIMATES

THE FACTS:

In The Climate Cycle the earth gets cooler and warmer over and over.
Minnesota has been in an Ice Age for the last 2 million years.
Most of Minnesota's present landscape was created by glaciers.
Deposits made hills; ice blocks formed lakes; heavy melting carved rivers.
When the climate was colder, glaciers covered much of the state.
When the climate warmed between the glaciers, Minnesota was tropical.

This graph* shows the climate cooling and warming for 2 million years.
* After Bray, <u>Billions of Years in Minnesota</u>.

Warmer periods

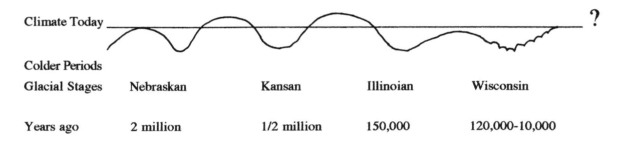

Glacial Stages	Nebraskan	Kansan	Illinoian	Wisconsin
Years ago	2 million	1/2 million	150,000	120,000-10,000

In small groups talk about the Climate Graph.

1. How often has it been colder?
2. How often has it been warmer?
3. Looking at the pattern, what do you think will happen next? Why?

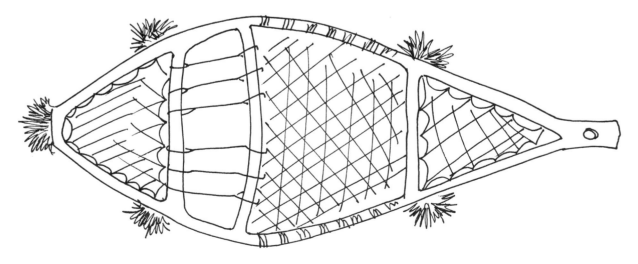

Why Do Climates Change?

Natural climate changes are caused by volcanoes, the tilt of the earth, and glaciers.

Human-made changes may be caused by burning gas, coal and oil, and by cutting trees.

Carbon dioxide can form a barrier that keeps heat from escaping the earth.

Gas, coal and oil give off Carbon Dioxide, CO_2.

Young, rapidly growing trees use CO_2. Dead trees give off CO2

We need SOME CO_2 (a greenhouse gas). Without any CO_2 all heat would reflect off the earth, and the temperature would be 20 degrees below zero!

GREENHOUSE ACTIVITIES:

Research and discuss these questions in small groups.

Where will you find reliable information?

There is so much controversy about the greenhouse effect and global warming, how will you know whom to believe?

Your report can contain both points of view.

1. Younger trees absorb carbon dioxide; dead trees give off CO_2. Should some old growth forest areas be cut and replanted with younger trees?
2. Is the temperature of the earth really rising?
   How much? How fast?
   Most temperatures are measured at airports.
   What effect does all the concrete have on the temperature?
   How could clouds affect computer models of global warming?
3. In the Tropical Rain Forest, what percentage of trees is growing rapidly?
   What percentage is mature? What percentage is dying or dead?

   Tipi
4. The cost of converting industry to non-greenhouse gases is several trillion dollars. If we spend the money on these changes, what other things would we have to give up?
   Does the evidence for the greenhouse effect support these changes?
5. What are alternatives to fossil fuels?
   What are the effects of solar and nuclear power?

List some other controversial questions (like the overall effects of Columbus coming to the New World, or the value of space exploration.)

Explain both sides of these issues.

IGLOO

Climate Story Activity:

1. Create and illustrate a story about the future climate in Minnesota.

What might cause the change? Why?
(Natural: Global Tilt, Glaciers, Volcanoes, Human-made: Greenhouse Gases....)
What would the temperature, seasons and precipitation be like?
If the ice caps melted, what would happen to the rivers and oceans?
How would the melting affect the big cities located near water?
What were the plants and animals like during the warm times?
Would they return? Would new species evolve? Describe them.
How would the people adapt and live in their new climate?
What will houses look like? What will the people eat?
How will the new climate affect the way people spend their free time?

2. Design-a-Tree Activity:
Design a new tree for a warmer climate with higher CO_2 levels.

Review plant characteristics and how plants grow.

Will it have leaves, needles or spines?

What kind of bark? Why?

Make your plant have both real and imaginary characteristics.

WIGWAM

3. Climate Homes Activity:
Traditional people have always used engineering skills to adapt their homes
to the climate.

Research and construct models of different kinds of traditional homes.

(Each student or small group can do one home.)

Tell about the people who made these homes.

Where, when and how did they live?

What basic math shapes did they use in construction?

4. The Climate Cycle:
In small groups show how the climate cycles through warm and cold times.
Each group can do one cycle.

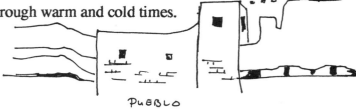

PUEBLO

Chapter 33

Motion/Force/Work

CONCEPT(S):
Change
Cause and effect
Interactions

TOPIC & THEME:
Motion/force/work.

QUESTION(S):
How did traditional people rely on motion and force to do work?

PROCESS & THINKING SKILLS:
Collect and organize data

INTEGRATIONS:
Social studies
Science
Art

MOTION -- FORCE -- WORK

THE FACTS:
Forces and the Laws of Motion are easier to remember if you think about a birchbark canoe.

1. The canoe just sits still if the water is calm and if no one is paddling it.
   When the canoe is paddled, it moves. It stops moving when paddling stops.

1st Law of Motion:
An Object at rest stays at rest until a force makes it move.
A moving object keeps moving until a force makes it stop.

What force acts on the canoe to make it move?
The paddling pushes the canoe forward.

What force acts on the canoe to make it stop?
Friction with the water makes the canoe stop if it isn't being paddled.

2. Paddled by one person, a light birchbark canoe can accelerate faster
   through the water than a heavy log dugout.
   A big paddle will push the canoe forward faster than a little one.
   A big wave will push a canoe sideways faster than a little wave.

2nd Law of Motion

An object's acceleration depends on the mass of the object.
An object's acceleration depends on the size and direction of the force acting on it.

3. When the person pushes the paddle backwards, the canoe moves forward.

The 3rd Law of Motion   Name_____

For every action there is an equal and opposite reaction.
What forces act on the canoe and paddler?
Make your drawing below, label the forces.

Thrust from the person paddling pushes the canoe forward.
Friction with the water slows it down.
Lift causes the paddlers' hair to flow out behind.
Gravity pulls the hair back down when they stop.
Work moves the canoe over the distance.
Energy in the paddlers' muscles does the work (moving the canoe.)
Machines help people do work. The paddle is a simple machine.
When the paddle is raised it has potential energy. When it swings down, it has kinetic energy (energy motion .)

    Kinetic is an old Greek work meaning "to move."
    Animiobide is the Ojibwe word meaning "it moves away."
    Bevege is Norwegian for "to move."
    Mouvoir is French for "move".

In any language, when something moves, it has energy (kinetic) motion.

THE ACTIVITIES:
Understanding and Communicating ideas -- models and language.

1. Airplanes and Eagles

   For transportation, airplanes are as important today as canoes were yesterday.

   Like the canoe, the airplane and eagle flight rely on the Three Laws of Motion and the Forces.

   As the force of air strikes different control surfaces, it causes the plane to move in different directions.   (The Second Law of Motion.)

   What is controlled by the ailerons?

   What does the elevator control?

   What does the rudder control?

2. Make a model and become a test pilot:

   Fold and fly a simple paper airplane.

   Record the distance and direction of each flight.

   Experiment: Add weight (paper clips) to the nose of the plane.

   Cut ailerons, rudder and elevator.

   What happens when they are folded?

   Make a class graph on the blackboard to show your results.

3. Many cultures have used picture-writing to convey their ideas.

   1.) Write the Law of Motion and explain how airplanes demonstrate it.

   2.) Make airplane or eagle drawings to explain:

       the Laws of Motion, Forces, Energy, Machines, and Work.

       Your pictures can be as detailed or simple as you choose.

   3.) Make up some simple picture writing for captions.

4. Make model airplanes and eagles from styrofoam trays.

   Explain how physics makes them fly.

5. Make Kites and model hot air balloons.

   Use the Laws of Motion and Forces to make them fly.

TRADITIONAL MODEL ACTIVITY:

1. Select a Traditional Object:
   In a small group select a traditional object that will demonstrate the Laws of Motion and Forces. Your object can be from any culture. You might think about: drums: eagles, windmills, sailboats, toys, or tools.

2. Check your idea. Jot down your results:
   How could we use this to show inertia ?
   How could this show the effect of mass and force?
   How could this show action and reaction?
   How could we use this to show:
   lift
   gravity
   thrust
   friction
   energy (potential and kinetic)
   work

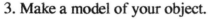

3. Make a model of your object.
   Make a poster to show how it explains the Three Laws and the Forces.

4. Explaining:
   The Ojibwe have a tradition of clear and strong public speaking.
   Use the model and poster to explain these ideas to the class.
   Teach these ideas to younger children using the objects and poster.

FIND OUT MORE:

Learn about the exciting dreams and work of Mary Ross, the first woman engineer employed by Lockheed Missles. Mary Ross is Cherokee.

How did Jerry Elliott High Eagle develop the inertial guidance system for NASA? (What IS an inertial guidance system?)

Meet a pilot (with airplane).
Ask a pilot to bring his or her small airplane to an air strip near your school so you can see the flight controls. Take a discovery flight!

Get education packets from Civil Air Patrol, Minnesota DOT, Cessna.
Explore student and teacher scholarships to Space Camp.

Chapter 34

Simple Machines

CONCEPT(S):
Survival
Change
Structures
Interactions

TOPIC & THEME:
Simple machines.

QUESTION(S):
How did traditional people use simple machines to make their work easier?

PROCESS & THINKING SKILLS:
Experiment
Predict

INTEGRATIONS:
Science
Art
Social studies
Math

SIMPLE MACHINES

THE FACTS AND ACTIVITIES: Illustrate the following ideas.
Teachers can photocopy these pages for students.

A LEVER IS A ROD RESTING ON A POINT (A FULCRUM).

Minnesota's soil is full of little stones and big boulders left by glaciers.
How could people plant crops or build houses with all those rocks?
They used levers to pry the stones, stumps and roots out of the earth.
Stick levers could be used to pry out the little stones.
Big log levers could be used to pry out the big rocks and stumps.
The longer the lever, the more efficiently it works .
Levers let you use less force to do more work.

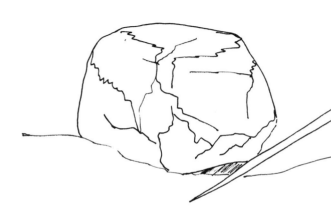

The Atala is a spear-throwing tool invented by many cultures.
It increased the power of the throw by 50%.
The longer the arm (lever), the longer the throw.
The atala "extends" the throwing arm, so the spear travels farther.
      Early ones were very simple notched sticks.
Later, people added weights and finger loops.
The atalas shown at the Jeffers Petroglyphs look like this.

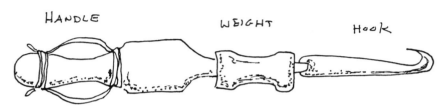

HANDLE   WEIGHT   HooK

AN INCLINED PLANE IS A RAMP USED TO RAISE AND LOWER THINGS.

Stepping from a canoe in the water to a high bank, people would have walked along a log.
The log ramp is an inclined plane.

Many cultures used travois to carry heavy objects when they traveled.
The travois only had one or two friction points. It was much easier to move the object than
dragging the whole thing along the ground where friction would really slow it down.

A Wedge has angled sides that come to a sharp point or edge.
   It's used to split or pierce things.   Here are some common wedges:
   Show how they work. (Use the back of the page if you wish.)

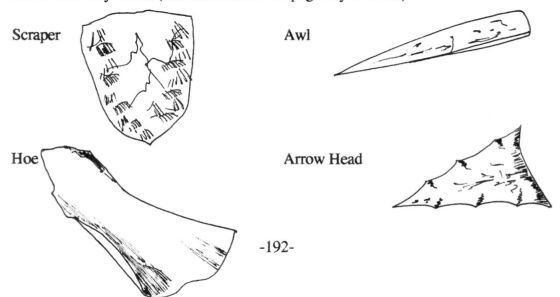

Scraper

Awl

Hoe

Arrow Head

A Screw is used to hold things together.

It is an inclined plane running around a rod.

The screw design was used in basket weaving and coil pottery.

Trails that wound around a mountain were easier to walk on than trials running right straight up the side of the mountain.

A wheel and axle made it easier to move things.
Eskimo people invented spinners to wind homemade cord.
This was easier than winding it around and around by hand.

Mexican people put wheels on some of their toys.
The wheels cut the friction so the toys could move faster.
The Asians invented the fishing reel and potters wheel.

Pulleys use a wheel and rope.

They are used to move things up and down and sideways.

(Illustrate at least one of the following uses.)

People of the Northwest tribes use pulleys to set up their huge, heavy totem poles.

Navajo people could use pulleys to raise the top bar of their weaving looms.

Incas used pulleys to help build their incredible suspension bridges over deep canyons.

SIMPLE MACHINES AND FORCES.

Snow Snake:

Woodland and prairie tribes played "snow snake." Players threw carved sticks on top of, or even under, the snow to see whose went the farthest.

The players who knew the most about the forces would win.

This is a snow snake:

How could its travel be affected by lift, thrust, weight and friction?

Make and Test a snow snake. After throwing your stick with friends, try to improve your design using ideas about lift, thrust, weight and friction.

NOTE: ALWAYS THROW AWAY FROM PEOPLE, NEVER TOWARD THEM!

Graph the results of your first and second design.

COMPLEX MACHINES are made from two or more simple machines.

Show which simple machines make up these complex machines:

Harpoons:

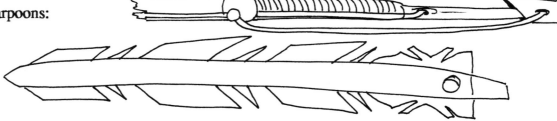

Spring and snare traps:

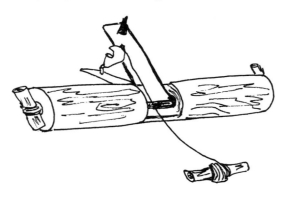

Drills:

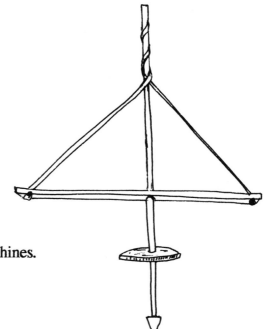

Invent your own complex machine from simple machines.
It should make a job easier. It can be funny.

3. MATH CHALLENGE: Invent traditional story problems for these equations:

Measuring Speed

Speed is Distance divided by Time: S = D/T

Example Question: What is the speed of a canoe going 12 miles down the Mississippi
River in 2 hours?

Answer: Distance of 12 miles divided by Time of 2 hours gives a Speed of 6 mph.
12 miles /2 hours = 6 mph

Measuring Work

How much work does it take to portage a canoe a quarter of a mile?

Work is Force times Distance: W = F x D
It's measured in Newton-meters.
For example: a small handful of clay weighs about 4 oz.
If you lift that clay one meter, it takes 1 newton-meter of force.
If you lift a three-pound pot one meter, it takes 12 newton-meters of force.
If you lift your three-pound pot two meters, it takes 24 newton-meters.

Try this Question:
If it takes a FORCE of 100 newtons to portage a canoe just one meter,
how much WORK does it take to portage the canoe a DISTANCE 400 meters?
(400 meters is about 1/4 mile.)

WORK = FORCE TIMES DISTANCE   (W = F X D)

W = 100 newtons x 400 meters
40,000 newton-meters = 100 newtons x 400 meters

Answer:
It takes 40,000 newton-meters of work to portage a canoe a quarter mile!

Make up some more story problems to measure work.

Chapter 35

Energy Types and Chains

CONCEPT(S):
Patterns
Structures
Components

TOPIC & THEME:
Energy types and chains.

QUESTION(S):
What types of energy are found in Northern Minnesota?

PROCESS & THINKING SKILLS:
Collect and organize data
Record
Infer

INTEGRATIONS:
Science
Art
Home economics

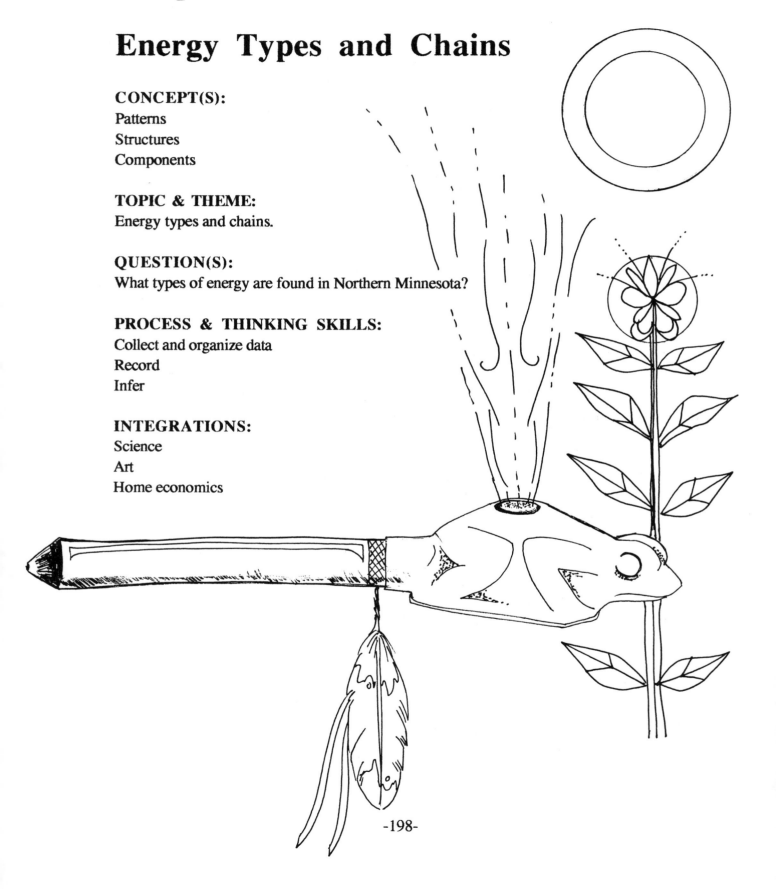

ENERGY : TYPES AND CHAINS

THE FACTS:

A spear ready to be thrown has <u>potential energy</u>.
The spear in flight has <u>kinetic energy.</u>

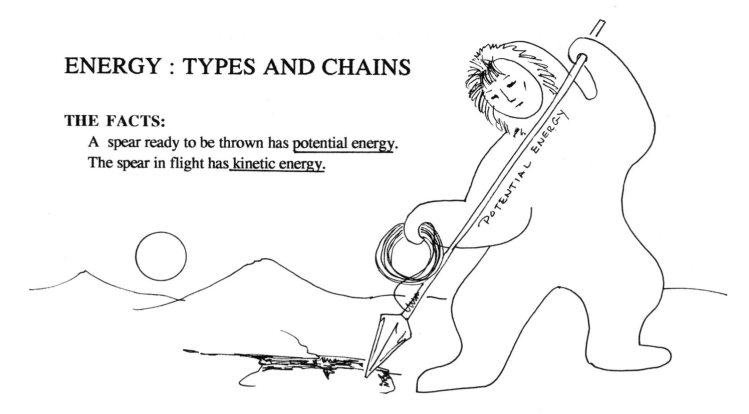

Birch wood contains <u>chemical energy</u> stored in the wood molecules.
When the wood is burned, <u>heat energy</u> is released.
<u>Light energy</u> from a fire or the sun is visible <u>radiant energy</u>.

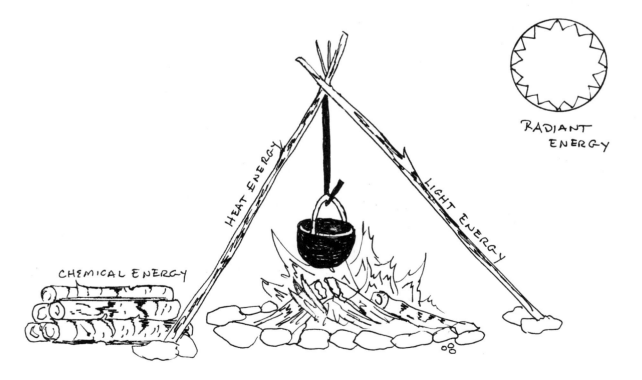

During a thunderstorm, animals run from the thunder and lightning. Running takes <u>mechanical energy</u>.

The lightning is caused by <u>electrical energy</u> traveling through charged particles of matter.

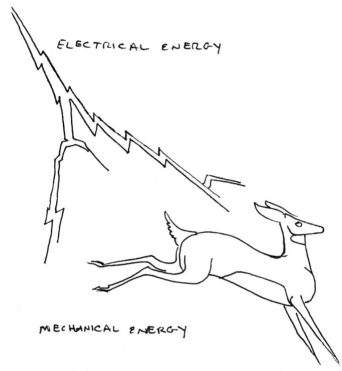

<u>Radiant energy</u> travels in waves across empty space, like waves on a lake can travel across the water.
There are several kinds of radiant energy: Light, Solar, X-Rays, and Radar.

<u>Solar energy</u> is radiant energy that comes from the sun.
Traditional people used it for warmth, to grow food, and to dry meat.

<u>X-Rays</u> are used by Ojibwe doctor Kathy Annette to find broken bones.

<u>Radar</u> uses radio waves that travel through gas, but bounce off solids and liquids. Alaskan bush pilots depend on radar information to locate bad weather and other airplanes.
Energy Chains: Energy can be transferred from place to place.

A person doing beadwork or embroidery gives off energy. She makes the needle move. The needle receives the energy.

This cooking pot of maple sap gets energy by direct contact with the fire -- **conduction.**

The bread propped up beside the fire gets energy from heat moving through the air -- **convection.**

Some radiation comes from the fire too.
It travels in invisible waves, and we can't see it.

Energy is changed and transferred along energy chains.
The wood fire is a good example:

RADIATION

CONDUCTION

CONVECTION

THE ACTIVITIES:

1. Energy in Pictographs
   Use words and pictographs to show each type of energy:
   Kinetic, potential, chemical, heat, mechanical, electric,
   radiant: light, solar, x-rays, radar.
   Use examples from traditional or Western cultures.
   Use words from English and your language.

2. Illustrate a real energy chain in pictographs.
   Describe the energy changes in a paragraph.

3. Illustrate an imaginary energy chain. Make it funny if you wish.
   (For example: An imaginary machine that runs on the steam from a
   cooking fire could erect a wigwam.)
   Describe the energy changes in a paragraph.
   Erect a model of the machine for fun.

Chapter 36

Energy Sources

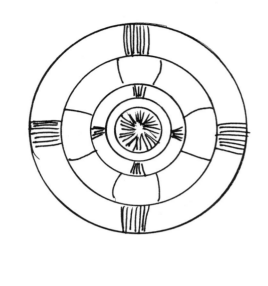

CONCEPT(S):
Relationships
Cause and effect
Components

TOPIC & THEME:
Energy sources

QUESTION(S):
What are the traditional sign and symbols for common energy sources?

PROCESS & THINKING SKILLS:
Collect and organize data
Record
Special relationships
Recall

INTEGRATIONS:
Science
Art
Language arts

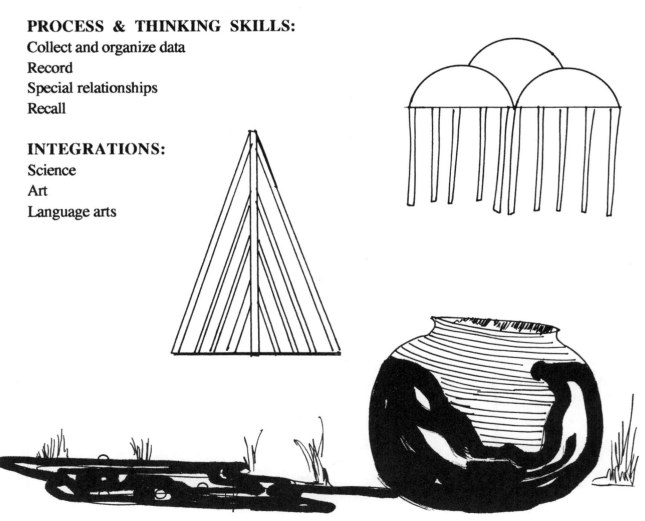

ENERGY SOURCES

THE FACTS AND THE LANGUAGE:

FOSSIL FUEL ENERGY:

Indians in Pennsylvania and near Los Angeles, California discovered oil and tar in open pits.
Oil is a fossil fuel, made from the decayed bodies of ancient plants and animals.

Tar is "bigiw" in Ojibwe.
Invent a symbol for "bigiw."
Draw it.

BIOCONVERSION ENERGY:

Biomasses like trees and trash can be converted to fuel.
Traditional people all over the world have burned wood for fuel.

Tree is "mitig" in Ojibwe.

Trash is "ziigwebinigan."
Invent a sign for trash.

WATER ENERGY:

Traditional people used water energy to move canoes and rafts.
Ancient Chinese used water to drive a clock.

Waterfall is "gakijiwan" in Ojibwe.

WIND ENERGY:

Prairie people built signal fires on the tops of tall cliffs.
Winds would rise along the face of the cliffs, carrying the smoke from the
signal fire high into the air.

There are many Ojibwe words for wind:

ombashi	He is lifted by the wind.
aanimad	The wind blows wildly.
gwekaanimad	The wind shifts.
gichi-noodin	It is very windy. There is a storm.

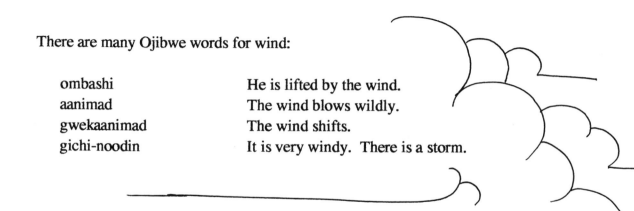

GEOTHERMAL ENERGY:

Traditional people around the world from the Americas to Finland to Rome have used naturally-heated pools of water for steam baths.

He takes a sweat bath, "madoodoo."
Invent a sign for geothermal energy.

SOLAR ENERGY

Many traditional people used their knowledge of the sun to design homes.
The Anasazi, ancient Hopi people, created designs that are still being used by architects today.

Sun is giizis in Ojibwe.
The sign for sun is:

NUCLEAR ENERGY

Today, scientists from many cultures are trying to find safe ways to use this valuable energy source. Uranium fuel has been an important source of income to some tribes of the Southwest.

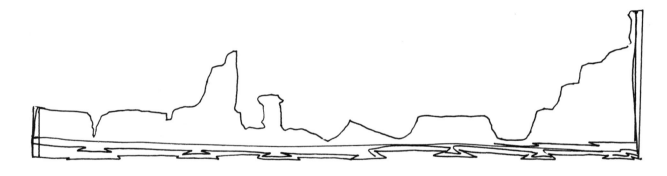

THE ACTIVITIES:

1. Using Energy Sources

   The class is divided into small groups.

   Each group is responsible for researching one energy source.

   Each small group makes two energy posters or dioramas.

   A. Show how any traditional culture used this energy source.

   B. Show how it is used today.

   C. Write the advantages and disadvantages of this energy source.

2. Extension:

   In a third poster or diorama show how this energy source might be used in the future.

3. Write a legend of how The People came to understand and use one of the energy sources.

4. Research Energy Careers among people of your culture.

5. Energy Engineers. Try to convince another class that your energy source is the best.

Chapter 37

Observing and Measuring Matter

CONCEPT(S):
Structures
Interaction
Components

TOPIC & THEME:
Observing and measuring data.

QUESTION(S):
1. What are some traditional material made of?
2. How can they be measured?

PROCESS & THINKING SKILLS:
Measure
Analyze
Record
Experiment
Predict
Collect and organize data
Observe

INTEGRATIONS:
Science
Art
Social studies
Math

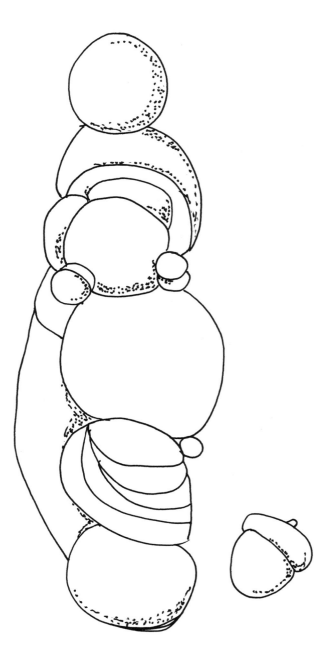

Natural Clay Concretions
Formed at Lake Superior
10,000-20,000 years ago.

OBSERVING AND MEASURING MATTER

THE FACTS:

    Ceremonial pipes are made of matter.

    (Matter takes up space. It is a liquid, solid, or gas.)

    A pipe is made from matter called pipestone.

    Pipestone is a beautiful soft red rock that is easily carved.

    The stone is a form of clay.

    Clay is a <u>compound</u> of aluminum, silicon and water.

    (In a compound the particles are joined chemically.)

    (In a mixture, they are just mixed together but not joined.)

Silicate is a molecule made up of atoms of silicon and oxygen.

Silicon and oxygen are elements.

The silicate molecule looks like a tent with a triangle base.

An atom of silicon is in the middle of the tent.

Four oxygen atoms are at the corners, like tent pegs.

The symbols for silicon and oxygen are Si and O

The formula looks like this: SiO_4

Traditional people smoked tobacco for ceremonies.

Tobacco is cut up for the pipe.

It is a physical change.

The tobacco is still tobacco.

When the pipe is smoked, the tobacco burns.

A chemical change takes place.

The tobacco becomes ash and smoke. It can't ever go back to being tobacco.

After the ceremony the ash may be sprinkled on the sand.

The sand and ash make a mixture.

There is no chemical reaction. It is possible to separate the particles.

(Sand itself is in the silicon family.

It has one atom of silicon and two atoms of oxygen, SiO_2.)

Today we use silicons for computer chips, spacecraft tiles and much more.

BLACKDUCK POTTERY

Clay pots are made of matter.
Raw clay is even softer than pipestone.
When a clay pot dries, a physical change takes place.
(Soak the pot in water, and it "melts" into clay again.)
When a clay pot is fired, a chemical change takes place.
The silicate turns to glass. It cannot ever be clay again.

Pottery was invented all over the world by different cultures.
Perhaps a woman from the ancient Blackduck culture daubed wet clay on
the bottom of a grass basket to hold water better.
She set her clay basket down beside the fire, the heat fired the clay.
She invented pottery for her people.

Good designs come from many things in nature.
The silicon atom would make a beautiful bead or pottery design.

Silicon has 14 electrons arranged in three shells.
The electrons circle a nucleus containing 14 protons and 14 neutrons.

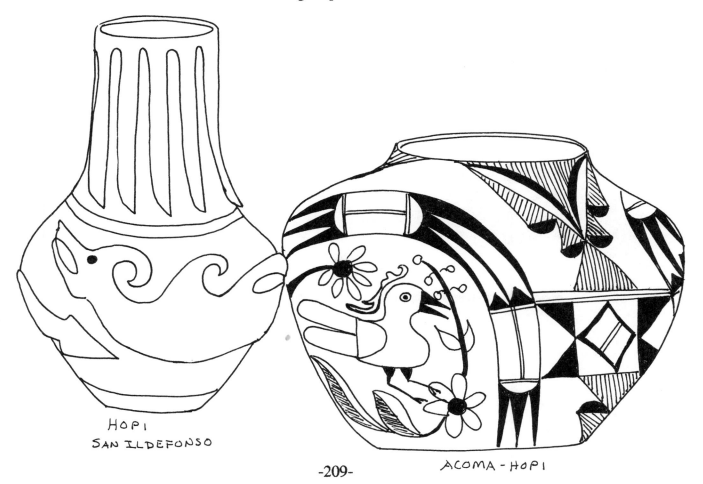

HOPI
SAN ILDEFONSO

ACOMA - HOPI

Traditional people observed and measured matter.

Solve a problem with the Scientific Method:
The scientific method is just a logical sequence of steps to solve a problem.

The Problem:
You want to carry water from the stream to the cooking fire, but your grass basket leaks.
Your problem is to design a basket that won't leak.

Predict:
You predict that daubing wet clay on the basket might hold the water better.

Experiment:
So you try it. You might try clay from several different places to see what works best.

Record:
You want to remember where you found the best clay, so you make a map of symbols to show where the good clay is.

grass basket   clay basket

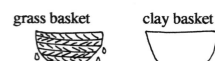

a two day canoe trip, the west side of the third lake, under a big pine tree.

Conclusion:
This clay makes a good sealer for my grass basket. It holds water well.

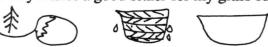

This often leads to a new question or problem:
I wonder if the clay would get harder in the fire?

Then the process starts over again. That is how cultures grow and change.

Measuring Matter the Traditional Way:

Matter is anything that takes up space -- solid, liquid or gas.
Maple sugar is a solid. Maple syrup is a liquid.
The vapor that comes from boiling down the sap is a gas.

Mass -- All matter has mass.
Weight can be measured in grams and kilograms.
Eagles, lakes and air all take up space.

Weight -- The amount of pull between objects.
Weight is measured in newtons. (Think in terms of hamburgers. A McNewton is a quarter
pounder. 1N = about 1/4 lb.)
(One kilogram is about two and a half pounds.)
The earth has more pull on an eagle than on a chickadee.
The eagle weighs more.
What if the eagle flew to the moon? (The moon is smaller than earth.)
The pull between the objects would be less. The eagle would weigh less.
On the moon, it might be harder for the eagle to sit on the rocks than to fly!
In space the eagle's mass is the same, but it weighs less.

Volume: The amount of space taken up by the mass.
Volume is measured in cubic centimeters and cubic meters.
A drum takes up more space than a drum stick. The drum has more volume.

Density: The amount of mass an object has for its volume.
Why does a canoe float?
A canoe has a lot of volume because it takes up a big space.
A canoe doesn't have much mass because it's made of very thin birch bark.
A canoe doesn't have much mass for its volume (not much density.)
That's why a canoe floats.

Why does even a small rock sink?
A small rock doesn't take up much space, so it has little volume.
But the rock does have a lot of mass. (It's packed with granite or sandstone.)
The rock has a lot of mass for its volume (a lot of density.)
That's why even little rocks sink.

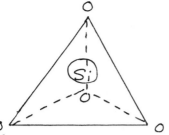

ACTIVITIES:

1. Make up math story problems about measuring clay particles.
   (5,000 of them fit on a line 1 centimeter long!)

2. Make a design based on the silicate molecule or the pipestone elements.
   Use good paper. Try colored pencils on white paper.
   Try colored paper on colored paper.

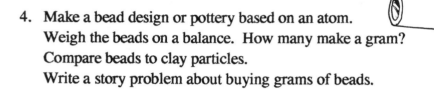

3. Use a balance to weigh a pipe to find out how many kilograms it weighs.
   Weigh several other pipes. Graph your results.

4. Make a bead design or pottery based on an atom.
   Weigh the beads on a balance. How many make a gram?
   Compare beads to clay particles.
   Write a story problem about buying grams of beads.

5. Use words and pictographs to write a traditional recipe.
   Use science measurements.
   How many liters of water and kilograms of wild rice would you need?

6. Do a simple observation using the scientific method.
   Use words and pictographs to record your results.

7. Write a creative story about an eagle who flies to at least two objects in space (one bigger and one smaller than earth.) Tell what happens, what weight problems he has and how he solves them.

8. Using natural and human-made materials, experiment with sinkers and floaters.
   Record your observations in words and pictographs.

9. Why would knowledge of mass, weight, volume and density be especially useful to traditional people of many cultures? Make up a story about such a discovery from your culture.

Chapter 38

Matter, Heat, and Energy

CONCEPT(S):
Interactions
Relationships
Change

TOPIC & THEME:
Matter, heat, and energy.

QUESTION(S):
Why was heat energy important to traditional people?

PROCESS & THINKING SKILLS:
Record
Experiment
Predict

INTEGRATIONS:
Home economics
Social studies
Science
Art
Math
Health

MATTER, HEAT AND ENERGY

FACTS AND ACTIVITIES:

Traditional people from all cultures have invented devices for making fire.
When food was roasted directly in the fire, the heat was transferred into it.
Later on, people invented pots and pans to cook food in.

People who placed pottery or metal pans on the fire also cooked with <u>conduction</u>. The heat went directly into the pan and then directly into the food. Particles in clay and metal are close together, so they make good conductors.

The pans would be hot to handle.
What could traditional people use for insulators?
The particles in insulators are far apart, so the heat doesn't travel easily through them.

People who placed food near the fire cooked by convection. The heat energy was transferred to the air around the fire, making it hot enough to bake bread.

People who cooked in leather or grass containers placed heated rocks into water inside the container. The rocks heated the water and the water heated the food. Would you call this conduction or convection?

Draw pictures to show cooking by conduction and convection.

Wigwams and cabins were heated by **convection**.
The fire warmed the air, which warmed the people inside.
Draw a picture of a traditional home from your culture.
Show and describe how the home is heated.
Heat the movement of molecules.

Pretend you are cooking maple syrup and put a spoonful in the snow to cool.
When you first take the spoonful of syrup out of the pan, it is the same temperature as the big pot
of syrup.   Syrup in the spoon cools much more quickly, so the big pot has more **heat energy**
than the spoon. **Heat** is the movement of particles. Heat is measured in calories. When you put
thin maple syrup in the snow, it cools quickly and becomes very sticky. That's because the
particles aren't moving as fast as in the boiling syrup. **Temperature** measures how fast the
molecules are moving.Temperature can be measured in degrees Celsius.
Draw a picture to show how temperature is different than heat.

Heat energy is measured in calories. In the days before people had cars, TV sets, snack food, and alcohol, people had very little diabetes, a disease of too much blood sugar. People had to work very hard just to find enough food to eat. They walked or ran everywhere. Even if they took a canoe or horse, they had to make the canoe or train the horse first. Life took a lot of work. People burned their food as fast as they ate it. The food was converted into heat energy (which is measured in calories.) It made the person warm in cold weather, and gave the person energy to do work and find more food.

How much heat energy do you burn?
Walk a mile and you burn 100 calories.
Drive a mile and you burn 4 calories.
Dance at a contest for an hour and you may burn 300 calories.
Sit in the grandstand and you only burn 15 calories.

THE ACTIVITIES:

1. Illustrate on the hand-out to show different uses of heat energy.
   (Teachers can photocopy the previous pages on Heat Energy.)

2. Exercise Heat-Energy Posters.
   In small groups make posters showing the calories burned in different activities.
   You may use magazine pictures, drawings or pictographs.
   Assemble the posters into a mural.
   Graph your information, and put it on the mural too.

3. Learn more about a chronic disease of your culture.
   Research the possible causes. Find out symptoms, prevention and treatment.
   Invite a health care person to visit your class to learn more.
   Use your knowledge to make a change.

4. Pretend you live in a traditional culture.
   You want to tell future generations the importance of exercise and good
   health. Make a pictographic story or wall mural to convey your message.

Chapter 39

Properties and Structures of Matter

CONCEPT(S):
Structures
Components

TOPIC & THEME:
Properties and structure of matter.

QUESTION(S):
What are the physical and chemical properties of traditional and non-traditional objects?

PROCESS & THINKING SKILLS:
Observe
Experiment
Predict
Collect and organize data
Record

INTEGRATIONS:
Science
Art
Social studies
Home economics

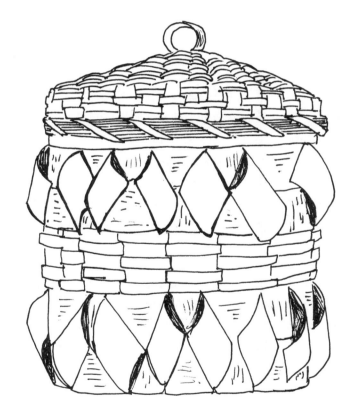

PROPERTIES/STRUCTURES OF MATTER

THE STORIES:

The legends of many cultures teach that each thing is special, having its own special traits and gifts and its own unique role in the universe. In many creation stories, a Creator makes the water, land and sky. The sun, moon, and stars light the sky. Rain and snow fall on the mountains and plains. The Life-Giver creates plants, animals and people. All things are special and each is connected to the others.

THE FACTS:

Different things have different properties.

Oak, black ash, tamarack and birch trees have different woods and barks.
Through experimentation traditional people found that they could use different trees in different ways: Tamarack roots can be separated into thin strands for weaving bags.
Black ash can be separated into thin strips for weaving baskets.
Oak is a hard wood that burns slowly, useful for keeping fires going at night.
Birch bark was stripped into wide sheets for building houses and canoes.

Chemical Properties:

We can find chemical properties when they change into something else.
Oxides: Ojibwe people found a red scum on the top of some springs. After it was dried and powdered, they used it for red paint. The "scum " was iron oxide.

Traditional people from Africa to the Americas have chipped petroglyph designs through the "desert varnish" on rocks. A light colored rock may contain chemicals that react with air, turning the face of the rock very dark. When the artist chips through the color, the light rock shows through. Desert varnish is an oxide. Oxygen reacts with the rock. There are many oxides.

Burning: Both coal and obsidian are black and shiney. Coal burns and obsidian does not burn. Burning is another chemical property. Substances are different because the atoms that made them differ. Each atom has its own special number of electrons that go around the nucleus. Oxygen has eight electrons. Calcium has 20. Copper has 29.

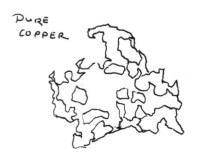

PURE COPPER

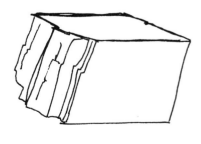

CALCITE

Elements

All things on earth (and in the sky) are made up of elements.
An <u>element</u> has only one kind of atom.
An atom is a tiny particle that is the basic building block of all matter.
When the copper culture people of Lake Michigan mined for copper a thousand years ago, they exposed pure copper sheets by cracking the rocks along the copper veins with fire and cold water. This pure copper contained only one kind of atom.

Each element has special properties.
Gold is very heavy, yellow and shiney.
Iron reacts with the air to make rust.
Sulfur has a bad smell.

When two or more atoms share or exchange electrons, they are called molecules.
Atoms can share electrons with atoms of the same or different elements.

When two oxygen atoms share electrons, they make O_2 , the oxygen we breathe.
When three oxygen atoms share electrons, they make O_3. That's ozone.

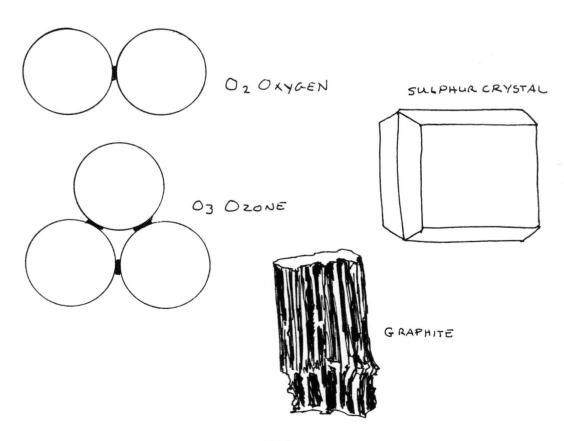

Compounds and Mixtures:

When different atoms react to form a new substance, it's a <u>compound</u>.

The natural pigments used for dyes are <u>compounds</u>.

When different substances are combined but do not react chemically, it's a <u>mixture</u>.

Elements in a mixture can be separated (like picking beads out of plate of sand.)

Elements in a compound cannot be separated easily.

If you mix morels with wild rice and salt you will have a very delicious mixture.

<u>Solutions</u> are mixtures in which one substance is dissolved in another.

Lake water is a solution of water and oxygen. The oxygen is dissolved in the water.

Fish "breathe" the oxygen.

Acids and Bases

Traditional people used acids and bases they made or found in nature.

Liquids are found as acids, bases or neutrals. Most rainwater and snow is slightly acid.

* Many plants are good sources of citric acid (Vitamin C).
* Black bubbling liquid in the mud near White Earth made a good black dye.
* The liquid was iron and acids. Women soaked bull rushes in this mud to get a shiny black color.
* Natural acids and bases were made by soaking wood or wood ash in water. These were used for medicines, cleaning or for setting dyes.

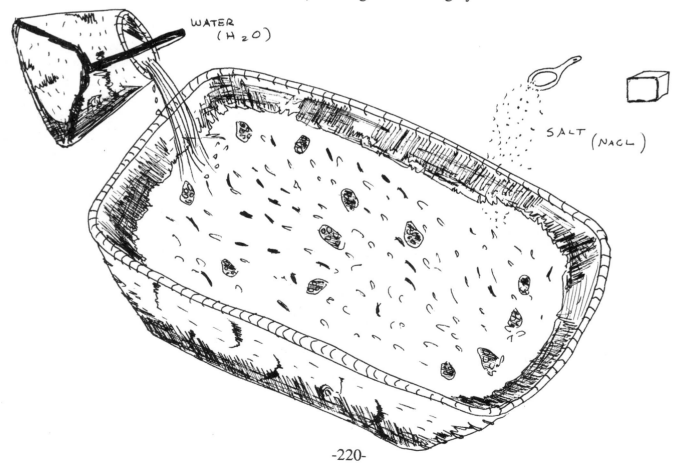

WATER
(H_2O)

SALT ($NaCl$)

THE ACTIVITIES

1. Observe the physical properties of natural and human-made objects:
   You might observe and record:
   State of the matter (liquid, solid, gas)
   color, odor, taste (ONLY IF YOUR TEACHER SAYS IT IS SAFE!),
   melting temperature, freezing temperature.
   *Graph your results
   *Write a fiction or non-fiction story about how traditional people could have used this
     knowledge.

2. Homemade paint. (Compounds)
   Gather safe household acids and bases (lemon juice, baking soda....)
   Collect flower petals, leaves, or bright vegetables (carrots, purple cabbage, tomato skins,
   blueberries, beets.)
   Use litmus paper to find out which are acids and which are bases.
   Special litmus paper will even tell you where they are on the pH scale.
   Chop up the petals into tiny pieces. You should have at least 2 tablespoons.
   In a small jar, pour a little acid over the petals.
   In another jar, pour a base over more petals.
   The liquid should cover the petals.
   Stir and let it soak for at least 24 hours.
   Record your results.
   Enjoy painting with the paint. You can paint something "real".
   Or you might want to paint a traditional design from your culture.
   (Some colors may be very pale, but some will give a good strong color.)

3. Homemade Mixtures
   Cooking is a good way to make mixtures.
   Use combinations of traditional foods to make interesting mixtures.

4. Homemade Solutions
   Mix traditional liquids:
   water and maple syrup
   Tea and lemon grass.
   Chokecherry and blueberry juice (add sugar or maple syrup for jelly.)

5. Make dazzling two and three dimensional designs based on the
   molecule structure of different compounds: (Snowflakes, quartz.)

Chapter 40

Changing States of Matter

CONCEPT(S):
Change
Interaction

TOPIC & THEME:
Changing states of matter.

QUESTION(S):
How do common substances in Minnesota change?

PROCESS AND THINKING SKILLS:
Observe
Analyze
Record
Measure
Infer
Experiment
Interpret

INTEGRATIONS
Science
Art
Social Studies

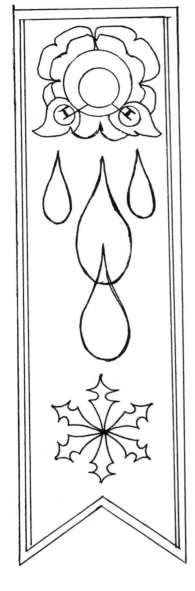

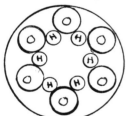

H_2O ICE CRYSTAL

WATER MOLECULE

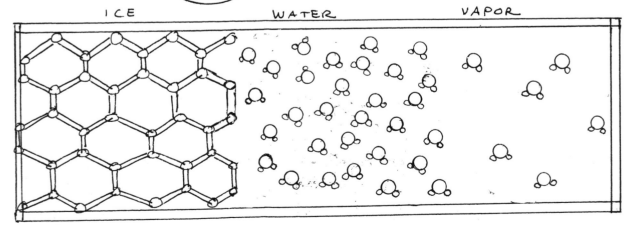

ICE   WATER   VAPOR

CHANGING STATES OF MATTER

THE FACTS:

How did people keep food fresh in the summer and winter? A hundred years ago there were no refrigerators or freeze-driers. Water was boiled out of liquid maple sap to make it thick. When all the water is out, sugar crystals form. Maple sugar is a solid. If you keep a cover on the kettle of boiling sap, the water vapor condenses as liquid on the lid. In winter people boiled dried blueberries and mixed in maple sugar and moose fat for flavor. Some things, like fat and butter, do not have crystals. They have a low melting point, and their "solid" shape is easily changed.

People dried berries, meat and fish in the hot sunshine. The liquid quickly evaporated out of the food, so it did not spoil. Fish was sometimes dried and powdered, then mixed with maple sugar and stored in birch bark makuks. It kept for a very long time. During the winter, Minnesota's natural ice box kept food frozen.

European settlers froze food in the summer, too. During winter, when the ice was thick on the lakes, they cut it into slabs and hauled it with horses to the ice house. The ice house was often at least partly below ground. It had layers of straw for insulation. Ice would stay frozen all summer. On the prairies, ice was stored in sod houses with layers of sod as insulation.

The water (or matter) in our story takes three forms (or states). In the winter it is solid ice, with the molecules rigidly arranged in crystals. In the spring it melts (at 0° C) to become a liquid. The molecules can move around in a liquid. In the summer, the water evaporates and becomes water vapor (a gas). Molecules are very active and far apart in a gas.

All these changes in the state of the matter are physical changes. The water vapor can always become water or ice again. Nothing new has been made. It's not as if the ice thawed and made a lake full of cranberry juice.

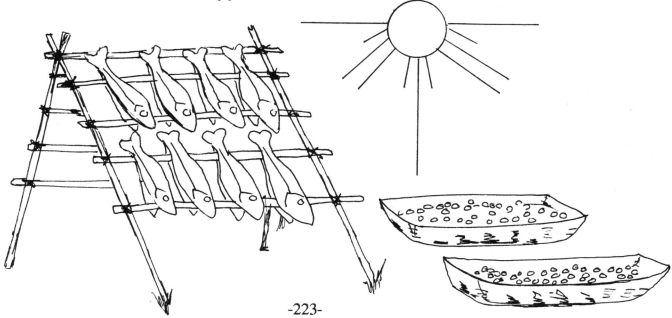

ACTIVITIES:

1. Collect a variety of ethnic Minnesota foods and natural substances.
Experiment to find their freezing points, melting points, and boiling points.
Graph your results. Try both bar graphs and pictographs.

2. Enjoy crystals through a microscope. You might try making crystals from sugar, salt, etc.
Discover the freezing point, melting point and boiling point of water with sugar in it.
Try it with salt. Compare your results.
Make posters with crystal designs to help interpret the results.

3. Experiment with home-made insulators and evaporators.
Students try to make the best insulator or evaporator.
Each student is given an ice cube.
The object is to keep your ice cube frozen the longest using available materials.
Try making evaporators too.
As a class see if you can determine the critical factor: thickness, color, type of material....
Record your results in an interesting way --
    * petroglyph designs to tell the story
    * short story (fiction or non-fiction)

4. With a partner, invent a game to teach the states of matter
This can be a board game, a card game, or a game with playing pieces.
Play the games in class. Then take them to a class of younger children to help them learn.

5. Paint a traditional style picture from your culture showing the states of matter. You may invent symbols if you wish.

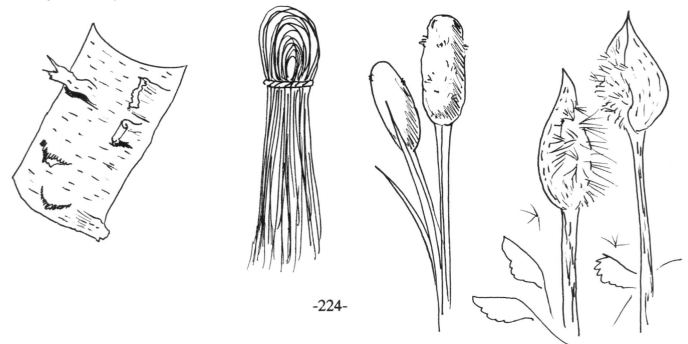

Chapter 41

Waves

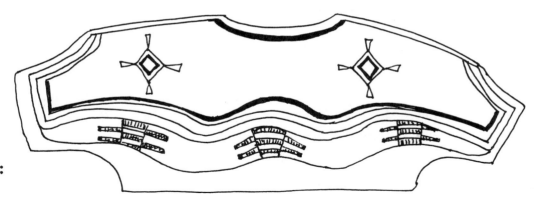

CONCEPT(S):
Structures
Components

TOPIC & THEME:
Waves

QUESTION(S):
How did traditional people use this knowledge of waves?

PROCESS & THINKING SKILLS:
Experiment
Predict
Record
Recall
Interpret

INTEGRATIONS:
Science
Art
Math
Language arts

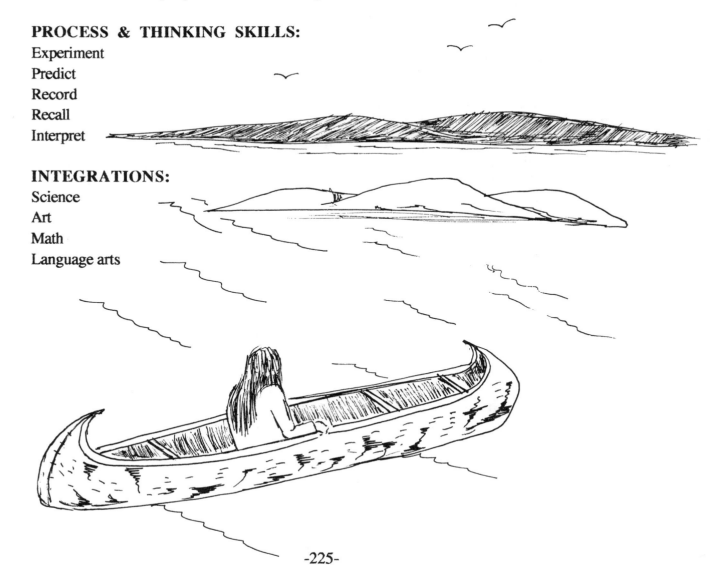

WAVES

THE STORIES: Why did traditional Minnesotans invent canoe paddles?

Maybe it happened like this: Some people wanted to cross Cass Lake to Star Island. They built a canoe, got in, and pushed off from shore. They glided through the water for a while because of the laws of motion. (Something moving will stay moving until it's stopped by a force.) After a while, the friction of the water against the canoe stopped it. Once the canoe was stopped, it just bobbed up and down in the water.

The people could see the waves moving under them to the island, but they couldn't get to the island. The energy of the wave could move across to the island, but the water and the canoe could not move with the wave. In order to make the canoe move through the water, people invented paddles, so they could push the canoe through the water.

THE FACTS:

Water waves and light waves are called transverse waves. Remember the canoe: Wave Energy Moves. Matter (water) does not move.

Traditional people of the Pacific islands experience dreaded tsunami. These enormous waves are so big they can wipe out entire cities. They can be caused by an earthquake in South America, thousands of miles away. There is tremendous energy in an earthquake. The energy travels through water in a big long transverse wave. Out in the ocean the tsunami wave length might be 125 miles long and only 1.5 feet tall. Because the ocean is so deep and so big, the wave might not seem very big to a ship that sails over it.

But once the wave approaches the land, its energy comes into friction with the shallower ocean floor. The wave length shortens and the height grows. There is no place for the energy to go, so the crest of the wave builds taller and taller. By the time it reaches shore, the crest of the tsunami wave may be 50 feet high, and traveling 500 mph! Nothing survives.

Remember the tsunami. The water molecules (matter) do not travel from a South American earthquake to the Pacific Islands -- like tiny sightseers. The energy of the earthquake is all that moves. Energy moves in waves.

Water waves are called transverse waves. ("Trans" means "across," Verse" means "in a line." Transverse waves travel "across and in a line.") Transverse waves travel through matter, but the matter doesn't travel. Light waves travel "across and in a line too." Light waves are special transverse electromagnetic waves. They can travel through empty space.

Traditional people had no mirrors. How could they see themselves?

THE STORY:
It might have happened like in this Greek myth: NARCISSUS

Long ago there lived an extremely handsome young man called Narcissus, who was loved by all the maidens. But he was cruel to them no matter how lovely or kind or amusing they were. Echo loved him more than anyone, but she had been enchanted by a jealous queen and could not speak to tell him of her love. She could only repeat his words.
"Come!" he called.
"Come, Come," she softly replied.
He followed her voice, but he scorned her love too. He stalked away proudly, not caring that he broke her heart.
The gods had had enough of this selfish young man's behavior. One day when he leaned over a still pool of water he saw his reflection -- and fell completely in love with it! He sat by the pool gazing hopelessly at his own beautiful face day after day. Finally he wasted away, calling "Farewell."
Echo stayed by his side repeating sadly, "Farewell, farewell."
Where he died a beautiful flower grew. This flower's name is Narcissus.

THE FACTS:

What is a reflection?
Light waves travel very fast (300,000,000 meters in one second -- about 11 million miles per minute) Light bounces when it hits an object. Light hits you as you look into the still surface of a lake. The light bounces straight down to the glassy lake. Because the water is so still, the light bounces straight back to your eye. That's why you can see your reflection. When the water is choppy, the light is bounced back at an angle, so your eye can't see the image.

What is an echo?
Sound waves travel slower than light waves-- 330 meters in one second (about 11 miles per minute).They are different than light waves. Sound waves are called compression waves. Compression means "to squeeze together." They can't travel through empty space. Molecules are squeeze and released to make sound waves. They need air or water or a solid to carry the energy. (In space there is light, but not sound, because there is no air to carry the sound wave.) An echo is reflected sound waves.

THE ACTIVITIES:

1. Make models or experiments to demonstrate and explain water waves, light waves and sound waves.

2. Draw diagrams or story pictures to explain what you learned about waves.

3. Find stories or art from your culture or another interesting culture that show an understanding of light or sound.
   Or write a new story explaining how and why people invented mirrors.

4. Do a traditional painting that shows wave movement in transverse or compression waves. Write a paragraph about your painting using some of these words: transverse, compression, light wave, sound wave, crest, trough, amplitude, wave length.

5. Find a picture and description of the Narcissus flower. Design a bead pattern of the flower reflected in the still pond.

PAPERWHITE
NARCISSUS

DAFFODIL
(NARCISSUS)

Chapter 42

Sound and Sound Waves

CONCEPT(S):
Structures
Cycles
Patterns

TOPIC & THEME:
Sound and sound waves.

QUESTION(S):
What can traditional instruments and animals teach us about sound?

PROCESS & THINKING SKILLS:
Compare
Spatial relationships
Observe
Collect and organize data

INTEGRATIONS:
Music
Art
Science
Language arts

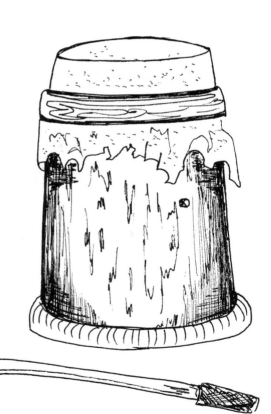

SOUNDS AND SOUND WAVES

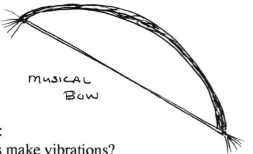

MUSICAL BOW

THE FACTS:
Three kinds of instruments are common to many cultures:
Sound is caused by vibrations. How do these instruments make vibrations?

Wind instruments are played by blowing -- flute, saxophone, trumpet, French horn, clarinet, trombone, recorder, bassoon, penny whistles, piccolo, pan pipes and tuba. The digereedoo is a wind instrument from the Australian bush. It's made from a eucalyptus branch. You hear its deep growling tones in movies about Australia. The accordion has keys that are struck, but the sound is made by wind in the bellows. Is it a percussion or wind instrument?

Percussion instruments are played by striking -- drums, rattles, gong, xylophone, marimba, tambourine, bells, chimes, and tambor. The hurdy-gurdy has strings that are struck with a turning wheel. Is it a string or percussion instrument? The organ has keys that are struck, but the sound comes through tall pipes. Is it a percussion or wind instrument?

String instruments are played by plucking or with a bow -- harp, guitar, the violin family, lap dulcimer, banjo, balalaika, harpsichord, zither, sitar and lyre. Pianos and hammered dulcimers have strings, but they are played by striking the keys. Are they string or percussion instruments?

THE LANGUAGE:

English	Ojibwe	Spanish	Norwegian
to blow	boodaajige	silbar	blåse
flute	bibigwan	flauta	fløyte
to string	naabidoo' -	encordar	snor
fiddle	naazhabii'igan	violin	fiolin
to strike	bakit'-	tocar	slå
drum	dewe iigan	tambor	tromme
sound	wiimbwewe	sonido	klang
music	madwewechigan	musica	musikk

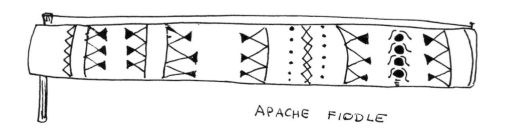

APACHE FIDDLE

THE ACTIVITIES:

1. World Music:
   Listen to music from several cultures. For each song try to identify what kinds of instruments are playing: wind, string or percussion.
   Listen again. This time make an interesting drawing by following the beat or rhythm with a crayon on big paper. Do different pitches make you feel like using different colors? Try it.

2. Community Music:
   Explore your community. Find people who play different instruments.
   Invite them to your classroom to play for you. Ask them to share any special songs from their culture. Listen for the different vibrations.
   Ask a guitarist to show you how he or she tunes the guitar using vibrations.
   Make a diagram drawing to show how the instrument produces sound.

3. Making Instruments
   Students will gather in groups of three.
   Each student will make a simple musical instrument -- wind, percussion or string.
   How will you change pitch in your instrument?
   How will you change intensity?
   Your instrument might sound like something in nature.
   Test your instruments. Modify them if necessary.
   Write a paragraph about your instrument.
   Include a drawing of your instrument.
   Use the "Language" words to label the drawing.
   (Use words from another language if you wish.)
   Make a group poster of your musical inventions.

3. Making Music
   Experiment with your instruments. Make up a simple song.
   String and percussion players can sing too.
   The human voice makes sound by vibrating vocal cords.

4. Musical Graphing
   Graph the kinds of instruments your class invented.
   Graph the different pitches.
   Graph the range of intensities.

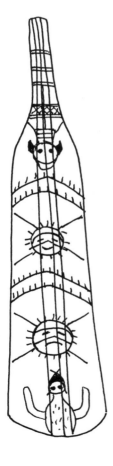

ESKIMO
GUITAR

Chapter 43

Sounds in Our World

CONCEPT(S):
Structures
Cycles
Patterns
Relationships

TOPIC & THEME:
Sound in our world.

QUESTION(S):
1. How are the sounds of Northern Minnesota produced?
2. How did traditional people of many cultures make and use sound?

PROCESS & THINKING SKILLS:
Collect and organize data
Experiment
Predict
Record
Observe

INTEGRATIONS:
Social studies
Art
Music
Math
Science

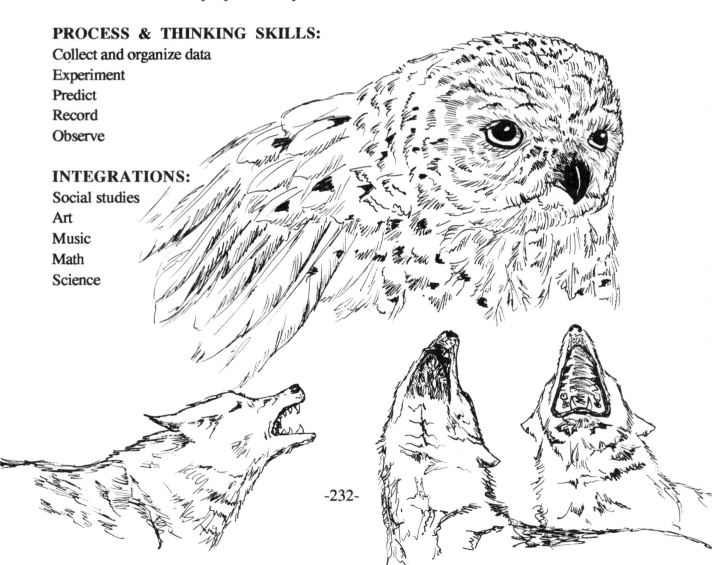

SOUNDS IN OUR WORLD

THE FACTS: Minnesota sounds are echoes from distant times and spaces.

HUMAN SOUNDS

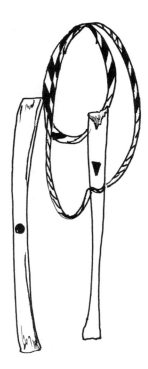

More than 700 kinds of musical instruments have been discovered in South America, made by traditional people.

Some Native American music has some qualities similar to Asian music:
* Music is "circular." There is no clear beginning, middle or end.
    (Western songs are linear with a start, climax and finish.)
* Drums, bells and flutes were respected ancient Chinese instruments.
    Stringed instruments were for more relaxed informal occasions.
* Vocals are harsh, with vocal cord tension.
    (Singers from the Asian country Tuva almost growl their songs.
    A singer can make his voice sing two notes at the same time!)
* Unison melodies are accompanied by strong rhythm patterns.
* Longer notes are held with a pulsating sound.
* The form is free flowing.

BIRD BONE
FLUTES

The traditional Ojibwe flute is made from soft, straight wood, like ash, box-elder, or cedar. It has six holes. (Frances Densmore's book, Chippewa Customs, has a complete description for making a flute.)

The Apaches invented the America's only stringed instrument, a bowed fiddle. The pitch was controlled by the tension on the string.

Native American music is a part of everyday religion and life.
Japanese warriors were expected to be good musicians and poets too.
Ancient Egyptians sang and played religious music on reed flutes.
They also played flutes and harps for banquet music.

Some African drums have the heads tightened by long strings. When the player squeezes the strings, the head tightens and pitch goes higher.

The Ancient Chinese played bells made from bronze and limestone.

MAMMALS

Mammals have a voice box high in the windpipe (near the tongue). The voice box has two vibrating vocal cords that produce sound.

Big cats (like lions and tigers) roar. Little cats (like a lynx) purr. Why? Big cats have bones in their throat that are attached loosely. They can vibrate a lot, and make a great big roar. Little cats have tightly attached bones, so they vibrate much less, making a purring sound.

Chipmunks make a low barking sound to define their territory. Sometimes all the local chipmunks get together (sitting by their nests) and bark for an hour at a time.

Fox squirrels scold by making a few long whines and 12 or 13 low grunts. Gray squirrels scold by making low grunts first, followed by high whines.

Flying squirrels give a "chirp" with a pitch that is so high, many people can't hear the frequency.

A coyote's howl (ow ow OOOOOOOOOOO) lasts about three seconds. On a piano the notes of the coyote's song (ow ow) start on **B**. The note (OOOOOOO) starts on an **F**, 1 1/2 octaves above the first note, then slides back down to the next **B**.

Timber wolves are bigger and have longer, lower pitched howls. The howl lasts 7 to 10 seconds. On the piano start on **G** and jump up the next **G**. Then glide down to a **D**. Then glide down to a **G**, and hold for three or four seconds. Glide down to the next **D** over three or four seconds.

Bats send out a high frequency sound signal, which bounces off its prey and back to the bat. The flared nose acts as a transmitter and receiver.

Elk have a bugling sound of high intensity.

When moose fight, clashing their antlers, it sounds like cars crashing into trees.

Beavers communicate with sound under water. The water molecules carry the compression sound waves like air. Remember, light can travel through empty space, but sound waves have to be carried by molecules of air, liquid, or a solid. When a beaver dives, his tail slaps the water, making an intense warning sound. The sound carries through the water.

BIRDS

Birds have calls or songs. Their Ojibwe names mimic their sounds.
     A call usually has a low frequency (pitch).
     A song usually has a high pitch or frequency.

* A mourning dove has a low, mournful call, "omiimii."

* A chickadee has a song, a pattern of notes sounding like "gijigaaneshii"

* The robin's song sounds like "opichi".

* The owl's call sounds like "goo koo ko' oo."

     Birds have a simple voice box low in the windpipe, near the lungs.
     They don't have vocal cords that vibrate. Instead, the voice box has
     two membranes that tighten to make a higher pitch or frequency and loosen to make a
     lower pitch or frequency -- just like a violin.
     Intensity is controlled by air forced out of the lungs.

* Geese voice boxes are more like wind instruments. When the air rushes through, they say
     "honk."
* Warblers have long thin voice boxes with thin, flexible membranes.
* Song sparrows can sing up to 20 different songs.
* One Brown Thrasher sang almost 5000 mini-songs in two hours!
     This was no tedious repetition. Half the songs were never repeated.
* Ruffed grouse make a "drumming" sound by beating their wings together.
* Woodpeckers make noise by hammering their beaks on wood or metal.
* Loons make four different calls with their special voice box muscles.
* The whooping crane's windpipe is four feet long. The trumpeter swan has a long windpipe too,
     coiled around the breast bone. That's why these birds can sound like trombones!
* The average bird sings 12 notes higher than the best human sopranos.

Can you sing and breathe at the same time? How do birds sing for so long without breathing?
They have many air sacks that supply air, so a bird can sing all day without turning blue!

THE ACTIVITIES:

1. Woodland Pitch and Frequency

   A cradle board, hung with long ropes from a tree branch, rocks slowly in the air. What if the mother tied the cradle with short ropes? Make a simple model and see what happens.
   Count the swings of a pendulum on a long string.
   Count the swings of pendulum on a short string. Try one in between.
   Try several different lengths and graph your results.
   Try random lengths and regular lengths.

   Make and play an instrument with strings of different lengths.
   Or
   Make an invention that relies on a pendulum action.

   Make a poster to show what you learned about pitch and frequency.

2. An Intense Minnesota Experience
   Collect natural items from Minnesota or objects from your culture.
   One at a time, make a sound with each.
   Rank the item on a decibel scale on the blackboard.
   A decibel is a measure of loud and soft.
   Graph your results.
   Evaluate your objects.
   0-45 decibels is OK. (That's about as loud as a car.)
   50-85 decibels is annoying.
   More than 85 decibels can damage your hearing.

   Make posters showing how natural and human made sounds can affect people.

3. Computer Music
   Find out more about computer music.
   How is it programmed? (Kids can do it!)
   How are artists blending traditional music from many cultures with their new computer interpretations?

4. Watch and listen to a tape of the American Indian Dance Theatre.
   Can you hear the sounds of nature in the music?

Chapter 44

Optics

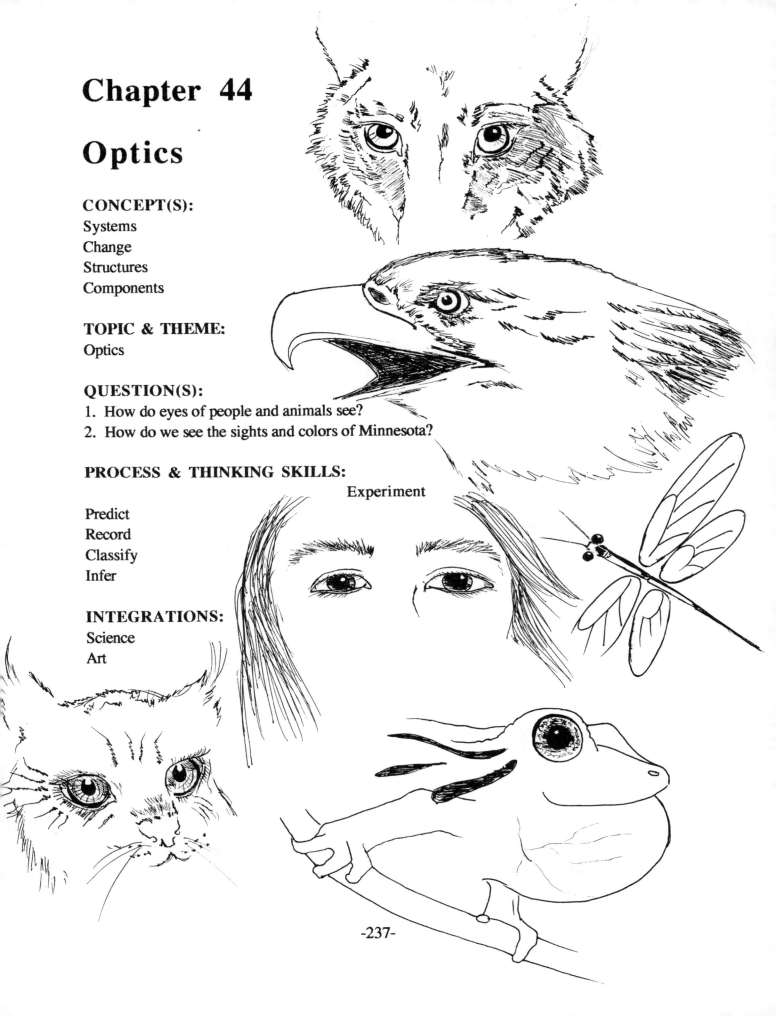

CONCEPT(S):
Systems
Change
Structures
Components

TOPIC & THEME:
Optics

QUESTION(S):
1. How do eyes of people and animals see?
2. How do we see the sights and colors of Minnesota?

PROCESS & THINKING SKILLS:

Experiment

Predict
Record
Classify
Infer

INTEGRATIONS:
Science
Art

OPTICS

THE FACTS: EYE CAN SEE YOU!

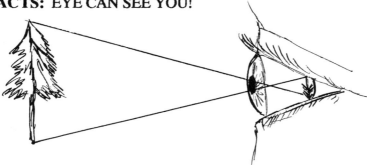

Animals use their eyes for different activities.
A goose just nibbles plants close to his face. Does he need good 3-D vision?
An owl must catch fast little creatures at night. How good is his 3-D vision?
Geese have flattened eye balls. The eyes are on the side of the head.
Owls have big round eye balls, like people. The eyes look forward.
Round, forward-facing eyes make it easier to see how far away something is.

Robins eat berries. Do they need to see color?
Owls hunt little gray mice at night. Do they need to see color?
The cones in the eyes of robins contain colored oils that transmit a color image to the brain.
The cones in the eyes of owls contain oils of only clear, pale blue and pale amber colors.
These are the only colors owls see.

Why do cats' eyes glow in the dark?
The eyes of cats have a curved mirror behind the lens. The mirror returns the light in a cone shape.
Behind the retina is a layer of highly reflective zinc.
The light bounces around in the eye so cats can see better at night.

Hawks have eight times more rods than we do. That means they can see eight times better.
The lens in your eye turns the image upside down. (The brain sets it upright again.) Mirrors
reverse the image. (Try to read something while looking at it in a mirror.)

HOW IS COLORED LIGHT MIXED?

Our eyes have cones that are sensitive to color. Some cones "see" green. Some cones see red-yellow-orange. Some cones see blue. When we look at a tree, green light waves enter the eye, and the green cones see green. When we look at the blue sky, the blue cones tell the brain, "blue." When we look at an red sunset, the red cones see "red."

When we look at a yellow flower, wavelengths of red are <u>added</u> to wave lengths of green. Remember the spectrum colors? Roy G. Biv (red orange yellow green blue indigo violet).yellow wavelengths are between red-orange and green. That's why mixing red and green light sends a "yellow" signal to our brain.

ACTIVITY: Make a model or drawing to visualize color vision.

HOW AND WHY: In small groups make posters or models to show:

WHY IS THE SKY BLUE?
Because blue wave lengths are easily scattered by dust in our atmosphere, while long wavelengths like red are less prone to scattering.

WHY IS THE LAKE BLUE?
Because it reflects the scattered blue wavelengths of the sky. Shallower water reflects green off the bottom.

WHY IS RED LAKE RED?
Suspended particles may reflect different colors, like red.

WHY ARE CLOUDS WHITE OR DARK GRAY?
Because each tiny drop of water reflects all the colors of white light. In white clouds, there are so many tiny drops of water that the colors are all reflected and the spectrum doesn't form. In gray clouds water drops are bigger and keep the sun from reflecting in the cloud. Black is the absence of color. No light - no color.

WHY IS THE SUNSET RED?
Because air and dust in the atmosphere bend (refract) light traveling through it.
At sunrise and sunset the sun is at the horizon, where there is more dust.
This refracts the white light more, and we see the red wavelength.

WHY DO BUBBLES, OIL FILMS, AND LIQUID CRYSTALS CHANGE COLORS?
Because the lightwaves are reflected from different thicknesses or layers of molecules. Bubble colors are formed from light being bent at both edges of the bubble skin. Oil films and liquid crystals must have a black background to absorb the other wavelengths of light.

Colors Mix Tricks

The colors of <u>light</u> behave differently than the colors of <u>paint.</u>

LIGHT	PAINT (PIGMENT)
White light contains all colors.	White is the absence of color.
Black is the absence of color.	Black contains all colors.
Primary colors of light are:	Primary colors of paint are:
red, blue and green	red, blue and yellow
Mixed Colors Are:	Mixed Colors Are:
Red and Blue = Magenta	Red and Blue = Violet
Blue and Green = Cyan (Turquoise)	Blue and Yellow = Green
Red and Green = Yellow	Red and Yellow = Orange
To mix colors of light, lights of different wavelengths are added. Mixed light colors are Additive.	To mix pigments, light waves are absorbed or subtracted. Mixed paint colors are Subtractive.

How are pigments mixed?   (COLOR THESE PICTURES)

Leaves contain colored pigments. When white light strikes a green leaf, the green wavelength is reflected back to our eyes. All the other colors of the spectrum are absorbed (subtracted) by the leaf.

Stained glass contains colored pigment. When white light strikes blue stained glass, the blue wave length is transmitted through the glass to our eyes. All other colors of the spectrum are absorbed by the stained glass.

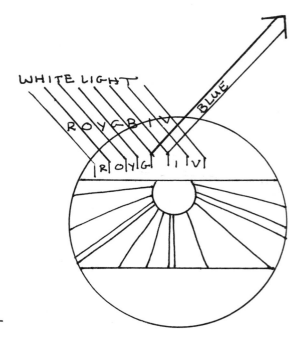

THE ACTIVITIES:

1. Construct Lenses

Cherokee Chemist Dr. Lloyd Cooke discovered petroglyphs of microscopic matter. How did ancient people see things that small? They might have used water drop lenses. Anything clear and curved can act as a lens. Try making a simple lens with a water drop: Have fun observing and recording   Adapted from the CESI Physical Science Source Book

1. Smear a thin coat of petroleum jelly on a clear piece of plastic (or microscope slide.)
2. Place two washers firmly on the jelly.
3. In one washer, put one or two drops of water. This lens is concave.
4. In the other washer, add enough water so it "curves" over the top.
   This is a convex lens.

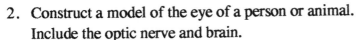

2. Construct a model of the eye of a person or animal.

Include the optic nerve and brain.

Mount it on cardboard.

You might make a detailed model that even shows the iris responding to light. Show how the lens and brain reverse the image twice.

3. To See or Not to See.

Lake water is usually transparent. You can see fish swimming under the water.

Light is transmitted through the water. Water is <u>transparent</u>.

Mud is <u>opaque</u>. You cannot see through it. Light is not transmitted by the mud.

Lake Superior Agates are often <u>translucent</u>. You can see light, but not images through them.

Collect natural and human made items that are transparent, opaque and translucent.

Make posters or bulletin boards of them.

4. Pin Hole Lens

Make a pin hole through black construction paper. Close one eye. Hold the pin hole up to the light (not the sun) a few inches from your other eye. Hold a skinny nail between your eye and the hole. Stare at the hole. You will see a shadowy nail, upside down in the lens.

Why does the nail look upside down? The nail makes a shadow on your eye, which the brain reverses for you.

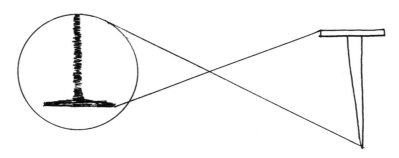

MORE ACTIVITIES:

5. Mixing Colored Paints AND Mixing Colored Lights
   Try mixing colored paint (red, yellow and blue).
   Try mixing colored light (red, green and blue),
   Use three flashlights with colored cellophane over the light.
   Record your results in a paragraph, pictograph, or drawing.

6. Exploring Traditional Opaque Painting:
   Traditional Indian style painting is done on dry colored paper (or hide).
   Opaque paint is used to paint beautiful, stylish designs and symbols
   of real things.
   TEMPERA (OR WHITE PAINT) IS ALWAYS OPAQUE. Light passing from the air to a
   particle of white paint is bent very sharply, so the paint becomes opaque. You can't see
   through opaque paint.

   Follow these steps. Use some of the new colors you mixed.
   1. Plan your painting. Do some sketches of your designs and symbols.
   2. Select a colored poster board.
   3. Lightly sketch your images on the poster board.
   4. Paint your designs with tempera paint.
   (Or you can add a drop of white tempera to watercolor.)

7. Exploring Transparent Painting

European watercolor paintings are painted on white, wet paper with transparent paint.
WATERCOLOR IS TRANSPARENT. When light passes from the air to the particles of paint, it
doesn't bend much. You can see through it.

Follow these steps: Use some of the new colors you mixed.
   1. Choose a habitat and plan your painting.
   2. Tape the paper to a piece of cardboard or to the table.
   3. Wet the paper with a damp paper towel. It should reflect light.
   4. Using a wide paint brush, paint the sky with watercolor paint.
      The sky can be many colors or just blue. (Don't use too much paint.)
   5. Paint the earth (and a lake or stream if you wish.)
   6. Stop and let it dry!
   7. Add details.

When your painting is dry, add plants and animals with opaque paint.
You can add a drop of white paint to your watercolors to make them opaque.

Chapter 45

Light and Color

CONCEPT(S):
Interaction
Patterns
Components

TOPIC & THEME:
Light and color.

QUESTION(S):
How are the light and colors of the north woods produced?

PROCESS & THINKING SKILLS:
Infer
Experiment
Predict
Recall
Record
Special relationships

INTEGRATIONS:
Social Studies
Science
Art
Language arts

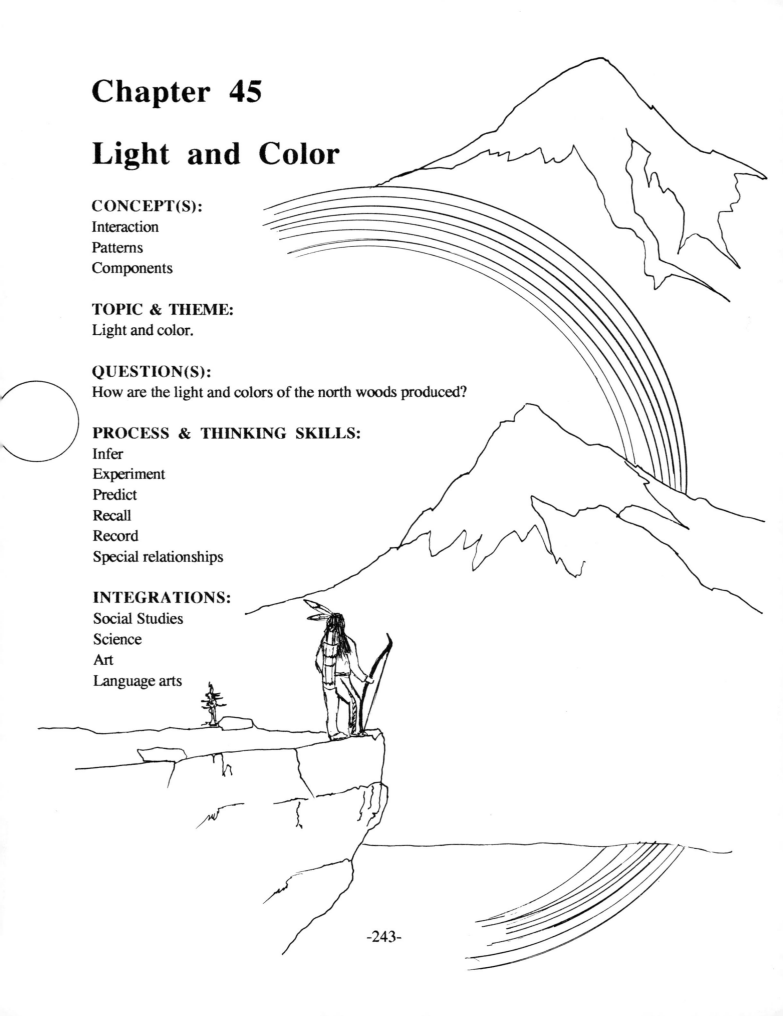

LIGHT AND COLOR

THE STORIES: The Rainbows of Lake Louise: An Assininboine Story

When the world was new, a tribe of giants lived in the beautiful Rocky Mountains of Canada. Their chief was a superb hunter. He was proud of all the animals he killed with his bow and arrows. And he was greedy. Instead of thanking the earth and the animals for giving him life, he was always scheming of ways to kill more -- more than he needed.

One rainy afternoon he watched the clouds, wondering if he had time for a short hunt between the storms. As he worked, the sun looked out from behind a cloud. A beautiful rainbow lit up the sky. Since the giant hunter was always thinking of hunting, he noticed the shape of the rainbow. "Now, THAT'S a bow!" he smirked. "With that bow I'll be the best hunter that ever hunted anything that ever moved!"

He immediately set off to climb the mountain under the rainbow. Yanking the beautiful rainbow out of the sky, he started back down the mountain. But with every step, the rainbow became more drained of color. By the time he reached camp, the rainbow's colors had faded and its strength was gone.

Furious, the greedy hunter smashed the bow against the mountain and threw the pieces in the lake. When the hunter had stalked away, the rainbow renewed its brilliant colors in the crystal water. Creator made a new rainbow for the Assininboine people. And still today they often see the rainbow colors in the sunrise and in the crystal clear waters of Lake Louise.

NOTE: FOR COLORS OF LIGHT AND PAINTS SEE OPTICS UNIT.

The Rainbow Legend: A Lakota Story

Long ago the wildflowers were talking and dancing in the warm sun on a summer afternoon. The sky was clear blue, the people in the village were happy. It was good to be alive. Red Prairie Rose and Indian Paintbrush spoke first, "This is all so lovely. I wish it could be forever."

Orange Butterfly Weed murmured, " Summer is almost over and soon.

Yellow Mullein, waved his velvety leaves sadly at the sky, "Soon winter will come. It will bring ice and snow, and we will die, Little Rose."

Green Cattail in the marsh swayed in the wind, thinking of the flowers' special friend, a little girl from the village. "At least the children will always be with us."

Blue Bonnet sighed, looking at the sky, "I wish, I wish we could go to the Land Beyond where the spirits of the people go when they die."

Mulberry (who delighted in sharing her delicious indigo-colored berries with the little girl), exclaimed, "Let's ask Little Sister to talk to the Great Spirit for us!"

Violet agreed, "Yes, we are only little flowers with very quiet voices. Maybe the Great Spirit will hear Little Sister."

Late that night, when the Moon of the Strawberries was full, Little Sister went to talk to the Great Spirit. "O Wakan Tanka, I am just a little girl, and my friends the flowers are even smaller than I, but we have hearts full of love for you, for this beautiful world, and for each other. It is hard to think of dying. They love the people so much. Would it be too much to ask for them to have a spirit place too?" As she waited very patiently for the spirit's answer, she cried silently, thinking of the sadness of the flowers.

Then the bird of wisdom spoke in the night. "Go to the flowers and tell them the Great Spirit loves them now and always. They will have their Land Beyond. When the Thunderbird comes with the next rain, tell them to look up in the sky. There will the souls of all their relatives who have gone before them."

Sister could hardly wait to tell the flowers. Soon summer was over and the Thunderbird brought the rain.

When the rain was over, the flowers looked up. Father Sun's bright rays streaked through the sky, and there -- more beautiful than anything they had ever seen before -- was a beautiful shining rainbow reflecting the love of Wakan Tanka.

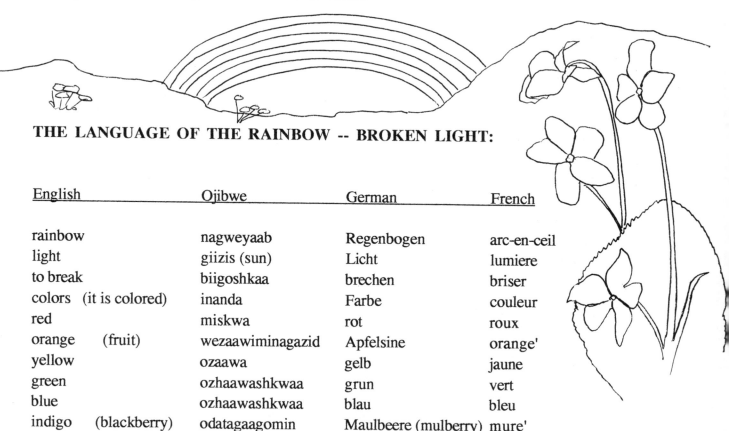

THE LANGUAGE OF THE RAINBOW -- BROKEN LIGHT:

English		Ojibwe	German	French
rainbow		nagweyaab	Regenbogen	arc-en-ceil
light		giizis (sun)	Licht	lumiere
to break		biigoshkaa	brechen	briser
colors	(it is colored)	inanda	Farbe	couleur
red		miskwa	rot	roux
orange	(fruit)	wezaawiminagazid	Apfelsine	orange'
yellow		ozaawa	gelb	jaune
green		ozhaawashkwaa	grun	vert
blue		ozhaawashkwaa	blau	bleu
indigo	(blackberry)	odatagaagomin	Maulbeere (mulberry)	mure'
violet	(blueberry)	miinan	violett	violette

THE ACTIVITIES:

1. The Refraction Game:

   Why is it so hard to spear fish in the water?

   How does it help to know how light refracts?

   Make a simple model of a pond.

   Make a fish on a cork and use a washer as weight.

   Looking into the water from the top, try to touch the fish with a pencil.

   Remember: Light rays change direction as they move from one material to another.

   Adapted from the CESI Physical Science Source Book

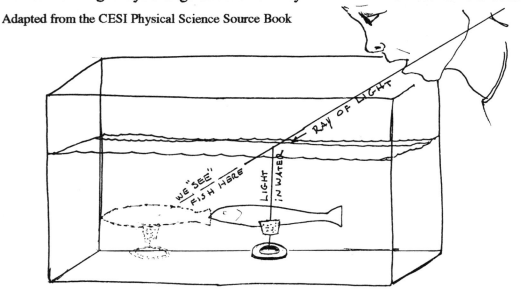

2. Painting a Rainbow:

   Paint a realistic or symbolic picture of a rainbow.

   You might want to paint a whole rainbow circle and then put a paper horizon over it.

   You can cut the paper to show trees, mountains, villages, cities, etc.

   Remember: the Rainbow is really a circle (Like the bow around the moon.)

   We only see the arch because the earth is so big, the horizon gets in the way. Sometimes from a mountain or an aircraft, we can see the whole circle.

   If you paint a double rainbow, the order of the colors is reversed!

   (This is because the second rainbow is a reflection of the first.)

   What is the color order in a triple rainbow? Why?

3. Writing the Rainbow

   Write a real or imaginary story about the rainbow using some science facts.

   Use the Languages if you wish.

   Remember: The rainbow is kind of like a hologram.

   The white light is separated by each drop.

   Each rain drop acts like a tiny prism. Our eye assembles the colors into a rainbow.

4. The Reflection Game:
   Place a small simple shape on your desk (like a triangle.)
   Stand a mirror up so that you can see the shape in the mirror.
   Looking at the shape in the mirror only (not the shape on your desk) try to draw the reflection of the shape you see. Try other shapes.
   For a real challenge try a star!
   Try the mirror at a different angle.

Remember:
   Light rays are reflected at an angle.
   Drawing the shape is usually easier for right brain people because they focus on visual things.
   It's harder for left brain people who focus on verbal things.
   (This can be frustrating. If you can laugh at yourself, it can be fun!)

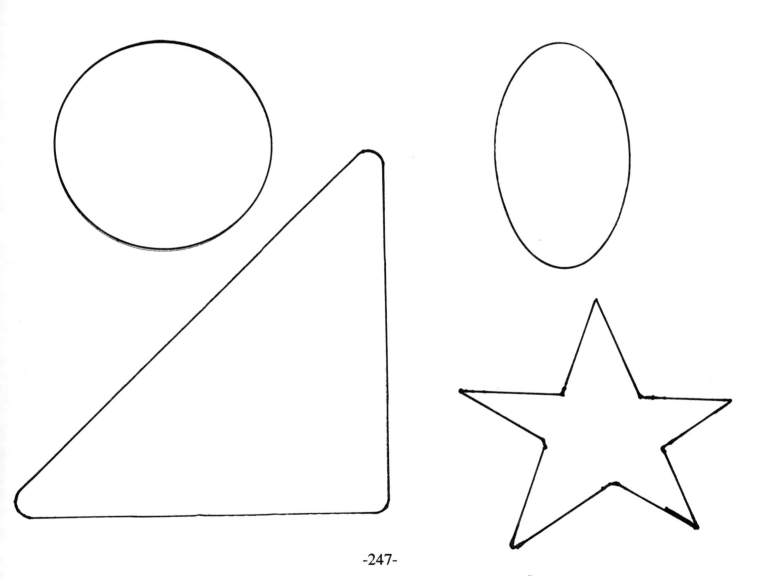

Chapter 46

The Electric Pow Wow

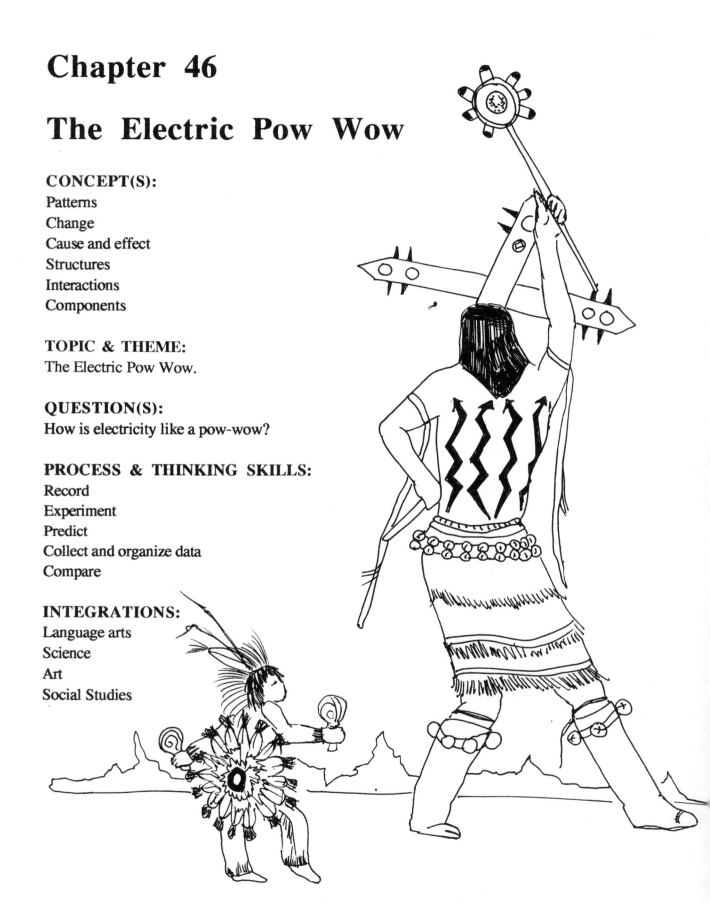

CONCEPT(S):
Patterns
Change
Cause and effect
Structures
Interactions
Components

TOPIC & THEME:
The Electric Pow Wow.

QUESTION(S):
How is electricity like a pow-wow?

PROCESS & THINKING SKILLS:
Record
Experiment
Predict
Collect and organize data
Compare

INTEGRATIONS:
Language arts
Science
Art
Social Studies

ELECTRICITY

THE ANALOGIES: Static Electricity -- Waasamo "He Sparks"

Bear Child woke up smiling. It was Pow Wow day! Cuddled up beside her was her favorite puppy. He did not yet have a name, and she had been thinking about it for two days. She murmured quietly to the little dog, asking him what names he liked, and telling him of her excitement for the new day and the celebration. As she talked, she stroked his long soft hair. The puppy raised his head, touching his nose to her finger. ZAP! Ouch! ARF! A little spark had jumped from her finger to his nose. "Well," laughed Bear Child, "at least now I have a good name for you. Waasamo -- he sparks!"

What Happened?

Friction from Bear Child's rubbing caused electrons from the puppy's fur to jump to her hand. After a while many many electrons (negative charges) piled up on the child's hand. When her hand was loaded with electrons, they all jumped to the puppy's nose, making a spark.

Electricity always moves from a negative charge to a positive charge. Two negative charges repel each other. Two positive charges repel each other. A negative charge and a positive charge attract each other.

THE ACTIVITIES:

1. Draw a cartoon strip of the story.
   Show the positive and negative charges.

2. Start an electricity story book.
   By the end of this unit, you will have several picture stories to help you learn about electricity. Draw a picture of this story. Use these words as labels: Electrons -- spark -- negative charges positive charges -- static electricity

The Electric Pow Wow
Dance Circle Atom and Static Electricity

An atom is a tiny particle that is the basic building block of all matter.

A Traditional Dance Circle is a good model of an atom.

In many dance circles, the drummers and drums are in the center of the circle (the **nucleus.**)

The drummers (**protons -- positives**) are in the center of the circle.

   Since they are all positives, why don't they repel each other?

   All the drummers are bound together by very, very strong clan ties.

The drums are the **neutrons.** (They don't have a charge, but add weight.)

The dancers going around the drummers are the **electrons --negatives.**

In an atom, the electrons are arranged in **shells.**

In a dance circle, there is often an inner ring (shell) of women dancers.

Let's say the women are the wives of the drummers. The want to be close to their husbands, and can't be budged out of the inner shell.

Dancers (electrons) on the edge of the circle aren't so involved. If they get hot and thirsty, they are **attracted** to the refreshment stand outside the circle. They leave the circle. After a while, if the refreshment stand is too crowded with dancers (negative electrons), they are **attracted** back to the drummers (positive protons), and return to the circle (spark).

This is like static electricity. The spark is like the dancers returning to the circle -- the movement of the outside or **free electrons.**

THE ACTIVITY:
Draw a picture of this story. Use these words for labels:

Positive Protons - Drummers
Neutral Neutrons   -   Drums
Nucleus - Circle Center
Negative Electrons - Dancers

Inner Shell - Women Dancers near the drummers.
Free Electrons -- Dancers on the edge of the circle.
Attraction - Refreshment stand
Electron Spark - Dancers Return to Circle

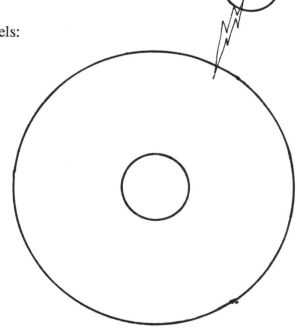

THE DANCE CIRCLE AND VOLTAGE

Voltage and Current

It's a perfect day for a pow wow. The sun is warm. There is a cool breeze. In the village, drummers (positive protons) gather and begin raising flags, singing songs, and beating the drums (neutrons).

The dancers (negative electrons) are fishing across the lake, but they hear the music, and they WANT to come to the pow wow. The drummers are very POSITIVE that the dancers will show up. The dancers are NEGATIVE because the fishing is so good, but when they hear the music, they really WANT to dance, so they jump in their canoes and head across the lake. (The drums are NEUTRAL. They don't care. They just make music.)

The "want" (urge) to go to the pow wow is **voltage.** The more the dancers WANT to get to the pow wow, the more voltage there is. The dancers -- all headed to the pow wow -- are the **current,** measured in **amps.** Many dancers go across the lake by canoe. They are a high current. A few dancers go around the lake on the foot path. They are a low current.

ACTIVITY: Draw a picture of this story. Use these words as labels.
Positive Protons - Drummers
Neutral Neutrons - Drums
Negative Electrons - Dancers (across the lake fishing.)
Voltage - WANT
High Current/ Low current - Many Dancers, Few Dancers

Resistance

People from miles around hear of the pow wow. They all want to come. If they canoe over on a still lake, it's an easy trip. There's nothing in their way. (**Low resistance.**) When current moves without resistance the path is a good **conductor.** But if they have to come through the woods, picking their way over dead trees, thorny wild roses, high hills, and little canyons, it's a slow and difficult trip. (**High resistance.**) They work hard, sweat and get hot. (Resistance in a wire makes it hot too.) Some of the people decide to camp or go home. When there is more resistance, there is less current. When current meets a lot of resistance, the path is a poor conductor, or good insulator. Resistance is measured in ohms.

ACTIVITIES:

1. Draw a picture of this story. Use these words: **Current -- Dancers**
    Low Resistance -- Smooth Lake -- Good Conductor -- Low ohms
    High Resistance -- Deep Woods -- Good insulator -- High ohms

2. Test the Resistance -- Collect natural and human-made materials.
    Using a simple ohms meter, test each to see if it is a good conductor or good insulator, or somewhere in between. Record and graph your results.

CIRCUITS AND SWITCHES

A foot path goes all around the lake, connecting the villages. It's like a **circuit**. Deep in the woods, Papa Bear hears the music too. He remembers the last pow wow he attended. After he chased the people away, he ate piles of fry bread, Navajo tacos, wild rice, venison, fish, and maple sugar. HE WANTS TO GO. (Papa Bear has high voltage, doesn't he!) So Papa Bear lumbers down the path to the pow wow. Papa Bear is traveling along the circuit.

But there's a problem. A steep little canyon cuts across the path. People have shoved a fallen tree over the canyon to make a bridge (**switch**) to cross. And that's just what they do. People on the path (circuit) see Papa Bear behind them. They run across the tree bridge, and drag it over to their side of the canyon.

Papa Bear is trudging along the path with a silly grin on his face. He's day-dreaming of pow wow left-overs. He doesn't even notice the tree is missing until he finds himself tumbling over the cliff. OOOOOOOOPS!

Papa Bear is knocked out cold until after the pow wow. The circuit is broken when the switch is opened. Seeing that Papa Bear is no longer a problem, the people put the bridge back over the canyon so more villagers can walk across. The circuit is closed and active again.

ACTIVITIES:

1. Draw a picture of this story. Use these words as labels.
   Open Circuit -- Bridge down -- Switch is open
   Closed Circuit -- Bridge is in place -- Switch is closed.
   Current -- people and Papa Bear

2. Make a simple switch as shown.
   Select a good conductor. Use the ohm meter to see what happens when the circuit is broken.

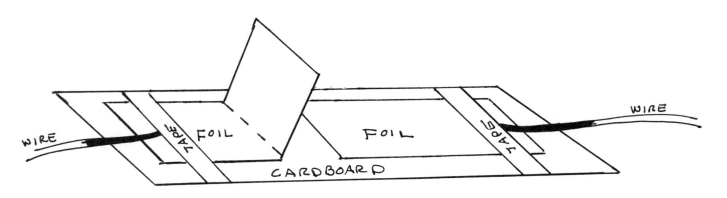

Adapted from *Comets Science*

AC AND DC CURRENT

Direct Current
After the pow wow some of the people take the south road to their village. They are all moving directly in the same direction.
This is Direct Current (DC).

Alternating Current
Some of the people take the north road to their village.
But when they arrive home, they find that a hunting party (bringing three buffalo) is headed for the pow wow village. So they turn around and go back to the site of the pow wow.
After they all eat buffalo and dance some more, they return home.

But they suddenly discover they accidentally lost an eagle feather at the pow wow village.
So everyone runs back to the village to look for the feather.
Bear Child suddenly remembers she packed it with her outfit.
So everyone returns to the village.

Current traveling back and forth is an Alternating Current.
(Alternating Current travels back and forth 60 times in a second!)

The Activities:
1. Draw a picture of the story. Use these words.
   Current -- People on the path
   Direct Current -- People going in one direction and staying put.
   Alternating Current -- People changing their minds (and direction.)

FINAL ACTIVITIES:

1. Write and illustrate your own analogies.

2. Create a play about Electricity using analogies.

3. Display your Electric Pow Wow story books.

4. Make a giant picture story.
   Each small group selects a different concept to illustrate on big paper.
   Display them.

5. Invite the community in to learn about the Electric Pow Wow.

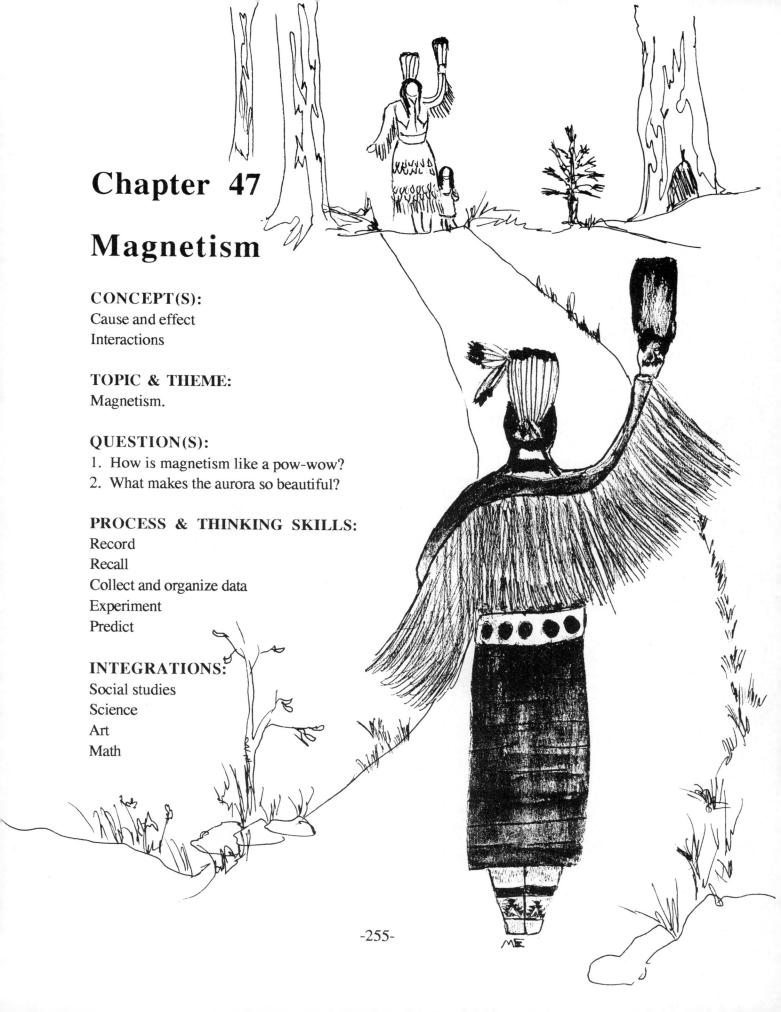

Chapter 47

Magnetism

CONCEPT(S):
Cause and effect
Interactions

TOPIC & THEME:
Magnetism.

QUESTION(S):
1. How is magnetism like a pow-wow?
2. What makes the aurora so beautiful?

PROCESS & THINKING SKILLS:
Record
Recall
Collect and organize data
Experiment
Predict

INTEGRATIONS:
Social studies
Science
Art
Math

MAGNETISM

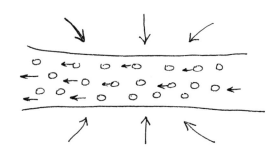

THE ANALOGIES:

Electricity Makes Magnetism

Dancers (negative electrons) walk along a path (current) to the pow wow.
Along the way they laugh, sing songs, talk happily, and call out to their friends in the villages along the way. The friends in the villages hear the dancers on the trail and they are PULLED toward the trail by the excitement and fun of going to the pow wow. **Magnetism is that pull.** Lots of laughing and talking people on the trail would have more pull than just a few stragglers. The pull around a current is a magnetic field. A big current has more pull than a weak current.

Magnetism Makes Electricity

There is a path beside a village. No people are on it. (No current.)
Women from the village cross the path several times a day to get water at the creek. Every time they cross the path, they wonder about taking the path sometime. Where would it lead? How far would it go? What would they see and learn along that path?

The line of women crossing the path is like a **magnet,** the path is like a **wire.** Every time they cross over the path, some of the women are tempted to go down the path. A few eventually do follow the path. As they move on the path they are like electrical current. The more times a magnet passes over a wire, the stronger current it makes. (More electrons move to the wire.)

ACTIVITIES:

1. Draw pictures of these stories for your Electric Pow Wow book. (Chapter 46)
   Use these words as labels:
   Current -- people (electrons) on the path
   Magnetism -- a pull toward the path

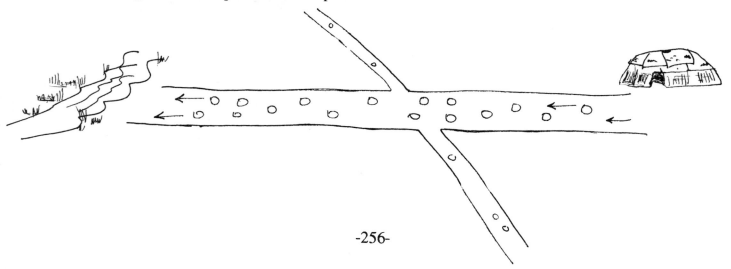

THE FACTS:

Nickel, Iron and Cobalt can be natural magnets, called lodestones.

People in Turkey and China discovered this thousands of years ago.

When a magnet is suspended, one pole will point North.

Two Thousand years ago the Chinese invented compasses. They put a polished lodestone on a polished table and watched its pole rotate to the North. Less than a thousand years ago, they started using compasses for navigation. The compass needles were slivers of lodestone.

Regular iron

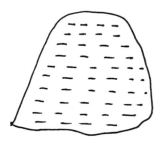
Magnetic iron

In regular iron the atoms are lined randomly.

In magnetic iron, many of the atoms are lined in the same direction.

Magnetic North is probably caused by electrical currents in the core of the earth. The magnetic pole has changed poles several times since Earth began. No one really knows why or how. A million years ago, the compass needle would have pointed South instead of North.

What happens if you break a magnet in half between the poles?

You have two little magnets, each having a North and South Pole.

Battery experts tell us the ancient Egyptians made simple batteries. (They don't know why.) We know this from lists of material and directions found in ancient Egyptian writing. They used zinc, copper and acid.

Some fish are living batteries! Their bodies produce strong electrical current for protection. Special cells have a special chemistry that lets them act like wet cell batteries. They are connected in series for more voltage. Torpedo rays can make 220 volts of electricity (twice as strong as the normal voltage in your house.) A human might not be killed by this charge, but he certainly would be knocked off his feet.

ACTIVITIES:

1. Magnet patterns in bead designs.
    Using a bar magnet and metal filings, look at the beautiful patterns the filings create around the magnet. **This is the magnetic field.**
    Make a bead design based on this design.

2. Invent a Silly Job Machine that needs at least one magnet.
    This is a VERY complicated and silly device used to do a simple task.
    Could you invent a Bed-Making Machine that uses a magnet?
    Brain-storm several other such machines. Select your favorite.
    Draw the machine. Can you make it into a cartoon?
    Tell how the magnet would work.

3. Make and test natural batteries
    Batteries need acid. Lemon juice is acid.
    Put a zinc nail and a copper nail in a lemon. Connect them with a wire.
    Test the battery with an amp meter.
    Try two, three, or four lemons connected in a series. What happens?

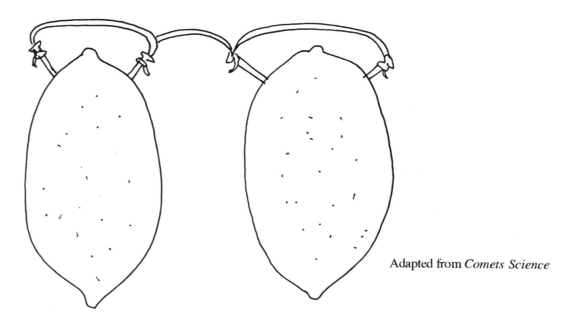

Adapted from *Comets Science*

4. What on earth would the ancient Egyptians DO with a low voltage battery?
    What would happen if they rigged them in a series?
    Write a science fiction story about how and why the
    Egyptians invented and used batteries.

AURORA

People of many cultures have created legends to explain the Aurora.

THE STORIES:

Eskimo (several stories)

Land and ocean are surround by an impossible chasm. A perilous pathway crosses it to the heavens. Only the best souls and ravens can cross. The feet of new spirits are guided lovingly by the light from the torches of the old spirits. This is the light of the aurora.

Most Eskimo legends says that Aurora lights are spirits of the ancestors. They lead a happy afterlife, playing football with a walrus skull. (The object of the game is to kick the skull in such a way that when the skull falls to earth, the tusks stick straight down into the snow.) One legend has the lights as walrus spirits playing with a human skull!

Yukon River Eskimos said the dancing lights were animal spirits -- leaping deer, graceful seals, breeching beluga whales, and jumping salmon.

The North Woods

In Wisconsin, the Menominne believe in a happy afterlife for ancestors too. The say the lights are torches for spear fishing.

The Canadian Ojibwe legend combines Static Electricity with its story. They say the Aurora is caused by many deer in the sky. Deer hide gives off static electricity sparks easily when petted.

European Stories

Vikings believed the Aurora was caused by fires glowing around the edge of the earth. Some believed that glacier frost caused the sky flames.

Medieval Europeans were terrified of the Aurora. The were convinced it was made of terrible battles, severed heads, flashing swords. During one aurora in France, ten thousand people made pilgrimages to pray for protection.

A Medieval German sketch shows candles flaming above the clouds, looking exactly like birthday candles!

The Sound of Lights. Eskimo stories say that the whistling and crackling sounds are the voices of spirits calling to people on earth. Greenland villagers say the sounds are made by spirit children twirling, dancing and playing in the snowy lights.

Scientists have not been able to record any aurora sounds. They think the aurora is too high for any possible sound to carry to human ears. What could make the sounds people associate with Aurora?

THE FACTS:

Scientists study the Aurora at the University of Alaska in Fairbanks. They use rockets and air transport planes loaded with instruments. Scientists have found that the aurora is a giant generator with a conductor and a magnetic field.

The magnetic field surrounds the earth, giving off lines of magnetism. The conductor is a solar wind of protons and electrons. The magnetic field lines around the earth "wire" the field to the solar wind as it moves around the earth. (It makes a gigantic closed circuit.) Like a battery, this circuit has a positive terminal and a negative terminal. The positive terminal is on the morning side of the solar wind. The negative terminal is on the evening side. (See the picture.) The current is mostly electrons. When the electrons strike the atoms and molecules in Earth's atmosphere, energy (light) is released. That's the light of the aurora.

How high is the Aurora? Jet planes travel about 7 miles above the earth.
The Aurora extends from about 100 to 300 miles above the earth.

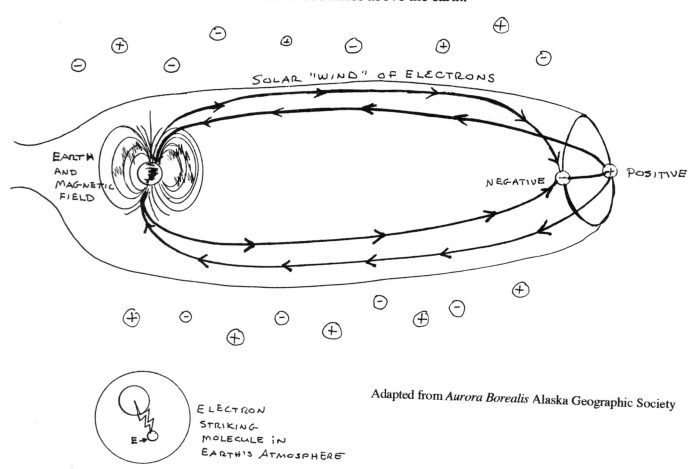

Adapted from *Aurora Borealis* Alaska Geographic Society

THE ACTIVITIES:

1. Write your own Aurora legend. Make it interesting, but use science facts. You might try an analogy.

2. Collect Aurora stories and language words from different cultures of students in your classroom. Illustrate the stories. Make a book for your school library. Include a page of the REAL Aurora story.

3. Watercolor Auroras. Transparent watercolor on a wet paper makes a beautiful aurora.

Follow these steps:
    1. Tape your paper to a piece of cardboard.
    2. Wet the paper with a paper towel.
    3. Add a stripe or two of colored paint in the sky.
    4. Tilt the paper up at an angle to make the color spread down the paper. When dry, it will look like Aurora curtains.
    5. You can add details with black ink when it is dry. TRY IT!

Chapter 48

Communication

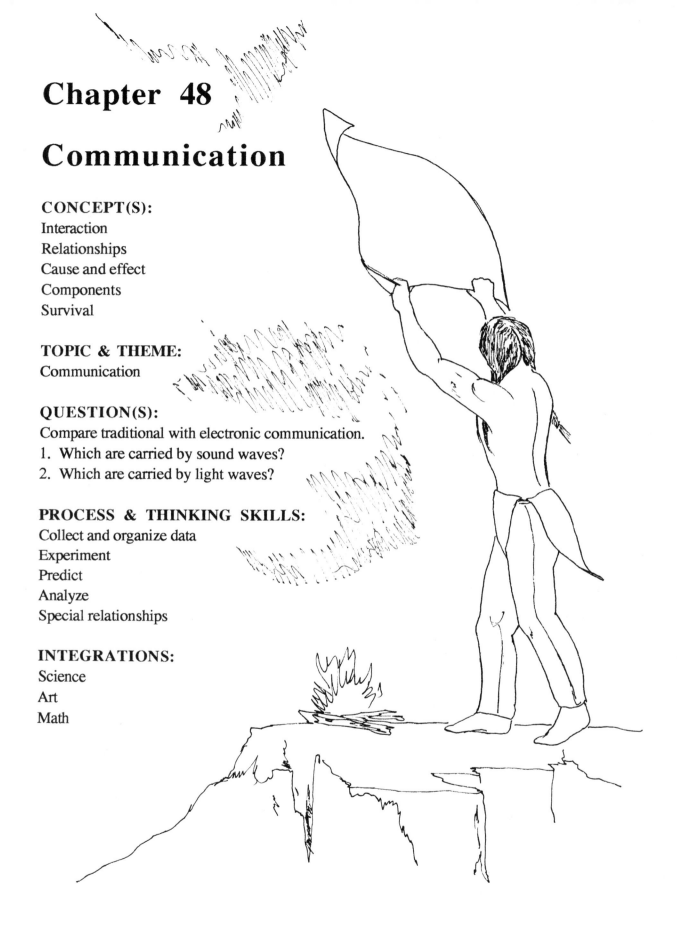

CONCEPT(S):
Interaction
Relationships
Cause and effect
Components
Survival

TOPIC & THEME:
Communication

QUESTION(S):
Compare traditional with electronic communication.
1. Which are carried by sound waves?
2. Which are carried by light waves?

PROCESS & THINKING SKILLS:
Collect and organize data
Experiment
Predict
Analyze
Special relationships

INTEGRATIONS:
Science
Art
Math

COMMUNICATION

THE FACTS: Many cultures used sound and light waves to communicate complex messages. Today we also use radio waves.

* Ancient people used drums.
  The drum was the transmitter; the listener was the receiver.

* They used smoke signals.
  The smoke was the transmitter; the observer was the receiver.

* Mirrors were also used.
  The mirror was the transmitter, and the observer was the receiver.

* When a traditional hunter placed his ear on the earth to hear a distant sound, like a herd of deer, he knew that sound waves carried over the land are interrupted by trees, mountains, air and other objects. Sound waves carried through the earth are not interrupted as easily. The deer hooves were the transmitters, and the hunter's ear was the receiver.

* The famous Navajo Code Talkers sent secret messages for the U.S. military in World War II. They were critically important to the success of the war because the Navajo language was so complicated, the enemies could not break its "code."
  The message was spoken in Navajo into a microphone.
  A small magnet in the microphone changed the voice into an electrical current.
  The current, changed into radio waves, was sent out by the transmitter.
  Hundreds of miles away, an antenna on the receiver picked up the waves.
  The waves were changed back into current.
  The current was changed back into sounds vibrations by a small magnet in the speaker.
  The radio operator, another Navajo, heard the code.
  Messages were passed secretly.

THE ACTIVITIES:

1. Dissecting Communications Equipment
   (OR Dissecting Small Motors)
   Collect worn-out telephones, tape decks, radios.
   (OR) Collect worn-out hair driers, alarm clocks, calculators.
   Carefully take them apart.
   What's inside?
   Can you find the magnets?
   Get a diagram of the device and identify everything you can.
   Draw it.

   Is there any way to simplify it and still make it work?
   (Good engineers try to find the simplest, most elegant design possible.)

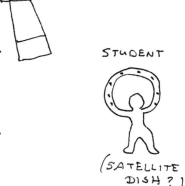

STUDENT

(SATELLITE DISH ?)

2. Find out more about the Navajo Code Talkers
   What is unique about the Navajo language that made it so hard to break as a code?

3. How and Why Pictographs
   Find out how other electronic communications work.
   Work in small groups or by yourself.
   Draw pictographs to show how a picture is sent and received for TV.
   For fun you can make your pictographs look really ancient, but be sure to
   make the information accurate.
   How does radar work?
   How do computers work?
   How do VCRs work?
   How do CD players work?

STAR
(ELECTRICAL
SPARK?)

EARTH / RIVER
(TV ? - COMPUTER ?)

4. How will people communicate in the future?
   Invent a fantastic future communication device.
   Make a prototype from cardboard boxes, string, wire, foil...
   (It doesn't have to work.)
   Make up a biography for the inventors (you or your group).
   Tell how they found a need and a solution.
   Tell what new technology you needed to discover for this to work.

SHELL

(RADAR?)

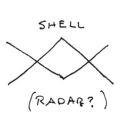

APPENDIX

MAKWA'S THINKING SKILLS

Makwa (Bear) finds food, shelter and water by using instinct and thinking skills. When you complete a *Waterdrum Science* Activity, record your thinking skills.

OBSERVE   I use my eyes to learn about

_____

ANALYZE   I break down complicated things into small easy parts:

_____

RECALL   I remember and use these facts and ideas:

_____

RECORD   I draw and write about the things I observe:

_____

INFER   I make these good guesses:

_____

MEASURE   I measure in metric:

_____

CLASSIFY/SEQUENCE   I can put things in groups and in order:

_____

COMPARE   I can tell how some things are different and the same:

_____

INTERPRET   I can record both accurately and in my own special way.

_____

THE CIRCLE OF SCIENCE

Use it every time to plan and record your science and invention projects.

The Circle of Life and the **Medicine Wheel** are two of many sacred circles.
The Circle of Science is an easy, clear way to understand scientific methods.
It was invented by Sue Dale Tunnicliffe in England; it is used by kids all over the world.
She calls it the **"Shape Sequence"** because things are done in a certain order.
You can decorate the shapes and the circle to reflect your culture.

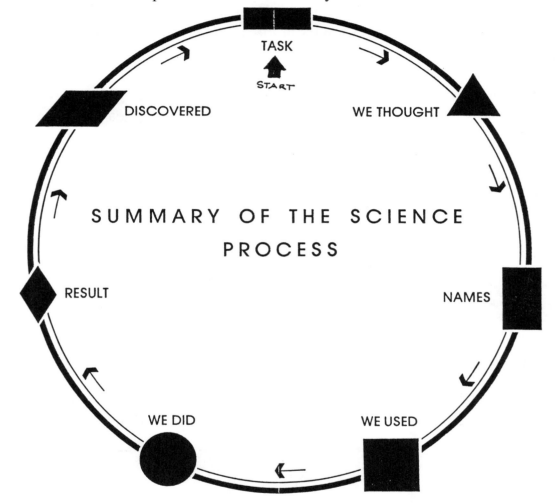

Used with permission of Sue Dale Tunnicliffe

Task (Identify the Problem), **We Thought** (Hypothesis), **Names** (Who is in your group?)
We Used (Equipment), **We Did** (Experiment), **Result** (Your findings based on what you did.),
Discovered (Generalization). A Discovery often leads to a whole new idea and Task--in a circle!
When you use the Circle of Science, you may use both words and pictures for your explanations.
You can make up pictographs for the ideas represented by the shapes.

WATERDRUM SCIENCE BIBLIOGRAPHY

* Suggested Reading

LIFE SCIENCE

Aquatic Invertebrates; Torstar Books, 1985

Barlowe, Dot and Si; *Who Lives Here?;* Random House,1978

* *Book of Mammals Vol 1;* Special Publications Division; Washington D.C: National Geographic Society, 1981

* *Book of Mammals Vol II;* Special Publications Division; Washington D.C. National Geographic Society, 1981

Brenna, Louis A; *Beginners Guide to Archaeology;* Stackpole Books, 1973

Crowley, Kate and Link, Mike; *Love of Loons;* Voyageur Wilderness Books, Voyageur Press Inc.

* Cruickshank , Allan D. and Cruickshank, Helen G; *1001 Questions Answered About Birds;* Dover Publication Inc., 1958

Domico, Terry; *Bears of the World;* Facts on File, 1988

Hazard, Even B; *The Mammals of Minnesota;* University of Minnesota Press, 1982

King, Barry G and Showers, Mary Jane; *Human Anatomy and Physiology;* W.B. Saunders Company, 1969

Macdonald, Dr. David-Editor; *The Encyclopedia of Mammals;* Facts of File Publications, 1985

* *Nature at Work;* British Museum, 1978

Queeny, Edgar M; *Prairie Wings;* Schiffer Publishing Ltd.,1946

Reptiles and Amphibians; Torstar Books, 1986

Robbins Wilfred W., Weir T. Elliot, and Stocking C. Ralph; *Botany-An Introduction to Plant Life*; John Wiley and Sons Inc.,1967

Rue III, Leonard Lee; *The World of the White-tailed Deer;* J.B. Lippincott Company, 1962

Schmidt-Nielsen, Kurt; *Animal Physiology;* Prentice Hall Inc., 1964

Steel, Rodney and Harvey, Anthony-Editors; *The Encyclopedia of Prehistoric Life;* Gramercy Publishing Company, 1979

Terres, John K and Knopf, Alfred A; *The Audubon Society Encyclopedia of North American Birds*; New York: 1980

Vaughn, Terry A; *Mammology;* W.B. Saunders Company, 1972

Wild Animals of North America; National Geographic Society,1979

Welty, Joel Carl; *The Life of Birds*; Saunders College Publishing, 1982

EARTH SCIENCE

* Bray, Edmund C; *Billions of Years in Minnesota;* The Science Museum of Minnesota, 1977

Dinwiddi, Donald, and Macfall, Russell P; *The Complete Book of Rocks, Minerals, Gems, and Fossils*; Popular Mechanics Books, 1978

Foster, Robert J; *Geology Second Edition*; Charles Merrill Publishing Company, 1966

Gilluly, James , Walters, A.C. , and Woodford, A.O; *Principles of Geology--Second Edition*; W.H. Freeman and Company, 1951

Goldsmith, Donald; *The Evolving Universe;* Benjamin/Cummings Publishing Company, 1981

Gross, M. Grant; *Oceanography;* Charles Merrill Publishing Company, 1967

Lewin, Roger; *Thread of Life*; Smithsonian Books, 1982

Miller, Albert; *Meteorology*; Charles Merrill Publishing Company, 1966

Miller, Albert and Thompson, Jack C.; *Elements of Meteorology*; Charles Merrill Publishing Company, 1970

Miller, Ron and Hartmann, William K; *The Grand Tour, A Traveler's Guide to the Solar System;* Workman Publishing 1981

* Mooney, Harold M; *Earthquake History of Minnesota;* University of Minnesota, 1979

Neph, John R; *The Adventure Story;* 1976 (Ancient copper mining.)

* Ojakangas, Richard W. and Matsch, Charles L; *Minnesota Geology;* University of Minnesota, 1982

Rapp Jr., G.R. and Wallace, D.T; *Guide to Mineral Collecting in Minnesota;* Minnesota Geological Survey, 1966

Setterholm, Dr., Morey, G.B., Boerboom, Lamons, R.C., J.J; *Minnesota Geological Survey*; University of Minnesota, 1989

Spencer, Edgar Winston; *Basic Concepts of Historical Geology;* Thomas Y Crowell Co. 1962

Weiner, Jonathon; *Planet Earth*; Bantam Books, 1986

* Wolter, Scott F; *The Lake Superior Agate*; Lake Superior Agate Incorporated, 1986

PHYSICAL SCIENCE

* Akasofu, S.-I *Aurora Borealis The Amazing Northern Lights*; Alaska Geographic Society, 1979 Write to: PO Box 93370, Anchorage AK, 99509, $ 19.95

Amdahl, Kenneth; *There Are No Electrons*; Ingram Co., 1992

Collings, Peter J; *Liquid Crystals*; Princeton University Press, 1990

Flanton, Ira; *Rainbows and Curve Balls*; New York: Wm. Marrow and Company, 1988

* Gonick, Lary and Huffman, Art; *The Cartoon Guide to Physics*; Harper Collins Publishers 1990

* Hazen , Robert M. and Trefil, James; *Science Matters-Achieving Scientific Literacy*; Doubleday, 1992

Hewitt, Paul G; *Conceptual Physics a New Introduction to Your Environment;* Little, Brown, and Company, 1971

Hecht, Jeff; *Optics*; New York: Charles Scribner's, 1987

* Macaulay, David; *The Way Things Work*; Boston: Houghton Mifflin, 1988

* Malone, Mark R-editor; CESI SOURCE BOOK *Physical Science Activities for Elementary and Middle School;* ERIC Clearinghouse for Science, Mathematics, and Env'l Education, 1987. Contact: Joanne Vasques Wolf, Mesa, AZ (602) 898-7815

Rossotti, Hazel; *Light and Sound;* Princeton University Press, 1983

Sherman, Alan, Sherman, Sharon, and Russikoff, Leonard; *Basic Concepts of Chemistry* Second Edition; 1980

* Walker, Jearl; *The Flying Circus of Physics with Answers*; John Wiley and Sons, 1975

WORLD ART AND LITERATURE

Baglin, Douglas, Mulins, Barbara; *Aboriginal Art of Australia;* Shepp Books, 1970

Bierhorst, John; *Doctor Coyote*; New York: Macmillan, 1987

Cowan, James; *Mysteries of the Dream Time;* Prism,1988

Davidson, Hilda; *Scandinavian Mythology*; Hamyln,1967

Davison, Basil; *African Kingdoms;* Great Ages of Man, 1966

* Dwayne, Corinne; *Loon Legends;* North Star Press,1988

* Hamilton, Edith; *Mythology*; Penguin Books, 1977

Ions, Veronica; *Hindu Mythology*; Hamyln,1967

Ions, Veronica; *Egyptian Mythology*; Hamlyn, 1968

Kapffe, Carl Andrew; *Paul Bunyan*; Hist Lord Associates,1984

Leach, Maria; *How the People Sang the Mountains Up*; Viking Press, 1967

Mac Cana, Proinsias; *Celtic Mythology*; Hamlyn, 1968

* Mayo, Gretchen; *Earthmakers Tales*; Walker, 1989

McAlpine, Helen; *Japanese Tales and Legends*; H.Z. Walck, 1959

Moskin, Marietta D; *Sky Dragons and Flaming Swords*; Walker, 1985

Piggot, Juliet; *Japanese Mythology;* Hamyln,1967

Temple, Robert; *The Genius of China*; Simon and Scuhster Inc., 1986

Vitaliano, Dorothy; *Legends of the Earth;* Indiana University Press-London, 1973

Weiss, Malcom E; *Skywatchers of the Past;* Houghton Mifflin, 1982

AMERICAN INDIAN EDUCATION
All are recommended

American Indian Science and Engineering Society (AISES)
1630 30th St. Suite 301, Boulder, CO, 80301 (303) 444-9099
An excellent source of materials, workshops, summer camps....

Cornelius, Carol; *Six Nations Teachers' Guide*; Akekion Press; Cornell Uni., Ithaca, NY

Hands On, Minds On; Science Activities for Children. AISES, Boulder, CO.

Lac Du Flambeau Native American Curriculum, Lac Du Flambeau School., Wisconsin

National Indian Education Association, 1819 H St. NW Suite 800, Washington DC 20006
(202)835-3001

National Organization of Fetal Alcohol Syndrome Phone: (800) 66- NOFAS

Navajo Division of Education: *The Beauty Way*, Window Rock, AZ, 1989

Our Voices Our Vision, AISES, Boulder, CO

Outdoor Science, Outdoor Math, University of Northern Arizona, Flagstaff

Science Activities for Teachers (Grades 5-12) AISES, Boulder, CO

Smith, Walter; *Comets Science*; Washington D.C. NSTA
(A big book full of profiles and career activities of minority women in science-tech fields.)

Smith, Walter S; Project Director; *Earth's Caretakers*; MASTERS PROJECT, Uni. of
Kansas; 1993

SACAI Curriculum (Science of Alcohol Curriculum for American Indians) AISES

Zastrow, Leona M.; *Learning Science by Studying Native American Pottery;* Santa Fe,
New Mexico: EPIC Inc. 1991 Write to: 202 Ojo De La Vaca, Santa Fe, New Mexico.

NATIVE AMERICANS

Agenbroad, Larry D; *Before the Anasazi;* Museum of Northern Arizona, 1990

* Benton-Bani, Edward; *The Mishomis Book The Voice of the Ojibway;* Red School House, 1988

Brown, Vinson; *Native Americans of the Pacific Coast;* 1977 Naturgraph Publishers Inc.

Bryan, Nonabah G; *Navajo Native Dyes Their Preparation and Use;* The Filter Press, 1940

Burland, Cottie; *North American Indian Mythology;* Peter Bedrick Books, 1965

Clark, Ella Elizabeth; *Indian Legends of Canada;* McClelland and Stewart Limited, 1960

Coe, Michael D; *The Maya;* Pelican Books Ltd., 1971

* Densmore, Frances; *Chippewa Customs;* MHS Press, 1979

* Densmore, Frances; *How Indians Use Wild Plants For Food, Medicine, and Crafts;* Dover Publications, 1974

* Dwyer, Corrinne A; *Loon Legends;* North Star Press, 1989

* Esbensen, Barbara Juster-retold by; *Ladder to the Sky;* Little, Brown, and Company, 1989

* Gilmore, Melvin R; *Prairie Smoke;* Minnesota Historical Society Press, 1987

Goldfein, Rosanne P.-editor; *American Indian Art;* Mary G. Hamilton, Autumn 1988

* Highwater, Jamake; *Arts of the American Indians;* Harper and Row Publishers, 1983

* Johnston, Basil; *Ojibway Heritage;* University of Nebraska Press, 1976

Kohl, John Georg; *Kitchigami Life Among the Lake Superior Ojibway;* Minnesota Historical Society Press 1985

Larned, W.T; *American Indian Fairy Tales*; Wise Parslow Co., 1935

Malotki, Ekkehart Lamotuaway'ma, Michael; *Earth Fire*; Northland Press 1987

Miles, Charles; *Indian and Eskimo Artifacts of North America*; Bonanza
  Books 1963

* Nichols, John and Nyholm, Earl; *An Ojibwe Word Resource Book*; Minnesota
  Archaeological Society, 1979

Peyton, John L; *The Stone Canoe and Other Stories*; McDonald and Woodward
  Publishing Company, 1989

Smelcer, John E; *The Raven and the Totem;* Salmon Run Book, 1992

Trimble, Stephen; *Talking with the Clay*; School and American Research Press, 1987

* Warren, William A; *History of the Ojibway People*; MHS Press, 1984

Wright, Barton; *Hopi Kachinas*; Northland Press, 1977

Vennum Jr., Thomas; *Wild Rice and the Ojibway People*; Minnesota Historical Society
  Press, 1988

Vogel, Virgil J; *American Indian Medicine*; University of Oklahoma Press, 1970

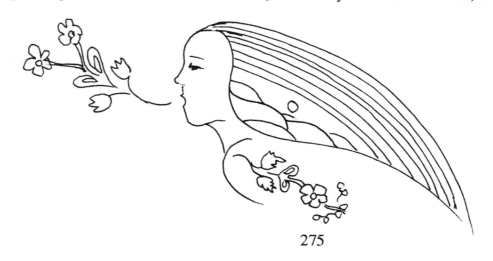

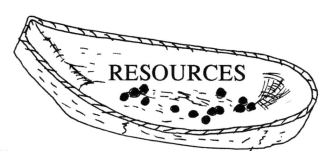

RESOURCES

MICROSCOPES:

Brock Magiscope Model 60. These rugged kid-proof scopes dazzle children and adults
with a crystal clear view of the micro-world.
For a Discount Contact:
Carolyn Petty 12014 Irvine Ave. NW, Bemidji, MN 56601, (218)243-2456

MUSEUM PUBLICATIONS:

Both are beautiful and brimming with information:
Native People Magazine,
Heard Museum, P.O. Box 36820, Phoenix, AZ 85067-6820

Plateau Magazine (Quarterly),
Museum of Northern Arizona, Route 4, Box 720, Flagstaff, AZ 86001

SKULLS, FEATHER AND FUR: Any local taxidermist.

ROCKS: and great pamphlets. Minnesota Geologic Survey (612) 627-4780
Concretions are for sale from Byron Buckeridge (715) 893-2321

VIDEOS:

American Indian Dance Theatre
223 E/. 61st St. NY, NY 10021
Phone (212) 308-9555

Beyond Tradition (Contemporary Indian Art and Its Evolution)
See splendid science and math connections in the artists' creations.
Jacka Photography
Phone (602) 944-2793 Phoenix, AZ

Taking Tradition to Tomorrow from AISES
(American Indian Science and Engineering Society.)
Meet ancient astronomers and agricultural researchers. See how American
Indian traditions are important to today's doctors, scientists and engineers.
AISES, 1630 30th St., Suite 301
Boulder, CO 80301 Phone: (303) 492-3400

ILLUSTRATION CREDITS

Front Cover Photography: Bemidji Indian Education

Student Illustrators:
Students are from the Chief Bug O Nay Ge Shig School, Bena, MN unless indicated.
Their art teacher is Roberta Lord.
Ranae Barrett 21, 63
Tara Barrett 65, 72, 76, Back Cover
Steve Ducheneau 55, 70
Mary Edwards (Pine Point School) 255, 279
Frank Graves 80, 130, 136
Greg Kingbird, 40
Tanell Lord 264-A
Barton Roy 8,15,82
Ranae Roybal 21
Ed Roybal 33
Roberta Roybal 31, 81, 277
Susan Roybal 136, 4
Cliff Jones 93
Emily Smith 80
Gary Smith 1, 2
Bradley Weaver (Pine Point) 268
Holly White 41, 64, 71

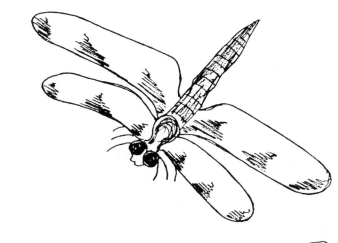

Principal Illustrator:
Lee White: 25, 49, 61, 85, 105, 163,
177, 184, 190, 200, 213, 254,

Artist: All other illustrations are by the author, Carolyn Petty.

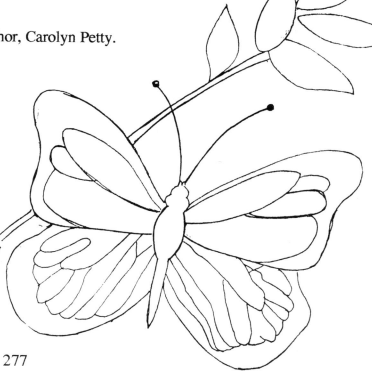

278